# ONE HUNDRED MONKEYS

# ONE HUNDRED MONKEYS

The Triumph of
Popular Wisdom
in Canadian Politics

## ROBERT MASON LEE

MACFARLANE WALTER & ROSS
TORONTO

FIRST EDITION

Macfarlane Walter & Ross
550 Queen Street East
Toronto, Canada  M5A 1V2

**CANADIAN CATALOGUING IN PUBLICATION DATA**

Lee, Robert Mason, 1956-
One hundred monkeys : the triumph of popular wisdom
in Canadian politics

Includes index.
ISBN 0-921912-00-5

1. Canada - Politics and government - 1984-   .*
2. Canada.  Parliament - Elections, 1988.*
I. Title.

FC630.L43 1989      971.064'7      C89-094619-1
F1034.2.L43 1989

Printed and bound in Canada

*To Marni*
*and*
*Jacqueline Jean*
*(born February 11, 1989)*

# CONTENTS

Acknowledgements     ix

1   *The Once and Promised Land*     **1**

2   *Voters and Other Strangers*     **18**

3   *The Whole Elephant*     **45**

4   *Millennial Anxiety*     **66**

5   *A Bit of Cleaning Up*     **84**

6   *Being There*     **104**

7   *Lord of the Ring*     **125**

8   *The Mo-Jo Mini-Bubble*     **141**

9   *The Dancing Topspin Masters*     **158**

10   *A New Way of Talking*     **172**

11   *Shaking the Booga-Wooga Stick*     **188**

12   *Dambusters*     **208**

13   *Exiting Confusão*     **231**

14   *One Hundred Monkeys*     **252**

*Source Notes*     **278**

*Index*     **279**

# ACKNOWLEDGEMENTS

The first step in learning about politics is to accept chaos; the second is to harness it. Each person who enters politics, or writes about it, must find his own way; but without the help of experienced and charitable guides, each would become lost.

For their generosity in sharing their knowledge of politics in general, and electoral politics in particular, I would like to thank the following who helped with this book: George Archer, Norman Atkins, Ron Basford, Derek Burney, Sharon Carstairs, John Chomiak, Peter Connolly, Tex Enemark, Pierre Fortier, Martin Goldfarb, Allan Gregg, Johanna den Hertog, Donald Johnston, Michael Kirby, Stephen Lewis, Marc Lortie, Peter Lougheed, Alan Lutfy, Art Lyon, Preston Manning, Paul Martin, Jr., Dalton Mc-Guinty, Peter McKenzie, Neil McNeil, Keith Morgan, David Morton, Harry Near, Howard Pawley, Bruce Phillips, Tim Ralfe, Lee Richardson, Robin Sears, and John Webster.

As these people are players of the game, some will find themselves painted in a flattering pose; some will not. My respect for them, beyond whatever foolishness is imposed on them during a campaign, remains undiminished.

As a writer of politics, I'm standing on the shoulders of giants. To my betters in the craft, who have been kind and instructive advisers in the national and provincial capitals, I owe thanks: Elly Alboim, Glen Argan, John Burke, Stevie Cameron, Robert Fife, E. Kaye Fulton, J. Douglas Goold, David Halton, Stephen Hopkins, Robert Hurst, Jamie Lamb, Don MacGillivray, Tim Naumetz, Marjorie Nichols, John Sawatsky, Val Sears, Jeffrey Simpson, Doug Small, Michel Vastel, Greg Weston, Les Whittington, and Hugh Winsor. Three others deserve special mention, as their insights are illuminated by esteemed friendship: Ron Graham, Roy McGregor, and Charles Gordon.

For opening their special areas of knowledge, I am grateful to Lorne Bozinoff at Gallup, Angus Reid, Richard Johnston of the

University of British Columbia, Ralph Heintzman at the Social Sciences and Humanities Research Council, and Derek De Kerckhove at the McLuhan Centre.

Lydia Miljan of the Fraser Institute provided fast, accurate media transcripts. Thanks for tapes and transcripts are also due to the staff of the CBC Radio programs *Ideas* and *Media File*.

The *Ottawa Citizen* provides me with a diverting alternative to a nine-to-five job. I am grateful for the leave of absence and the valuable experience, in Ottawa and elsewhere, which made this project possible. Special thanks are due to the indefatigable Keith Spicer; to Scott Honeyman, who is a wise man; and to Graham Parley, one of the finest newspaper editors I have known, and the only kind one. A number of the *Citizen's* staff provided useful advice: Norman Provencher on the markets, Nancy Gall on fashion, Martin Cleary and Alje Kamminga on sport, Jay Stone on meaningful trivia. Steve Proulx, the wizard of the hard-drive library, often reached into the nöosphere and brought back useful results.

This book was commissioned and published by John Macfarlane, Jan Walter, and Gary Ross. These three individuals possess a rare clarity of vision, singularity of purpose, and dedication to the craft. They are also blessed with an abundance of humanity.

Gary Ross, my editor, deserves particular thanks, for the expert and tireless manner in which he brought this book to completion. His effort was extraordinary, his judgement sound, and his eye keen. The book could not exist without him.

I.M. Owen, who copy-edited the book, saved me from many embarrassments by his careful and well-informed reading of the manuscript.

Finally, to my wife, Marni, whose life was so disrupted by my labour and her own, and who bore both with good cheer and unfailing confidence, I offer my love and admiration.

It is fashionable in a book such as this to credit others for any wisdom it may contain, while accepting personal blame for any errors. As this is a political book concerned primarily with an election campaign, however, I will say this about any distortions, errors, or half-truths: I only hope I gave as good as I got. In the immortal words of Gordon Grant, Ottawa bureau chief of the Canadian Press: I stand by most of this stuff.

# ONE HUNDRED MONKEYS

# CHAPTER 1

# THE ONCE AND PROMISED LAND

*Let's sing a song of long ago,*
*When things could grow*
*And days flowed quietly.*
*The air was clean and you could see,*
*And folks were nice to you.*
RANDY NEWMAN

THE REGION OF ESTRIE IS ABOUT an hour and a half east of Montreal by car. The area is called "L'Estrie" on tourist maps, but most English-speaking residents continue to call it "the Townships," or, more properly, "the Eastern Townships." In French, the translation is "Cantons-de-l'Est." Many English-speakers believe this is a direct rendering of "Townships of the East." It isn't quite; the word "canton" has distinct resonance in Swiss French, referring as it does to an autonomous territorial division. The distinction is subtle but telling. For an English-speaker, a township evokes a kind of shire. For a French-speaker, a canton evokes a kind of province. The residents of a canton undoubtedly feel more sovereign than the residents of a shire, though neither group may be aware that the other's reference means anything more than, say, "this place, here."

In life and in politics, much confusion grows out of the names of things.

Donald Johnston awoke on an August day in 1988 when

1

the sun was shining over the Loyalist country. In early morning, the sky had been silvery with mist rising from the surrounding valleys; before long it was a burnished estival blue. Johnston had dressed carefully for the day. He wore sandals, a pair of cut-off trousers, an old cotton T-shirt, and a flat-brimmed straw hat. The hat was battered and ragged. Plaits of straw extended beyond what was once the rim, and there were holes on the ridge of the crown, where it had worn through.

The pathetic old hat gave Johnston the air of one who was at once eccentric and unfortunate. The casual visitor could have mistaken him for a painter who had taken to these hills on account of the light, or some doddering patriarch who had been removed from society. Either view would have had some ingredient of truth. In fact, Johnston was in political exile. Some months earlier, the former Liberal cabinet minister had written a "Dear John" letter to his leader, whose name actually was John.

"Regrettably during the past year," it began, "our relations have been deteriorating." The letter set forth Johnston's disagreement with the Liberal leader's policies. It pointed out the dangers to their party presented by such a course. It concluded that the leader had been deceived by bad advisers, and made an appeal to his principles: "I cannot believe you are on a course which satisfies your personal philosophy." The leader had responded to this private message by embarrassing Johnston publicly — he had him removed from the front bench of the Opposition. Two days later, Johnston had left the Liberal Party.

Technically, then, Johnston's exile was self-imposed. He was not idle; he had taken working papers to the cottage, and his phone was often busy. But he admitted, to himself and others, that this was a place better suited to doing no work at all. Perhaps he felt the higher air and the solitude would offer some new illumination on the problems confronting him.

Johnston moved onto the screened verandah of the cottage, where he could look down the lawn toward the pool. "Heather," he called. Johnston's voice is soft, and it warbles slightly in the higher registers, but it carries well. His wife looked up toward him. "Heather, we have a guest."

Heather Johnston had been swimming, and raking leaves from the pool. She set down the floating rake and started up to the cottage. Exercise and sunshine had invigorated her; she strode with a broad gait, a slight, active woman with alert eyes and a clever smile. So ruddy and lively she seemed, surrounded by farmsteads and the flecks of distant cattle, that she might have come from putting up hay, ready now to lay in jars of preserves. "I'll put on some corn," she said.

Her presence seemed to have a rousing effect on Johnston. He followed his wife into the cottage, opened the door of a fridge and rummaged around inside. He found a beer, decided against it; the day seemed to call for a light chianti. He brought it back to the verandah and pulled the cork. He cleared his papers into a neat pile on the big wooden table and poured three glasses. The burst of chianti mingled with the smell of drying hay — someone nearby had already started baling.

The smell of drying hay is a powerful stimulant, a goad from the laziness of July to the commitments of August. Johnston called through the screen to his wife. "Heather, have we called Ron?" he asked. From inside she replied no, not for a long while. "We should call him up," he said.

Johnston talked about this and that, but the conversation rambled, the verbal equivalent of shuffling papers. Heather Johnston came out of the kitchen with a bowl of corn on the cob.

"It's peaches and cream," she said.

"That's the best," Johnston said.

It was time to ask him what he was doing here.

Johnston's fortunes had been tied to those of the Liberal party for a decade. He had served in two cabinets, run for the leadership, and established himself as one of the half-dozen most distinguished and influential Liberals of his day. He'd picked a hell of a time to decamp. It had been four years since the Liberals had put in their most dismal electoral performance in history, having been buried beneath the record Tory landslide of 1984. Johnston's party was in disarray. The leader had just suffered yet another attack on his right to govern the party; the Liberals were in debt some $5-million; and their four years in opposition had done little to persuade Canadians to return them to office. A fall election seemed inevitable. This, surely, was the time for all good Liberal men to come to the aid of the party.

Johnston explained that he was there primarily because of two issues. One was called free trade. The other was called Meech Lake. If, as many people believed, free trade was destined to be the centrepiece of the election campaign, then Meech Lake would be the vacant place-setting at the table, the unseen guest whose presence is acknowledged but seldom mentioned. Both were fundamental to the future direction of the country, but neither was well understood by the public — Meech Lake because politicians talked about it so little, free trade because they talked about it so much.

MEECH LAKE WAS an agreement that had been negotiated by a Conservative government fond of calling its federal-provincial agreements "accords." The word not only has the advantage of being spelled identically in French and English, it also evokes equanimity and balance. Thus, the Canadian government used the same marketing techniques in choosing a name for its domestic power-sharing arrangements that a Japanese automobile manufacturer used in naming one of its models. With both the Honda Accord and the Meech Lake Accord, the seller is seeking to reassure, and to beguile, the buyer. In one case, the product is an automobile. In the other, the product is a constitution. The Honda marketing people realize, however, that a purchaser wants more than a family sedan. The purchaser may want to bring order to his chaotic life; he may want peace for his jangled nerves; he may want to reconcile himself to the frightening pace of modern life. So he is sold not a car but an Accord.

Similarly, Canadians wanted more than just a constitution. They had one of those already. But the one they already had — it was just then celebrating its sixth birthday and was getting broken in — meant less to them than the acrimony that had surrounded its unilateral patriation by Pierre Trudeau. Quebec had refused to sign the agreement. The other provinces wouldn't sign it unless a clause were introduced that allowed them to get out of it. Whenever they met to discuss it, the premier of Quebec sulked and smoked cigarettes while the premier of Alberta angrily threw his papers around the room. Canadians evidently didn't want a constitution as much as they wanted peace. So they were sold not a constitution but an accord.

Donald Johnston had decided to assume the role of consumer advocate. He kicked the tires of the accord, so to speak, and looked around under the hood. He didn't think Meech Lake was a very good buy. Far from an accord, he believed, it was a document

4

that spelled the destruction of Canada. He compared it to Dieppe, and Gallipoli, and wondered how the politicians responsible for all these travesties had lived with themselves. "Maybe too many people are coming into political life and into positions of authority without due regard for the enormous responsibilities," he said. "It's not games-playing. It's the lives of twenty-five million people and the future of a significant industrial power."

The Meech Lake Accord had been signed by all the provinces and had brought Quebec into the constitutional framework, as the Conservative prime minister, Brian Mulroney, was fond of saying, "with honour and enthusiasm." The prime minister had achieved the agreement by sequestering the provincial premiers at his Meech Lake retreat, north of Ottawa, one April night until they signed. A neologism was born. The word "meech" immediately entered Ottawa parlance as a verb, meaning to bludgeon an obstacle into submission, as in, "The request was outside the department envelope, but we meeched it in time for P and P."

To meech his constitutional accord, the prime minister had had to grant — or appear to grant — certain powers to Quebec in exchange for its signature. This raised the hackles of other premiers, who felt Quebec was already the darling of the Canadian Confederation and demanded concessions of their own. Quebec then wanted whatever the others were getting. The prime minister, by training and inclination a negotiator, deftly handled this unexpected development. He gave everyone what they wanted. Even his political adversary, the former prime minister Trudeau, admired this manoeuvre: "What a sly fox!"

Of course Trudeau, being a sly fox himself, may have had his tongue in his cheek.

The provinces did not get everything, mind you — had the premiers meeched a few hours more they might conceivably have emerged with provincial powers as yet undreamed of — the right to make appointments to the federal cabinet, say, or joint command of the armed forces. But to Donald Johnston's mind, what they did receive was quite a shopping list. To begin with, he believed, they had gained effective control of the legislature and the judiciary — two of the three main branches of the modern democratic state. They did not get the third branch, the executive, but they got good solid hunks of it. They got control of its spending power and its immigration, and they got a voice at formal meetings to chart national economic strategy.

Johnston was not being a wild-eyed zealot in interpreting the accord. His analysis was consistent with the prime minister's avowed view of the country. "I believe in a federalist state you should govern, to the extent humanly possible, in harmony with the provincial governments," Mulroney was on record as saying. "It is not always easy, I know, but you should go the extra mile to try and accommodate that, because the process of accommodation ensures that major decisions can then be made in a spirit that allows for economic growth and prosperity."

There is nothing intrinsically wrong with giving things away — the white-bearded gent of popular myth does so eternally. Nor is it necessarily wrong to give away significant powers, if a ruler feels it to be in the best interests of his country. But Johnston's reading of the new constitution had revealed to him a gift far too dangerous to be put in the hands of the provinces. It was the gift of self-determination. Each province would be able to break away from national programs and establish its own, with the federal government merely writing the cheque. More to the heart of the matter, the document meant that Quebec would be able — not only able, but required — to become French, while the rest of the country became English. This was a departure from the bilingual Canada Johnston had worked long and hard to achieve, a shift to linguistic dualism. "It's a legitimate option," he said, gnawing on a cob of corn. "But my major problem is that the debate is simply not taking place."

Johnston's understanding of the new constitution was certainly shared by the provinces that benefited from it. Quebec claimed it got more from the accord than it had dared hope; Alberta claimed to have been doubly blessed, by installing the provincial premiers as members of an annual board meeting while at the same time gaining a commitment to change the Senate further in the province's favour.

But the federal government had argued that the new constitution changed little, except that it had been signed by Quebec. "The Meech Lake Accord advances the cause of stronger minority-language rights in this country," said the minister of federal-provincial relations, Senator Lowell Murray. "It is thus perverse to cite language as a reason for not proceeding with it."

Murray also insisted the Supreme Court and Senate had

not been handed over to the provinces, merely opened to "negoti-ation and compromise." As for immigration, he said, the agree-ment would appear to give the provinces control over their levels. But the Charter of Rights would still ensure that immigrants, once accepted into Canada, could move anywhere they liked. As for spending powers, he said, the agreement changed nothing at all — provinces were already paid to administer federally mandated social programs, such as medical insurance, while meeting na-tional objectives.

SUCH A DISPUTE was possible only because the sort of thinking that went into naming the Meech Lake Accord had infiltrated the document as a whole. The only tangible, demonstrable, universally agreed-upon feature of the agreement was that Quebec had signed it. The founding fathers of the new constitution had stood on the shores of Meech Lake. Before them, the lake was still. The inclu-sion of Quebec had calmed the waters and brought about the pretence of peace. Beneath the surface, however, was a maelstrom, dangerous and unseen. The premiers were like mariners who read the tides but not the currents, and who later bicker when their charts prove inadequate.

The first ministers had originally agreed to recognize the existence of a "French-speaking Canada" and an "English-speaking Canada" as a "fundamental characteristic" of the country. That had been changed to read, "the existence of French-speaking Ca-nadians, centred in Quebec but also present elsewhere in Canada, and English-speaking Canadians, concentrated outside Quebec but also present in Quebec." That, they said, was Canada. From there, they agreed that "Quebec constitutes within Canada a distinct society." But nowhere was the distinctiveness of Quebec defined. It could have meant that Quebec was the homeland of French Canadians who are "centred" there. Or it could have meant that the province is distinct because English-speakers are "also pres-ent." Both terms are used to describe Quebec, and both terms accurately reflect the province. They both mean, more or less, "this place, here." As Lowell Murray remarked, the agreement simply "recognized our linguistic realities."

Linguistic realities are harmless enough. One can say that a tribe is "centred in the forest," and that a forest is a place where "tigers are also present." Taken together, the two descriptions

7

present a more complete view of the forest than either on its own. There is no contradiction. A problem might arise, though, if an order were issued to "protect the forest." Would the order be meant to protect the tribe from the tigers, the tigers from the tribe, or both from incursions by outsiders?

This was the problem posed by the Meech Lake Accord. The first ministers had agreed to "preserve" the "fundamental characteristic" of Canada. Quebec, in addition, was charged with not only preserving but promoting its distinct identity. This sounded more positive and more open-ended; it's just that nobody knew for sure what it meant. The English version of the agreement said that all the Canadian governments "affirmed" their roles in preserving Canada, which implied a pre-existing condition that was merely being continued. The French version dropped the word "affirmed," which implied that the agreement created new roles. It looked fishy, but nobody quite knew what that meant, either.

The pattern was repeated down the line. The first ministers had agreed to fill the Senate — the upper chamber of the legislature — with names the prime minister would choose from a list provided by the provinces. This was a major change from the existing system, in which the governor general — representing the head of state, the Queen — would summon senators after consulting with the prime minister. In fact, the governor general never demurred, and appointing the upper chamber was just one of many head-of-state powers enjoyed by the prime minister. Under the new system, this power would flow past the prime minister to the premiers. Or would it? The accord didn't say what would happen if the prime minister found all the names unacceptable. He could refuse to name anyone. Rather than giving the premiers a presidential power, the prime minister seemed to have placed them in the position of presidential advisers. Or had he? Nobody knew for sure.

The first ministers agreed that any province could negotiate its own immigration levels with the federal government. But what did this mean? Nowhere did it say whether these negotiations had to be concluded. The federal government would pay Quebec to receive and process its proportional share of immigrants — plus five per cent, lest a declining birth rate render the province less distinct. But what did this mean? Once inside the province, immigrants were guaranteed the right to move anywhere they liked in Canada. Quebec was guaranteed three seats on the Supreme Court, and all the provinces were given the right to submit names from which the prime minister must draw new judges. But what did this mean? What if the names were unacceptable? What if three provinces submitted names for one vacancy?

Provinces would also be paid a reasonable compensation by the federal government if they chose to opt out of a new national shared-cost program that fell under their jurisdiction. In return, the province would have to carry on a program or initiative compatible with national objectives. No one had the foggiest idea what this meant. No one knew, for instance, whether a national dental plan would be considered a new program or an extension of Canada's existing national medical-insurance plan. If a dental plan was considered new, then no one was certain whether the province's obligation to carry on a "compatible" program meant something like the national program, or merely something that did not conflict with it. If it had to be something like the national program, then no one knew whether the requirement to meet national "objectives" meant it had to meet certain standards or just certain goals. If it meant certain standards, then no one knew who would determine whether the compensation paid to the province was "reasonable." Constitutional experts who studied this clause came away with radically different views of its meaning. Some felt it would result in a crazy-quilt pattern of national programs, with the federal government a mere signer of cheques. Others felt it entrenched and furthered federal powers. Still others felt it struck a balance between provincial autonomy and national standards.

Could the Meech Lake Accord mean so many things, and still mean anything at all?

"WHEN I USE A WORD," Humpty Dumpty told Alice, "it means just what I choose it to mean, neither more nor less."

"The question is," said Alice, "whether you *can* make words mean so many different things."

"The question is," said Humpty Dumpty, "which is to be master — that's all."

The prime minister was a clear adherent of the Humpty Dumpty school of constitutional interpretation. In November, 1985, in Halifax, he had agreed to the premiers' demands for "full provincial participation" in the free-trade talks with the Americans. To the premiers, this meant they would direct the negotiations, determine what was negotiable, and approve or reject the final deal. In the presence of the prime minister, one of the premiers, David Peterson of Ontario, declared: "The bottom line is that the negotiator will receive his instructions from the first ministers." The prime minister peered over his Ben Franklins; he had already had a flare-up with the premier over a financial matter, and so he let it pass. Within hours, though, he was declaring that the role of the federal government was "unchallenged and undiminished" by the agreement. He was then asked what was meant, exactly, by "full provincial participation." (As it turned out, it meant that the provinces were briefed on the progress of negotiations and asked for their opinions, but had no direct influence on their outcome.) "It means," the prime minister replied, in his best Humpty Dumpty manner, "what it says it means."

That the prime minister relied on goodwill to resolve the questions of meaning in his constitutional agreement was shown by his many references to Confederation as being a "conversation" and a "continuing dialogue." In Saint-Hyacinthe, Quebec, that summer, he said his approach to federal-provincial relations was "characterized by trust and serenity."

It was not a hopefulness shared by all. Pierre Trudeau, whose suspicious instincts had been honed by a period in office marked by provincial duplicity and blackmail, saw great danger in the language of the constitutional amendments. "It is an old legal principle that legislators do not engage in empty rhetoric," he said. "That can happen, but not when writing laws.

"Either the phrase 'distinct society' means nothing, or it means something. We have made peace with Quebec by letting it believe that 'distinct society' means two nations. If the courts hold that it does have that meaning, Canada is doomed. If they hold otherwise, Quebec will have been tricked, and the howls of protest will strengthen separatism. One way or another, Meech Lake may mean the peace of the grave for the Canada we know and love."

Donald Johnston couldn't have said it better himself, and he didn't. Seated on the porch, allowing his head to loll back and his eyes to close, he quoted Trudeau's words: "The peace of the grave."

Johnston sorted through his papers for the 1987 report of the Commissioner of Official Languages. "The part that got so much attention in here was the part about anglophones being humiliated," he said. The language commissioner had said in his report that the "salvation of French, in Quebec or elsewhere, must surely lie in positively asserting its own demographic weight, cultural vigour and innate attractiveness, and not in humbling the competition." He was referring to a provincial law which made it a punishable offence in Quebec to display a commercial sign in English. His point — that making the display of English illegal was "humbling" (the French version translates as "humiliating") to the English minority — was lost on the Quebec government; the assembly immediately voted to censure the commissioner. This led to a great controversy.

But in another part of the report, the language commissioner spoke about the Meech Lake Accord. While he called it "a major step in the right direction," he too was troubled by its language. "What may look like a difference of a couple of syllables could affect the general language equilibrium in this country." The fact that the Canadian language situation was complex, he reasoned, was no reason for "fudging it," particularly if fudging led to a constitution that permitted two nations. Most Canadians, he said, "remain firmly opposed to a straight territorial solution to Canada's special linguistic dilemma as being, in the end, a recipe for national suicide."

"That's what caught my eye," Johnston said. "He's warning us of the Belgian example."

Johnston stood and walked over to the screen that encloses his porch. During his decade in the Commons and in the cabinet he had represented Westmount, a privileged English enclave in Montreal. He himself was bilingual — he had taken his law degree at Grenoble — and the French language was not frightening to him. But the sight of the valley made him reflect. "Here you have eight or nine hundred thousand people excluded from any debate about their future," he said, referring to the English minority in Quebec. "People assume the English are fat cats. Well, the real fat cats are either bilingual or becoming bilingual. They can afford to send their kids to special schools, or to leave the province. But the farmers in this valley are English-speaking. Always have been. They don't have those kinds of resources. They haven't a chance.

"But John Turner is convinced he will alienate Quebeckers if he says a word against Meech Lake, because his Quebec lieutenant tells him this is the most popular thing since the tin can."

Johnston let the words sour in his mouth a moment. "Since the tin can," he repeated bitterly.

FREE TRADE BETWEEN Canada and the United States gave rise to a labelling problem similar to the one created by Meech Lake. Critics of free trade called it "the Mulroney-Reagan Trade Deal." Proponents toyed with calling it "fairer trade" and "freer trade," as the words "free trade" had poor historical connotations in Canada. Eventually, they settled on the "Canada-U.S. Free-Trade Agreement." Critics of the deal reasoned that neither the Canadian prime minister, Mulroney, nor the U.S. president, Ronald Reagan, was as popular with Canadians as the country he led. Similarly, a "deal" connotes something less forthright, more clandestine and self-serving than an "agreement." The "Mulroney-Reagan Trade Deal" evoked negative sentiments among Canadians; the "Canada-U.S. Free-Trade Agreement" evoked positive ones. Although the government officially adopted the latter name, the issue was never really settled. Opponents continued to use the "Mulroney-Reagan Trade Deal," and probably always will.

In another time, perhaps, such a squabble would have been of little consequence, a treaty by any other name being a treaty. As we approached the dying decade of the second millennium, however, a thing contained by a name was often less significant than the name itself. The trend was so ubiquitous it was seldom noticed. Civic leaders borrowed military terms when they wished to convey a sense of action; a committee became a task force, even though it was still a committee. The military borrowed medical terms to lend a sense of healing to an act of destruction; a bombing became a surgical strike, even though it was still a bombing. Medicine borrowed the language of accountants to apply a sense of fiscal prudence to acts of political revolt; extra billing became balanced billing, even though it was still a violation of medicare.

The military tends to be most creative in the use of camouflanguage, but nowhere is it more widespread than in politics. This is not because politicians are more devious than other skilled practitioners, but because any practitioner must use tools that do the job. If the finance minister, Michael Wilson, wished to amend the taxation system, he knew he would have better luck calling the proposed amendments tax reform instead of tax change, reform carrying an in-built sense of correction. Enough tax reform may mean less fiscal restraint, which is another way of saying spending cuts. Enough fiscal restraint may mean deficit reduction, which is not reduction at all but growth at a slackened, though still dizzying, pace. And so on.

Often the first battle in promoting (defending) a government action is the battle over (choice of) words. Often, if the battle is not settled quickly, it drains much of the energy of the participants. For example, the pro-life (anti-abortion) groups, whose views differed sharply from the pro-choice (pro-abortion) lobby, began calling the unborn the pre-born, while their opponents continued to use the word fetus. The reason is simple: a fetus does not contain the same potential as a pre-born. A fetus is a noun, a pre-born is an adjective posing as a noun, with a verb in there bursting to get out. A fetus gets nowhere. A pre-born gets born.

Now, either this is all nonsense, and the energies spent agonizing over such things are wasteful; or it is meaningful, and the energies spent are necessary. It may not matter a jot what free trade is called; it may matter so much that the name alone becomes a deciding factor in whether it gains public acceptance. In either case, the effect of attaching one name rather than another should be measurable. This, at least, is what Richard Johnston thought.

RICHARD JOHNSTON — no relation to Donald — is a professor of political science at the University of British Columbia. Together with three other professors, André Blais of the University of Montreal, Jean Crête of Laval University, and Henry Brady of the University of Chicago, he designed the 1988 Canadian National Election Study. It was the largest publicly sponsored election survey ever undertaken in Canada, funded by the federal government's Social Sciences and Humanities Research Council. Roughly eighty Canadians a day, 3,600 in total, were asked their views on a number of subjects. The weekly sample was accurate to a margin of error of 4.5 per cent. Johnston decided to use this tool to measure the importance of a name.

Half the members of his sample group were asked whether they approved of the trade deal negotiated by the Mulroney government — the "Mulroney trade deal." The other half were asked whether they approved of the trade deal negotiated by the government of Canada — the "Canada-U.S. trade agreement." The respondents were chosen at random; the results, if the name meant nothing, should have been identical. They weren't. In the first half of the campaign, roughly five per cent more people approved of "the Canada-U.S. agreement" than approved of "the Mulroney deal."

The election campaign Johnston was monitoring included a live, televised debate. After the debate, the proportion supporting "the Mulroney deal" was fourteen points lower than the proportion supporting "the Canada-U.S. agreement." Fourteen points is a lot in a Canadian election. It's the difference between winning and losing.

In the weeks following the debate, one more remarkable thing happened; the two different treatments appeared to carry less and less weight. It mattered less which "deal" respondents were asked about, the Canadian one or the Mulroney one. By election day, those given the Mulroney treatment were actually slightly more disposed to favour the deal.

When Richard Johnston looked around for an explanation of this strange behaviour, he could not point to the trade deal itself — not a word had changed since he began polling. Neither could he reason that people understood more about the deal than when the election campaign began. If that had been the case, the responses of the two groups would have shifted in the same direction. They hadn't done so. Nor did it make sense to link the results with overall Canadian acceptance of the deal. If overall acceptance had increased, the approval rating in both groups would have improved in the last part of the campaign. In fact, almost all the improvement had occurred among the group given the Mulroney treatment — those asked about the "Canadian" deal remained about steady.

Neither the deal itself, nor knowledge of the deal, nor acceptance of the deal, could explain this behaviour. The only possible explanation was that Mulroney's name was no longer a liability. That could have been because Mulroney himself had changed — unlikely, but possible — or because attitudes toward him had changed. When Johnston checked, he found his survey results fitted that latter explanation perfectly. In all ways the researchers could check, the prime minister's own scores had paralleled the attitudes of the "Mulroney trade deal" group. As the prime minister's popularity went down, so did people's willingness to accept the "Mulroney trade deal." As his popularity increased, so did their acceptance of that deal. The "other" deal, meanwhile, the one signed by the government of Canada, was immune to shifts in attitude toward the prime minister.

When a substantial percentage of voters cast their ballots, in other words, they weren't voting on whether they approved of free trade with the United States. They were voting on whether they liked the name of the agreement.

DONALD JOHNSTON knew that the battle to seize control of the name of the free-trade deal was well worth the effort. He also knew what kind of campaign that would mean. In his letter of resignation to the Liberal leader, he had predicted: "[Other issues] will be touched upon in the election campaign, but the debate will be dominated by the two remaining issues, namely, the free-trade agreement and Mulroney's credibility." Johnston had no way of knowing the extent to which the two issues would be linked. But he warned Turner, fairly accurately: "Your anti-free-trade profile will cost you the next election. Shirley Carr [the Canadian Labour Congress president] and her followers will applaud you and agree with you but they will not vote for you. The end result could be a national polarization of left and right, with Liberals a spent and irrelevant political force. . . ."

The letter went on at some length. At his cottage, though, Johnston was more succinct. "It's a tragedy to see something like this polarized into a debate over sovereignty and reach levels of hysteria on both sides," he said. "The real issue should be, should Canada go for the deal and work the next five years to improve it, or is it such a bad deal that it should be abandoned? If it's not a bad deal for Canada, we should sign it. My own inclination is that the deal should be done, and then we sit down and point out to the Americans how, on both sides, the provisions could be improved. It's certainly no worse than what we have now. It might even be better."

Johnston had little more to say about free trade, other than that he saw it as a commercial arrangement which should be tested. He said that he saw less opportunity of price advantage for the consumer than of choice advantage. (He had slipped into talking like that, instead of saying, "Things won't be a lot cheaper, but there will be more to choose from," which is more the way he usually talks.) It was surprising, then, when he uttered a simple prophecy: "The election campaign is going to be about the sale of our sovereignty. That's why I sound so bitter about it, and I am. The sale of sovereignty. On a trade deal you can terminate if you don't like it."

AS THE AFTERNOON drew its long shadows on the lawn, Johnston returned to the subject of Meech Lake, offering more salted observations. "Western Canadians feel screwed by Ontario and Quebec, and they're right," he said. "The only solution seems to be a Triple E Senate." This was a term referring to change in the upper house, favourable to the hinterland. "What an inducement to Senate reform, telling those guys to come to Ottawa twice a year to run Canada" — those guys being the provincial premiers. "Imagine a social-democratic party approving a constitution that means they will have no role in social programs whatever." This was a reference to the New Democratic Party, which had endorsed Meech Lake. "We talk about free trade undermining our social programs. I don't think it will — under Meech Lake we won't have any!"

Johnston was offered the encouragement that perhaps, as people knew more about Meech Lake, they would like it less. Yes, he said, that matched his observation. There hadn't been an unkind word about Meech Lake in the Quebec broadcasts or newspapers, yet a recent poll showed that support for the accord was dropping in the province.

"How does that happen?" he asked. "Take with television. We all know the importance of television. Yet I've come to the view that, no matter what people do on television, somehow the people are a lot more intelligent than we think.

"There are things out there," Johnston added, "that are beyond our comprehension."

This was something he had observed throughout his political career. "I sensed it in my own riding. One day there was no problem, then all of a sudden there would be a change. We'd have a problem on our hands." It seemed to be happening more lately. He'd seen it in the 1984 campaign, when the Conservatives had swept the country, gaining the largest majority in Canadian electoral history. In Johnston's leader's riding, Vancouver Quadra, voters were poised to elect the Conservative candidate just days before the poll — all the surveys confirmed it. The only explanation for John Turner's victory appeared to be a last-minute "sympathy vote." But how could that happen?

"Have you ever heard about the hundred monkeys?" Johnston asked. "It was an experiment. These scientists taught one set of monkeys to wash their food before eating it. It was sweet potatoes. They taught these monkeys to wash their sweet potatoes, and then they observed that their parents were also doing it. Soon every one of the hundred monkeys on this island — they were on this island — were washing their sweet potatoes.

"Then they found these other monkeys on another island. And they were all washing their sweet potatoes, too! Within that species, something had communicated itself."

It wasn't political science, but it was tantalizing. Donald Johnston had found himself in a political climate in which things were no longer what they seemed. In which the constitutional order of the country was being determined by the Meech Lake Accord, a document whose ambiguity was the source of both its acceptability and its peril. In which external relations were determined by the Canada-U.S. Trade Agreement, a document whose acceptability seemed predicated less on substance than on presentation. In which things could mean exactly what you chose them to mean, depending, as Humpty Dumpty said, on which was to be master. The tools of communication had been beaten into scrap; debate about the substantive issues had become a symphony of euphonious but insignificant sounds. Any election campaign conducted in such a climate would be a recipe for bedlam, an invitation to absurdity, a dialogue of the mute.

And Donald Johnston had faith in the ability of the electorate to find its way through the muddle, using nothing more than a kind of popular wisdom, arrived at by some unexplained form of learning supposedly observed by scientists in an obscure experiment related to him by one of his staff. Johnston must have caught something resembling alarm in his listener.

"Just because a phenomenon hasn't yet been explained," he said, "doesn't mean that it doesn't exist."

# CHAPTER 2

# VOTERS AND OTHER STRANGERS

*We are in great haste to construct a magnetic telegraph from Maine to Texas, but Maine and Texas, it may be, have nothing important to communicate.*

HENRY DAVID THOREAU

IF YOUR JOURNEYS BRING YOU into contact with those who make it their business to help others get elected to public office, you will soon come upon an American magazine called *Campaigns and Elections*. You will find it hardly anywhere else: it is not sold on newsstands, not advertised in mass-circulation newspapers or magazines, not included in clearing-house come-ons. The Parliamentary Library in Ottawa has a complete collection, but most people cannot browse through the Parliamentary Library.

The magazine pops up in the most telling places. Robin Sears, the chief strategist for the New Democratic Party's 1988 election campaign, has a respectable collection on his bookshelf. John Webster, who directed the Liberal campaign, is a subscriber. Pierre Fortier, who ran a secret high-tech operation for the Conservative campaign, is a devoted reader. All are avid consumers of the magazine, yet all describe it in oddly removed terms, from "kind of scary" to "some interesting ideas." *Campaigns and Elections* is the *Playboy* of the political world; those who buy it claim they really have no use for it but find the articles thought-provoking.

Not only does this magazine have an impressive readership list, it draws advertising revenue from imposing sources. One issue contains a glossy spread advertising NBC News, several full-page ads from AT&T, one from General Dynamics, another from IBM, another from the National Newspaper Association.

Most of the ads, though, are from companies normal people have never heard of, selling products they had no idea existed. Some of these companies sell what was once known as constituency knowledge, voter contact, and fundraising. Changing America, Inc., sells what the advertisement bills as "Jesse Jackson's Secret Weapon." Wax earplugs? Anti-dandruff shampoo? No. Changing America, Inc., "provides Democrats with a wide range of direct mail and telemarketing services, including donor acquisition. . . acknowledgement. . . resolicitation. . . list maintenance. . . and monthly sustainer programs."

Rexnord Data Systems, whose clientele includes the Republican National Committee, the National Republican Senatorial Committee, four state Republican parties, and Republican Lieutenant Governor Scott McCallum, boasts a "multi-million-dollar computer facility" to help candidates get "the winning edge — keeping campaign and finance lists current for direct mail, Get-Out-The-Vote, fundraising, and issue- or candidate-related telemarketing." Another firm, Voter Contact Services, has compiled information on sixty-six million voters, and has them "matched for phones, probable ethnic origin, gender and carrier route."

Other companies specialize in what political parties once called campaign management. The most cleverly titled product is Hannibal, computer software for Democrats. (It helps get the elephants over the mountain.) Peripheral Visions, Inc., offers a "constituent management system designed exclusively for Apple MacIntosh" known as "The Party Animal."

Not all the products are computer-oriented. Politicians who already have, as one blurb reads, their "voters on diskette," may wish to know what the electorate is thinking. "If you're a Republican candidate on the way up," advises Hill Research Consultants, "you need a pollster who's headed in that direction, too." In another ad we learn that AT&T, the telephone people, are also there to help: "I think the voters are with me on that," says the candidate, Don Walley, in one AT&T ad. On the facing page, Don is pictured outside a balloon-bedecked campaign headquarters, consulting with an aide.

"Come on, Don," says his campaign manager, a competent-looking woman with a set jaw. "Polling a dozen people at a rally doesn't mean you know your whole constituency." Of course, Don. Get with it, Don. Call AT&T, ask about the Consultant Liaison Program, and find out how helpful AT&T can be "to your telemarketing operation and, ultimately, your campaign."

Having prudently polled, mailed, and telemarketed, the candidate can then find the appropriate company to help him send the appropriate message to the electorate. Chances are, the candidate is simply repeating to the electorate what the electorate previously said in the poll, but if you're as incompetent as Don you can't take any chances. These firms range from video-production companies to specialists offering advice in "crisis management" (which concerns itself with managing not the crisis but the attendant publicity). The candidate must tread carefully in choosing these companies: only a careful reading reveals, for instance, that the firm selling "issue conscious, campaign sensitive image profiles" is selling photographs.

Some people, like Don's Valkyrian campaign manager, are recognized for their service to democracy by the Pollies, America's Oscar Awards of voter manipulation. The Pollies, sponsored by the magazine and the American Association of Political Consultants, have become, we're assured, "a major post-election media event in Washington." Awards are offered in several categories, including radio, television, and newspaper advertising, fundraising campaigns, even down to the best "letter, postcard and/or collateral" in the category of "Persuasion/Getting Out The Vote." In this context, "collateral" can mean just about anything — for a hint, look up the helpful *Campaigns and Elections* article on the legal uses of "street money" on election day. Or collateral could be an expensive insert, or "premium," placed in a fundraising letter. Many Canadians have received in the mail a plasticized card from the Liberal Party of Canada. The card resembles a credit card, or a membership card, except that it is not good for credit, or membership, or anything else. Its sole purpose is to get you to open the letter. That's collateral.

20

THE EDITORIAL content of *Campaigns and Elections* is no less interesting than the advertisements. In "The Best Defense Is a Good Offense," subtitled "The secrets to launching — and deflecting — 11th hour attacks," the campaigner is warned about the first problem with negative advertising — how to make ad hominem attacks appear to be simple, guileless "comparative advertising." The article goes on to describe, in delicious detail, how you can leak damaging information about an opponent without the leak's being traced back to you. It's just the sort of article Don's with-it campaign manager would lap up. The snotty bitch. Why *can't* Don talk to real people who care enough to come out to his political rally? No wonder she wears her hair in a bun.

One issue of the magazine carries an interview with the former presidential candidate Pat Robertson. He was an intriguing character in U.S. politics, a television evangelist with fresh — some would say dangerous — ideas. But in *Campaigns and Elections*, the interviewer wanted to know if "your defeat [was] a strategic failure to target and get out your vote?"

"If I had to do it again," Robertson admitted, "I'd take a slightly different tack and emphasize TV more." And, presumably, call AT&T's Consultant Liaison Program. Robertson's advice to the aspiring president: "Avoid extraneous issues, and be very, very careful about what is said. Don't become involved in anything that is even remotely controversial. . . . The thing above all is to service press needs."

One article considered whether a particular candidate for public office lost the election because of his decision to record his advertisements on videotape rather than the classier but more expensive 35-millimetre film. In a similar vein, another piece offers a "do-it-yourself kit" of media consulting, with the subhead: "You can improve your TV presence with a home video camera and a VCR." Key points: Sit up straight, smile, keep the hand gestures high and tight, and "keep your legs under your chair." Come on, Don, get those feet off the desk.

Once seated, legs squarely under the chair, the American candidate-in-training is urged to "concentrate on the tough issues, such as abortion, tax hikes and gun control. Try to give a 15-second response to each; your manager should time your answers on a stopwatch."

Now, what's troubling about all this is not that some media

consultant wrote it. What's troubling is that so many candidates have read it.

IN THE ISSUE of *Campaigns and Elections* that happened to appear during the 1988 Canadian general election, the publisher of the magazine felt moved to write an editorial. Dismayed by the selection of the "clearly unqualified" Republican vice-presidential candidate Dan Quayle in the U.S., the publisher wrote: "We are in the business of helping candidates win elections by reporting on advances in political technology and technique. Yet, are we now part of the problem? Do good campaigning skills make substance unnecessary?"

Odd question, rather like the editor of *Guns and Ammo* asking whether the proliferation of Saturday Night Specials was linked to an increase in crime. Perhaps, from time to time, the publisher of *Soldier of Fortune* wonders whether his magazine is linked to news of another lout in green fatigues massacring Asian schoolchildren. How would he put his worries in print: "Yet, are we now part of the problem? Do good survival skills make Asian kids redundant?"

In his fretting over Quayle, the publisher need not have cast further for his answer than the nearest television set. There, during the televised 1988 Republican national convention, one of America's top journalists was assigned the task of finding out about Quayle, whom George Bush had just nominated as his running mate. The journalist, Diane Sawyer, is paid about $1.2-million (U.S.) a year for her contribution to the democratic process. In previous times, that contribution could have been described as the informing of the electorate and the questioning of those in authority. Now, it obviously means something different. Sawyer chose as her interview subject the nominee's wife.

SAWYER: Hello, Mrs. Quayle.

MRS. QUAYLE: Hello.

SAWYER: And congratulations, since this is the first time we meet you. I think we might as well ask you what a lot of people on this campaign seem to be saying is a *major issue*. Does your husband look like Robert Redford and do women lap that up?

MRS. QUAYLE: He's far better looking than Robert Redford, number one, and of course he's attractive, but women are more interested in what he's done for jobs and the economy than in his looks. I give women far more credit than that.

SAWYER: Do you think the "pretty face" factor, I guess — just another pretty face is what they'd say if it were a woman — do you think that affects women at all?

MRS. QUAYLE: No, I think it's more what's behind the pretty face. He obviously comes across as someone. . . .

And so forth. Such an exchange, in present-day electoral politics in the United States, would not strike the average viewer as unusual. Nor was this preoccupation limited to television. Newspaper reports invariably mentioned Quayle's resemblance to the film actor Robert Redford, although the *Washington Post*, in its style section, chose instead to debate whether Quayle ought to be compared to Redford or to the television talk show host Pat Sajak. And it was a magazine, *Vanity Fair*, that first ran the apocryphal story about Quayle, the law student, watching the Redford movie, *The Candidate*.

According to the magazine, Quayle decided after seeing the film to run for political office. The magazine quoted a classmate, who said Quayle had remarked that he was more handsome than Redford and that, with skilled packaging, he could be a success in politics. The story gained currency, despite being denied by Quayle. To anyone who would listen, Quayle said he didn't see the movie until a few weeks before his election to the Senate. On the balance of evidence, there is no prima facie case for dismissing Quayle's version. But his version was widely ignored; it didn't coincide with the popular conception. Everyone knew Quayle was nothing more than a storefront mannequin. Everyone knew he had been cynically chosen as a running mate to offset Bush's low appeal among female voters. But was everyone right?

The conservative columnist George F. Will had spotted Quayle early on as a senator on the move, and had written dispatches praising the politician's concerns and ideas. But even Will became dismayed by his behaviour during the campaign. Quayle, said the columnist, offered only "itsy-bitsy slivers of ideas... ideological lint."

Will blamed Quayle's coneheaded campaign on his undue reliance upon "handlers." He related the story of Quayle's appearance before a convention in New Orleans. "Jim Baker, Bush's head handler, is in ABC's anchor booth with David Brinkley and Peter Jennings, waiting to be interviewed. ABC's cameras are covering

Quayle's arrival at the Superdome. Baker, off camera, tells Brinkley and Jennings that when Quayle walks past the waiting journalists, he will say. . . and Baker recites virtually syllable for syllable what Quayle does say moments later. The pupil on the short leash gets a gold star."

Given all this, the question posed by the publisher of *Campaigns and Elections* revealed more than a touching naïveté. It also exposed a dangerous, and widespread, misconception about technology. Many people, the publisher included, hold to the innocent view that technologies are merely new tools applied to the same old job. Such people are living in a fool's paradise. Some technologies, admittedly, only make the same old drudgery faster, easier, or simpler. But other technologies change the nature of the job itself. The publisher's question was pointed in the right direction: it just didn't go far enough. As the Quayle example shows, "good campaigning skills" not only make substance unnecessary, they render substance obsolete. With such a self-evident case before him, the publisher ought to have gone further and asked: "Do good political technologies make campaigns unnecessary?"

If by "campaign" we mean the obsolete notion of a contest of ideas, if we mean the struggle between candidates to give voice to the unexpressed groaning of the people, if we mean a rational debate, the answer is yes — political technologies do indeed make campaigns unnecessary. Such campaigns still exist, in dusty civics texts and in the quixotic prose of newspaper editorial writers, but they are seldom fought in modern industrialized democracies.

Which brings up the relevant question about *Campaigns and Elections*. Why is it so popular here, in Canada, among those who make it their business to help others get elected to public office?

AT THE SAME TIME that the United States was choosing its national leader on the basis of whose running mate was prettier, whose salute to the flag snappier, or who looked sillier in the turret of a tank, Canadians were involved in a serious national debate about the future of their country.

Canadians prided themselves on the conduct of their national campaigns, and were naturally proud when *Time* magazine, in its cover story on the northern election, praised Canadians for their electoral conduct. In a comparison titled "How to Have an

Election," *Time* remarked that Canadian election spending was limited to $6.6-million per party, compared with the $140-million cost of an American presidential campaign. It said Canada's leaders "met for six hours in real debates, hurling questions directly at one another," unlike the controlled theatre of the U.S. presidential debates. Canadian voter turnout was seventy-five per cent, compared with just fifty per cent in the U.S.

Canadians could also reflect that their campaigning was less image-conscious. "It is implausible to imagine that anyone like our twenty-seventh President, the multi-chinned, three-hundred pound William Howard Taft, could be put forward as a presidential candidate in today's world," the American scholar Neil Postman wrote in his book *Amusing Ourselves to Death: Public Discourse in the Age of Show Business.* "The shape of a man's body is largely irrelevant to the shape of his ideas. . . ." Quite. But Postman goes on to argue that, in a visual, post-literate culture, television *does* make the body shape relevant to the successful conveyance of ideas.

For some reason, this is not entirely true in Canada. Taft would have no difficulty as a member of Parliament, could quite easily sit as Speaker, and would not find his appearance an insurmountable obstacle in seeking the party leadership. The leader consistently chosen as the most popular by Canadians in 1988 was also the least telegenic. Ed Broadbent, the leader of the New Democratic Party, has eyes that bulge from their bony sockets, sopping lips, and whistling nostrils; it is the face of a benign pit bull terrier. The country's most prominent newsreader on television is balding. The last guy had glasses so thick the neighbourhood kids could have used the lenses as hockey pucks. One of his former colleagues, a respected Parliament Hill reporter, was as fat and pink as a twenty-pound lobster, which put him in the same weight category as the cabinet minister who helped negotiate the free-trade deal with the Americans.

Irregularity of features was commonplace in Canadian public life, and did nothing to detract from the obvious competence of these people in their respective fields. All ranked highly in public esteem and were effective in presenting their ideas, the two elusive grails of the electronic age. This was a source of quiet pride to Canadians; it distinguished their public discourse from the entertainments to the south. It represented one of the many comparative advantages of the Canadian way of doing things.

Canadians would be deluding themselves, however, if they believed the influence of technologies had left their electoral process unchanged. They have merely escaped one, peculiarly American, manifestation of technology — the necessity of resembling a movie star. They have not escaped the technology itself, nor its more sweeping implications.

For one thing, the idea that image is unimportant in Canadian elections is only partially true. While Broadbent was not classically handsome, he was compatible with the medium of television in the sense best understood by Marshall McLuhan. Broadbent had learned to moderate the pedantic pitch and swell of his speaking style, to dress casually well, to appear more comfortable in his own skin — to become a "cool" performer for a "cool" medium. He could be anyone's uncle, or benign employer; his image was reassuring, unspecific, non-threatening.

Turner, though better looking, presented a "hot" image that was wrong for television. Words danced out of him like spit out of a skillet; his gestures were the incoherent flailing of a wrung chicken; his eyes were burning coal tips on the rail line from hell. His image was precise, dagger-like, ominous. Most viewers of the debate had watched enough television to recognize Turner as a potential Mutant Ninja Turtle from Outer Space; at any moment his tight layer of artificial skin could melt away, revealing two red lava pits set in a screaming face of slime. Turner was trapped in his persona, and Canadians weren't entirely comfortable with the idea of his getting out.

Mulroney's image, though very different, was no less a handicap. Mulroney faded into the wallpaper. If Broadbent's image attracted, and Turner's repelled, Mulroney's created a magnetic field of indifference between himself and the viewer. His face, on television, was a blank sheet. Nothing was written on it, and the concern of Canadians was that virtually anything could be.

It could be argued, of course, that all these impressions were misleading. Broadbent had the most activist agenda of the three leaders; in contrast to his soothing image, he planned real change. Turner's behaviour, in the face of repeated attempts to unseat him as party leader, belied his excitable image — he was, in fact, remarkably calm under pressure. And Mulroney's bold decision to introduce a free-trade policy that had defeated previous prime ministers was a sign of determination, not weak-mindedness.

Such an argument makes for interesting after-dinner discussion but has nothing to do with the realities of a campaign — certainly none of the leaders would waste time debating the matter. All recognized the futility of trying to correct the record, compared with the convenience and efficacy of fixing the image. All had taken steps to improve their self-projection — Turner, removing his shoes, prostrating himself and practising deep-breathing exercises; Mulroney, sequestering himself in a hotel room with video cameras to improve his ability to convey sincerity; Broadbent, revamping his wardrobe to appear better suited, so to speak, to the role of prime minister. All recognized the direct link between image and the ability to draw voter support.

Certainly, no one could ignore this link after the 1960 U.S. presidential debate. John F. Kennedy's victory over Richard Nixon was no accident, and had been planned by his advisers from the point of view of style. "The studio was quite warm," a former Kennedy adviser has recalled. "We thought maybe it should be cooled down a little, and we decided not to do that, just leave it the way it is, because Nixon is the kind of person who sweated a lot. And when the debate started it became clear, not only his make-up was bad, but the warmth of the studio was making him sweat a lot." Nixon's haggard appearance, his lack of make-up, his light suit against a light background, his shifting from a bad leg — all combined to yield the seminal lesson in image politics.

But of all the effects campaign technologies have wrought on public discourse, this emphasis on personal image is the least important and the most benign. It is as harmless as an old copy of *Vogue*, though every bit as instructive. Observing that image is important to the modern campaign is rather like commenting on the decline of trench-digging in modern warfare. While it is true that trench-digging is passé, a military historian would be missing the bigger picture if he were to notice only the loss of this skill, without noticing the technological developments that rendered obsolete the whole notion of fixed-front battlefields. Concentrating solely on the importance of image in politics carries the risk of failing to notice the larger issue of how technologies have altered the strategy, conduct, and usefulness of campaigns generally.

THE PRIMARY TECHNOLOGIES employed in a modern election campaign — television, advertising, and public-opinion surveys — have been in use in their present form for about thirty years. The secondary technologies — videotape, satellite transmissions, electronic mail, facsimile telecopiers, the computer — are younger, and have had the effect of enhancing and extending the impact of the earlier ones. Ready access to relatively inexpensive computer hardware and software, for instance, has made possible the overnight monitoring of shifts in public sentiment, as detected in opinion polls. The use of videotape and satellite transmissions — not to mention portable, lightweight cameras — has broadened the reach of television, allowing images to be gathered outside studios and broadcast to the public several times a day. Electronic mail and the facsimile machine have strengthened and speeded up internal party communications. While these later technological innovations all helped to make the "job" of campaigning easier, it was the earlier ones that changed the nature of campaigning itself.

While each of the technologies has an influence deserving of consideration, it was their combined effect that made such a dramatic impact on the 1988 federal election in Canada. Basically, the campaign saw one party — the Progressive Conservatives — bring to perfection a system of campaign management that cyberneticists would describe as a closed feedback loop. The same technologies and the same instincts drove the other parties to attempt the same thing; the Conservatives just did it better. As nearly as is possible in human affairs, they accomplished the creation of the self-sustaining, self-checking, self-fulfilling campaign.

Election campaigns have always required a division of labour between strategy and execution. Strategy formulation can be pictured as a process running from the ground up, from the masses to the party leadership. Campaign execution can be imagined as proceeding from the top down.

In the pre-technological age, the party machine acted as mediator on the strategic side. Election platforms were determined by party manifestoes at annual conventions of delegates who represented the "grassroots" sentiment of the political association. The platform was then incorporated into the theme of a campaign by a platform committee, and reflected in the speeches of the party leader. The leader was responsible, on the execution side, for reflecting this platform back to the people. The leader spoke down to the people; the people spoke up to the leader; the party was the intermediary.

The leader was not in command of both flows; political dialogue depended at the local level on the constituency organization. The riding was responsible for mobilizing and canvassing public support, raising funds, and getting out the vote. This meant the party rank and file possessed much of the information, and therefore wielded much of the clout, during a campaign. "The most important officer in any well-ordered Election Army, other than the Candidate, is the Poll Captain," wrote Senator Arthur Roebuck, advising party workers in 1945. "This is not flattery; it is the literal truth, because it is within your power to poll the vote upon which the success of your Candidate, your party and your Cause depend, and because if you and your associate Captains fail in this, the whole campaign is a failure."

The party leader was unable to monitor the progress of the campaign with the same sensitivity as a poll captain, who had canvassed the vote in his riding and knew with some accuracy its weaknesses and strengths. Similarly, voters did not have as clear a perception of the national leader as of the local candidate, whom they were likelier to have seen or heard for themselves. To a degree, this led to the conduct of separate campaigns, one at the national and the other at the local or regional level. The relative consequence of each to the outcome of the election has always been a matter of debate, but that is not at issue here. The significance of the arrangement was this: once launched, the national campaign was conducted in relative isolation from the voting public. Clues to its progress were provided by the party machine.

The local or regional party apparatus was expected to transmit its information upwards. Given the vagaries of human nature, the size of the enterprise, and the inadequacy of the tools, such communication was rusty; the arrangement did, however, enhance the importance of the local constituency organization. During campaigns, leaders toured the country — first by train, later by air. Part of the purpose of the national leader's tour was to make contact with the local party, in order to gain a sense of "how the campaign is going." The other purpose was to bring the national campaign down to a regional level. The leader sometimes did this by addressing local audiences on matters of national concern. But he also, to an extent that would appear remarkable today, spent time talking to voters about local concerns. His ability to do so usefully depended on the efficiency of the local party, which would brief him before his engagements. In this sense, the national campaign was also "driven" by the party rank and file.

The leader's ability to monitor the progress of a campaign was limited. There was no nightly national television, there were no published polls. Travel was relatively slow — even by air, a journey from Halifax to Toronto could, with stopovers and delays, entail a gruelling twelve or twenty hours. Newspapers arrived days after publication. In this environment, the role of the party in monitoring the effectiveness of the campaign, and in providing tactical advice, was crucial. Organization meant organization on the ground. The party that could provide accurate, timely information from all regions was at a distinct advantage.

A sense of the relative impotence of the party leader, and of his reliance on the party apparatus, is given by Dalton Camp in *Gentlemen, Players, and Politicians*. On February 19, 1957, Camp drafted a campaign strategy memo for the Conservative leader, John Diefenbaker, on the subject of the approaching general election. The memo contained the following passages:

"Newfoundland — They do not think federally and could not reasonably be expected to. . . . They are of course extremely anxious to have the chief or, failing that, a federal member of substance who will stress the federal aspects of politics. . . . The chief's visit in March will have a tonic effect. . . .

"Quebec — Now that Normand is busy again, we shall be getting accurate reports on individual ridings. The Quebec district picture will be much clearer after Perron returns. . . .

"Ontario — We are informed daily as to progress in Ontario through both Harry Willis and Dorothy Downing. . . .

"Saskatchewan — Personal 'on the ground' intelligence has been lacking, but the chief's tour should produce a great deal of helpful information. . . .

"Alberta — Much the same as Saskatchewan. . . .

"British Columbia — When Davie Fulton returns, he will no doubt have a great deal of information for us. You and I have discussed this to-day and are, I believe in mutual agreement as to the need of more extensive conversation with the B.C. members. . . .

"Yukon and North West Territory — We are in remarkably good contact with Erik Nielsen who seems very keen and also reliable."

The idea of a national political party entering a federal election with only a foggy notion of the Quebec situation — until, that is, Normand gets busy and Perron returns — seems somehow rustic. One can only imagine the importance of Normand, Perron, Davie, Dorothy, and Harry to the national campaign.

TELEVISION WAS to spell the death of the party machine as a tool of campaign strategy. Partly this was because television would enhance the role of leader, partly because television compresses time and eliminates distance. Camp had no way of knowing it, but this was the last election in which the Normands and Davies would be quite so important.

Before television's entry into ordinary households, the number of Canadians who had actually seen the national leader was estimated in the tens of thousands. Today, most Canadians "see" the prime minister several times a week. Liberal prime minister Louis Saint-Laurent had won the election in 1953 by touring the country by train, lecturing groups of schoolchildren, and visiting housewives. In a Canadian Press dispatch, he is described as having "refined the whistle-stop art to the point where he could give lessons to Harry S Truman, the old master." J. Murray Beck, in *The Pendulum of Power*, describes Saint-Laurent's habit of stepping down from the train at a time when other politicians used the observation car as their speaking platform: "Instead. . . he preferred to mingle with the people at the station and then deliver a short speech, using a hand microphone hooked up to a loudspeaker on the train platform."

Saint-Laurent, like so many silent stars who could not make the change to the talkies, was unprepared for the introduction of television in 1957. He disliked the new medium, feeling that political broadcasts were contrived and staged, which of course they were. They were also effective, which Saint-Laurent's free-time party political broadcasts were not. In the words of one observer, Saint-Laurent "read his text with scarcely a glance at the camera, and he looked much older than usual." His Conservative opponent, John Diefenbaker, took to television like a moth to a porch light. Diefenbaker was featured in all the broadcasts; he was the young crusader, the energetic champion, the dedicated lawyer.

Compared with party political broadcasts of today, of course, those appearances were dull fare. Before the 1958 Broadcast Act amendments allowed greater flexibility, politicians were prohibited from any dramatization, any dialogue, from anything other than a single-speaker presentation. Diefenbaker's little monologues tended to dwell on the specific and the mundane: "My fellow Canadians, the welfare of agriculture and of the farmers of Canada affects the welfare of all Canadians. . . I ask you to support your local Progressive Conservative candidate. . . to the end that farmers shall receive their fair share of the national income." The language, of course, reflected the literate age — "to the end that farmers shall" does not have the same zip as the post-literate "PC Now!" Still, next to Saint-Laurent, Diefenbaker was electric.

The singular effect of these first political broadcasts on most Canadians was to make them realize there was any opposition to Saint-Laurent at all. Something similar happened in France in 1965. Before that year, Charles de Gaulle denied his opposition access to television entirely, regarding it as a branch of government. Forced by legislation to open the airwaves to all-party political broadcasts, de Gaulle himself refused to participate, instead filling his time slots with a ticking clock. The voters ignored the clock, but were enthralled to see de Gaulle's political opposition for the first time. They denied him a governmental majority.

Those who bewail the advent of television as being somehow anti-democratic should consider this — in its early days, television nearly always worked to the disadvantage of the incumbent, and made changes of government possible. In Canada, France, Great Britain, and the United States, the advent of television brought with it the defeat of long-governing political parties. Even in its infancy, the medium showed its supremacy over the strategic might of the party machine.

Dalton Camp was enthusiastic about the prospective use of television in 1957, limited though it was to a "talking head" on regional networks. He wrote in his campaign memo: "The Prime Minister [Saint-Laurent] does not like the medium. This affords us the opportunity for a certain advantage."

Camp went on to give his reasons for favouring television. Considering that his thoughts were recorded thirty years ago, they were remarkably prescient. "The medium cannot be used to wage an argument and to win one. What it does do is to create an impression, and it is always possible to leave a good impression, whereas it is difficult to leave a message. It is very nearly as simple as this. The question that begs at every occasion of a political television broadcast in the viewer's mind is, 'Do I like and do I trust him?' Speech material and technique of delivery, which answer this question affirmatively, are what we must seek. . . ."

Television, then, had broadened the observation-car platform to include the entire country. In these circumstances, a leader required information appropriate to a larger audience. The content of his message had to change — no longer could he restrict his remarks to foresters in British Columbia, or fishermen in the Atlantic provinces. He was required, more often than not, to speak to national audiences on national concerns.

As the emphasis of campaigning shifted from the local candidate to the national leader, and the leader's emphasis shifted from regional concerns to national ones, a new need developed. Television had not yet created the global village, but it had almost instantly created a national riding. This in turn prompted the need for a national equivalent of the local riding's poll captain. The need was quickly filled by the public-opinion pollster. If, as Roebuck said, "The efficient Poll Captain is a Kingmaker," then the national pollster was king.

THE 1957 ELECTION and Diefenbaker's subsequent landslide victory in 1958 taught the Liberals that the old-fashioned, Saint-Laurent, whistle-stop style of campaigning was poorly suited to the television age. As part of a general overhaul and modernization of party operations, the Liberals looked to the United States, where the pollster Lou Harris had been instrumental in Kennedy's victory over Nixon in 1960. Probably no single decision would have greater impact on Canadian politics in the 1960s and 1970s than the Liberals' decision to draft Harris as an adviser to their 1963 campaign.

Harris, fresh from Kennedy's "board of advisers," was a walking example of the pollster's particular blend of scientific know-how and medieval alchemy. In 1962, at a time when computers were expensive and poorly understood, Harris had convinced CBS Television and IBM to co-operate in an experiment in computer-assisted vote projection. The project cost $250,000, an astronomical sum in those days, and even at that could afford only a small sample of voter intention. Still, according to J. Leonard Reinsch, a Kennedy adviser and mastermind of the 1960 debate: "The computer often correctly predicted the winner — even before the polls closed. That set off a torrent of arguments over whether computer results should be aired. The uproar has continued even to this day. . . ."

Harris polled Canadians and provided his Liberal employers with results that often contradicted both their "gut reaction" and their internal party advice. Although the party had used Lester B. Pearson's international accomplishments as a central part of the Liberal platform, these accomplishments, Harris warned, were regarded by the voters with indifference.

Harris was replaced in 1965 by another American, Oliver Quayle, who was in turn replaced by a young Toronto market researcher. Martin Goldfarb had developed a friendship with a rising Liberal Party strategist, Keith Davey. The relationship between Goldfarb the pollster and Davey the strategist was to be long and fruitful. As Davey has recalled: "There is no secret to winning elections, but too many academic journalists and politicians make it seem complicated. . . . Having determined the best issue, then that becomes the issue of the campaign. Polling is extremely useful in making this determination."

Davey placed the pollster in a position previously occupied by the party machine — between the populace and the leader. Although policy itself was, and still is, generated by party conventions, the choice of which policies to emphasize as election issues had fallen out of the hands of regional party organizers and into the hands of the pollster. Similarly, the pollster replaced the party as tactical adviser in mid-campaign. If a leader wished to "put his ear to the ground," he no longer had to visit a riding or wait for Normand to return; he merely consulted his pollster.

The pollster, then, was in direct competition with the party for the attention of the leader. As David C. Walker observed in *Canadian Parties in Transition*, "In an electoral system that requires an overwhelming amount of work in constituencies covering all corners of the country, political parties have seen themselves as the principal contributors to election victories and have expected, in return, to have a special bond with their leaders. . . . Pollsters enter this partisan arena at a much different level. Their understanding of the political world is based on analysis of voter attitudes and behavioural patterns and not on contacts with the party's rank and file."

Part of the pollsters' success in entering the inner court depended on their methods. Pollsters are a bit like spies; they slip into the general population. They plant questions in people's minds and heed every murmur of praise or grunt of dissatisfaction; then they slide back into the leader's presence, to whisper their findings in his ear. Because they work the shadows of strictest confidentiality, pollsters demand, and nearly always receive, direct access to the party leader.

But the largest part of the pollsters' success grew out of their indisputable usefulness — given the broad reach of political messages in the television age, their advice was, on a national scale, more accurate and more timely than anything generated by the rank and file. Pollsters made it possible for the leader to complete his own loop of information, between himself and the public; the responsibility for the setting of strategy and the monitoring of the campaign thus shifted from an unwieldy "party machine" to a tidy coterie of "backroom boys." Leaders were quick to latch onto this arrangement because it allowed them to consolidate their control over the campaign.

Once the pollsters arrived, the strategic contribution of the party to an election campaign was no longer required. This development had nothing to do with the pride, vanities, or lust of particular leaders; it was an institutional change, not a personal one. Indeed, because it was driven by technology, it took place in spite of the stated intentions of those who, like John Turner, resolved to "democratize" their party operations.

"NO ELITES! NO RAINMAKERS!" cried Turner when, in 1984, he assumed the leadership of the Liberal Party. Turner vowed to return the Liberals to their grassroots, to dismantle the coterie that had assumed control of campaign operations.

For a while it appeared he would succeed. Policy conventions during the next four years produced a host of Liberal promises, which could be carried into an election campaign. These were released on September 28, just three days before the 1988 election was called. They took the form of a forty-point manifesto. Party workers will offer this as evidence of the grassroots renewal of John

Turner; they will say it represents the democratization of the party platform; they will say the party still determines the strategy of the campaign.

When Liberal workers say this about the forty points, ask them to name five of the points. Ask them to name one. And ask them whether the crucial decisions of when to release the platform, whether to release it at once or in stages, and whether ever to refer to it again, weren't still made by the party's small, élite strategy committee.

The committee members were anxious to reassure "old guard" Liberal supporters that the party still maintained a left wing. So the progressive, left-wing platform was adopted. The committee members did not, however, wish to alienate the "soft" Conservative vote that could be lured back if the Liberals stuck to a moderate course. So they released the platform before the campaign, with the intention of striking a reassuring conservative note during the campaign itself. "Since Goldfarb's polling showed that Liberal support was already strongest amongst women, ethnics and people over 35," Senator Michael Kirby recalled in *Election*, "much of the party's campaign would be directed at men, younger Canadians and middle-income earners."

In other words, the Liberals wanted it both ways. They needed a policy platform, but they didn't want it to mean anything in particular, since meaning carries the potential of being understood, and understanding leads to decision, and decisions can go either way. It was the sort of thinking introduced to politics by the television age: as Dalton Camp had so early observed, it is better to leave an impression than a message. Turner himself confirmed this when he released the platform. Though it consisted of forty tangible promises, which could be priced, weighed, and considered, Turner presented it as a platform of "visions and values."

Voters were limited in their ability to digest the policy platform. The package was too thick, and the crush of events would soon preclude any serious analysis. Some reports noted that Turner seemed to have taken a shift to traditional Liberal themes of nationalism and concern for the disadvantaged. Others noted that just one of the items — universal, state-supported daycare — would cost $5-billion, this coming the day after Turner had loudly berated Mulroney for making twelve billion dollars' worth of promises in the Tories' sixty-nine pre-election handouts. In any case, the platform was quickly forgotten. The party leader could point to it when convenient, or never point to it again. How often during the campaign did John Turner affirm his commitment to fifty-per-cent Canadian ownership of the oil-and-gas industry? It was there in the platform; it existed, yet did not exist.

More important than the content of the Liberal platform is what happened to it in the hands of the strategy committee. Clearly, the party no longer spoke from the ground up in establishing which policies to stress in the campaign. This despite Turner's stated intention to restore the grassroots, do away with the rainmakers and the backroom boys. Turner's intentions were good, but had nothing to do with the reality of a modern campaign. When the leader's poll captain — the pollster — listens to the grassroots, he is listening not to the party but to the public at large.

TELEVISION HAD initially given the leader a greatly enhanced image. This higher profile led to the need for better information; the need to control information led in turn to the need for command of strategy. On a scale ranking the relative importance of the party in determining campaign strategy, the New Democrats would place first, the Liberals second, and the Progressive Conservatives a distant third. It is no coincidence that this scale corresponds inversely with the parties' ability to conduct a modern, responsive campaign. On the strategy side, the political party is an anachronism.

But the parties have not disappeared. By the measures of membership and revenues, party participation has never been healthier in Canada — despite a decrease in many of the conventional rewards of partisan activity, such as attention from the leader or patronage. Some commentators have suggested that television now controls agenda and voter turnout at the polls, a notion that led Arthur Schlesinger Jr. to remark: "Television has replaced the political party."

This is, I think, to confuse the effect of a thing with the thing itself. Television did eliminate the usefulness of the party in campaign strategy. Image is power, and the leader needed control of the image. But television did not become the party itself. The party just moved — from the strategic, ground-up side of the system to the executive, top-down side. The party is there, and it is just as crucial to electoral victory. Only now, the party is hiding.

The rise of television and pollsters, while eliminating one function of the political party, created another. Campaigns now had to be coherent. On the lowest level — that of image — ridings had to present the same "face" to the electorate. The viewer was able to travel vicariously with the party leader from place to place, and it was important that the campaign image be consistent. In the late 1960s and early 1970s, all parties began to adopt manuals instructing campaign managers what colours to paint the candidate's poster, which slogan to print on party banners, even where to place the candidate's mug on party materials.

This function, known as constituency servicing, was presented in the form of "assistance" from party headquarters to the scattered ridings. But its purpose was to impose the same visual theme across the country, and it was just one of many forms of discipline the party strategy committees would impose on the rank and file. From a preoccupation with the visual theme — remembering that image is the most superficial indicator of technological change — all parties found it necessary to extend their reach to items of substance, such as campaign technique and policy.

The riding-services package produced by the Liberal Party in 1988 filled a loose-leaf binder four inches thick. Called *Ready, Set, Go!* it included sections on campaign management, budgets and the Elections Act, instructions for the candidate, organizing special events, canvassing, communications, getting out the vote, and how to employ women and youth. Separate inserts told the riding how to find a candidate and how to recruit volunteers, and gave instruction in "demographics and message development," polling, and poll analysis. Finally, it included instructions and samples of the visual theme — an exploding maple leaf in fire red above the word "Liberal," typeset in Goudy extra bold.

No detail is too small for national party headquarters to specify. Beyond providing advice on campaign management, the package instructs candidates on their behaviour: "Dress neatly and do not be too flashy. . . . Have someone observe you and point out any nervous and distracting habits you may have, for example, jingling coins in your pockets, scratching. . . . Avoid doorstep debates, as they are counter-productive." It is not just a matter of dressing the candidate up — he is shown where to go and what to do. Workers are instructed not to disturb homeowners before nine o'clock in the morning or later than nine at night. They are shown the right way of using polls to determine average margins, switch votes, stay-at-homes, and expected performance.

And the Liberal services package was a short piddle compared to the Conservatives'. The Tories ran three-day candidate colleges in Ottawa, hosted by Norman Atkins and known as Norm's Boot Camp. The school gave candidates the motivational boost of an evangelical retreat, the self-confidence of a Dale Carnegie course, and the sales enthusiasm of an Amway convention; all conducted with the forced bonhomie of a gathering of the Moose Lodge. It must have been hell, but it was thorough: "What I liked best was the videos," said one new candidate. "Like the one that showed you how to go door-knocking."

This preoccupation with control extended to thought control as well, or, as the parties like to put it, "policy briefing materials." Each party instructed its candidates on the accepted line on any policy issue; this task fell to the national campaign committee known as "communications." The committee's purpose was to ensure that candidates would all be "singing from the same hymn book," thereby assisting the leader in the delivery of his message to the public. This approach enabled the parties to send forth a homogenized brigade of candidates, or, as the Book of Common Prayer puts it, a "noble army of martyrs."

Party organization, then, had switched from organization on the ground to direction toward the ground — to ensuring that the message determined by the strategy committee would be congruously and dependably reflected in all ridings. If this meant that the conduct of campaigns no longer responded to, or reflected, regional concerns, so be it — this was a necessity imposed by television and polling. If it effectively removed the electorate's access to one important vehicle of dialogue with the leadership — the party — so be it. If it was the first step in the creation of a nation of impotent political voyeurs, well, say hello to politics in the post-literate age.

WHEN CANADA developed its two-way video information system known as Telidon, pundits were quick to envisage the possibility of an established, permanent plebiscite. The joining of television to computer meant that voters could register, from their homes, their reaction to any legislative initiative. The more enthusiastic seers predicted that the technology would render Parliament obsolete. What was the use of the elected representative acting as middleman when the executive could take its orders directly from the electors themselves? Technology would restore the political order to some romantic notion of Athenian democracy, with the entire country a single city and all its citizens legislators.

What these prophets failed to realize is that voting is, in itself, not participatory democracy. It is the final act of democracy, just as sexual communion is the final act of courtship. But the sexual act, stripped of its preamble, quickly loses its meaning. So with the vote. To be denied any participation in the complex give-and-take of policy formulation, and then asked to judge the results, is to be given a choice without meaning. This is precisely what happened with the new, post-literate electoral model.

Although Canadians were able to observe the political process as never before, and although their "vote" was sought regularly through the "plebiscite" of the polls, they found the distance between themselves and the political process increasing. Rather than enjoying a more intimate political dialogue, they found themselves confronted with a hot line to strangers. The technologies did not create an actual dialogue, such as that between a community and its riding association, but the illusion of a dialogue, between everyman and the disconnected electrons of a television image; or between individual voters and the disembodied voices of polling field workers — those individual voters, that is, lucky enough to be polled at all; given the statistical science of polling, very few of us actually have to be listened to. Our chances of being polled in Canada during a campaign are slim indeed. Only about one voter in 15,000 is consulted for each national poll. In short, the ability to communicate does not guarantee that a real conversation will take place — particularly if the new technology means you must talk to those far away, instead of those close at hand.

The public's disenchantment with its electoral irrelevance showed itself during the 1988 campaign in two ways: the quite remarkable rise in non-partisan special-interest groups that sought to circumvent the party political process, and the decline in loyalty among the party rank and file. In their book *Absent Mandate*, the political scientists Harold Clarke, Jane Jenson, Lawrence LeDuc, and John Pammett identify Canadians as "flexible partisans." Only about a third are core supporters of a particular party; for the rest, "party identification does not constitute a highly stable, long-term, psychological tie." Voters will become quite excited by a particular issue or leader, and volunteer their services in support of a campaign, but are just as likely to endorse another party's candidate in the next election: "They often respond swiftly to short-term changes in the political landscape."

This volatility was of great concern to the party leadership. No leader likes to have his future determined by the roller-coaster of public opinion; by the vagaries of whether, on voting day, he happened to be ratcheting up the Matterhorn or plunging over the Drop of Doom. When Keith Davey was the Liberal campaign chairman, the aim of polling was to monitor public opinion accurately on a variety of issues. The strategy team would then attempt to make the focus of the campaign whichever issue was most favourable to the party. His motto was, "Determine the best issue and make it yours."

Allan Gregg, the Conservative pollster, brought a new discipline to polling. He found it was possible to create the issue. "It used to be an election was won by the ability to determine what the question was in the minds of the public," Gregg said. "Now, through the technology of polling and television, it makes it increasingly able to set the question in the mind of the electorate — what they believe they'll be deciding on election day."

This fundamental change in electoral strategy — from sensing the right issue to imbuing any issue with the right meaning — was made possible by the research techniques developed for product marketing. Rather than merely monitoring voter intention, pollsters found they could conduct research — known as psychographics — that unearthed the underlying hopes, fears, and emotions of the public. Product-marketers found their success improved when they appealed to the psychological needs of the consumer; so that, for instance, an automobile could be marketed to represent power and influence to a target audience of young working-class males who possessed neither. Or, as with the Honda Accord, to represent harmony to a target audience whose lives were discordant.

Public-opinion polling had long been able to generate vast amounts of information about voter attitudes and preferences. Allan Gregg's particular genius was to invest these numbers with his own insights. In doing so, he was following the lead of the advertising agencies. "Computers still disgorge vast amounts of research material; the desktop terminal is to an advertising researcher's office what a pot of pencils is to a writer's or art director's," wrote the British journalist Eric Clark in *The Want Makers*, his book about the advertising industry. "But the romance has faded a little; the research pendulum has swung increasingly to trying to find out less about numbers and more about what people want, how they tick — and how to capitalise on it."

This was Gregg's approach precisely, and the meaning behind his remark when he said of politicians, without a hint of humour or irony, "The biggest differences between selling Brian Mulroney and selling soap are that soap doesn't talk and its competitors don't say it's a crock of shit."

THE PROCESS of applying psychographic research was described in 1984 by Joel S. Dubow, the communications-research manager of Coca-Cola. The company, you may recall, engineered a breakthrough in the world of advertising and psychological motivation when it sold a carbonated soft drink as "It." Coca-Cola never bothered to explain what "It" was. That was the inspiration of the campaign. It allowed the consumer to load his own value or meaning onto "It." Whatever "It" the consumer needed, well, Coke was "It."

Dubow, according to Eric Clark's book, described Ivan Pavlov as the "father of modern advertising." Pavlov was a behaviour theorist, and Dubow explained the connection as follows: "Pavlov's unconditioned stimulus was a spray of meat powder which produced salivation. . . . But if you think what Pavlov did, he actually took a neutral object and, by associating it with a meaningful object, made it a symbol of something else; he imbued it with imagery, he gave it added value. And isn't that what we try to do in modern image advertising?"

It is important to remember those three steps. First, the object must be neutral; second, it must be associated with a meaningful object; third, it becomes a symbol for something else. The Coca-Cola man had described, in concise fashion, the three key elements of conducting a modern political campaign. The psychographic research methods shifted the pollster's burden from monitoring public opinion to triggering its responses. Having discovered a pool of sentiment in the populace, the pollster could suggest ways in which an issue could be presented to target that sentiment to the best advantage. His job was no longer unearthing what the question was in the minds of voters; it was in phrasing the question for them.

One corollary of this process was the necessity of stripping political dialogue of intrinsic meaning. It was the first of Pavlov's three steps: take a neutral object. After all, if Coca-Cola were not just a neutral soft drink but rather, say, a highly charged figure such as the Ayatollah Khomeini, it would be harder to market as "It." Political discourse, particularly at election time, tended to become vague and non-specific. So far as possible, the candidate wanted to be "It" rather than the Ayatollah. This was accomplished partly through the avoidance of loaded, meaningful language in the discourse of politics. The desired political climate was a kind of disinterested peace, a happy mindlessness, onto which any desired meaning could later be transcribed.

In the 1984 campaign, the Conservatives ran ads about their leader which said: "He's dedicated himself completely to the job at hand. . . . I like his ideas. . . . He's positive all the time. . . . He's making me proud to be a Canadian." Taken one at a time, these comments are benign pap; in combination they are like mental novocaine laced with Victory Gin. "I like his ideas. . . ." Come on. Brian Mulroney is a likable fellow, great for a laugh and to light up your smoke. He'd be a hit with Bertie Wooster and the crowd at the Drones Club, but Jeeves would probably find his company less than edifying. The last person to quibble with that assessment would be Mulroney himself. "I've always said," Mulroney had always said, "the two great cultural monuments are the Pyramids and the Laval law school library even though I've visited neither." "He's positive all the time." Sure. So is Vanna White. Do you want her to be prime minister? "He's dedicated himself completely to the job at hand." Vanna, too, when she turns the letters, is completely dedicated to the job at hand. "He's making me proud to be a Canadian. . . ." So is Vanna White.

The murder of meaning and comprehension as useful campaign tools was fairly easily accomplished. What followed was the step of endowing essentially neutral concepts such as free trade with meaningful associations. This is where the art of campaigning, in the flickering light of the New World democracies, had taken us by the autumn of 1988. Our arrival at this juncture meant several things. It meant one no longer had to wonder what the backroom boys were up to; one could see on the six o'clock news. Manipulations were necessarily manipulations on a grand scale. Political strategy was conducted under the very noses of the electorate, and the focus of political reporting had shifted from the back room to the living room.

The conditions were set in 1988, possibly for the first time in Canadian politics though certainly not the last, for the management of a bunker campaign. The bunker is a conceptual model only — campaigns offer far too many independent actors, too many unexpected events, too much (in its literal sense) chaos, for any such model to function perfectly. Still, the technologies allowed the party leadership to read the disposition of the electorate; after each day's salvo of media coverage, leader's tour, and advertising, the reading would be taken again. The resulting information would be used to fine-tune the azimuth and range of artillery for the next day's barrage. A party that had all its soldiers in line, that was flexible enough to follow a moving target yet disciplined enough to maintain order in the ranks, would be able to succeed in the campaign's object. The object was not votes. The object was to imbue the exchange with meaning. Wherever the meaning went, the votes were sure to follow. The crucial step, though, was the second one — the loading of meaning onto the neutral object, making it a symbol for something else.

This was where the real struggle for victory in the campaign of 1988 was to be waged. Only one party would succeed in bestowing its meaning, and thus its symbols, on the minds of one hundred monkeys. Only one party would see this meaning and these symbols mysteriously transmitted to the monkeys on all the other islands. The 1988 election, which many agree was about free trade, was an intricate and multi-layered contest about a great many things; but free trade, as we shall see, was not one of them.

CHAPTER 3

# THE WHOLE ELEPHANT

*The real fun is working up hatred*
*between those who say "mass" and*
*those who say "holy communion"*
*when neither party could possibly*
*state the difference between,*
*say, Hooker's doctrine and*
*Thomas Aquinas' . . . .*

C.S. LEWIS

PARLIAMENT IS STILL VIEWED BY many Canadians as a vital microcosm of the nation, a coliseum to which each region sends its single-combat warrior to battle in the cause of truth. Purified by the fire of ideas in the cauldron of the House of Commons, legislation issues forth to the good of the country.

Not quite. In truth, it's the sort of place where Albert Cooper, a Tory backbencher from Alberta first elected in 1980, once sat down in the middle of his own speech. Nobody was listening. He wasn't going to change anybody's mind. Nobody cared. So, in effect, he walked out on himself.

It's the sort of place that led Bill Blaikie, a Manitoba New Democrat first elected in 1979, to reflect: "I think one of the reasons a lot of people run for Parliament is that they feel they have something to say. I always thought that if I could just get to say these things in the House of Commons, that would be significant, it would matter. . . . However, since I have come to Ottawa, every-

45

thing I say is suspect, if it is listened to at all. So there is this incredible frustration. What ought to be the pinnacle of exchange of ideas is in fact the black hole in which nobody listens to anybody."

It's the sort of place that caused Barbara Sparrow, a Conservative MP elected by the voters of Calgary Southwest in 1984, to say, "I am absolutely amazed at how little input private members have into the formulation of legislation, policies, and/or regulations. It appears to me that most of the time we are told what a minister will be announcing in forty-eight hours and we do not have access, any means to study or contribute or change the finished product. But members must go to their constituencies to explain and support the decision of the government. Sometimes this is extremely difficult."

Sparrow's problem was that she still clung to the notion of politics as an exercise directed by the party, through its elected representatives, up to the leader. She had not realized the extent to which the equation had been flipped. The growth and complexity of government had undoubtedly contributed to the disenfranchisement of the MP, but technology had played the major role. The pollster having replaced the caucus as mediator of grassroots opinion, and television having imposed the need for party conformity, parliamentarians were no longer needed to legislate. All they did was legitimate.

And even in this legitimating role, MPs had no independence. They were expected to vote as the party whip directed — unless the party leader were generous enough to call a "free vote." If this restricted the role of the private member on the government side of the House of Commons, it was even worse for opposition backbenchers. They had been reduced, in the language of King James, to "sounding brass and tinkling cymbals."

By the time Brian Mulroney became the eighteenth prime minister of Canada, the concept of "executive federalism" had long since excluded the unwashed masses of parliament from legislative authority. Mulroney found himself with the largest government caucus in Canadian history, most of whom had no role in determining legislation. Since Mulroney knew the devil makes work for idle hands, he decided to endorse the McGrath report, which proposed giving members of parliament new powers.

James McGrath, a former MP, had spent seven months

investigating the role of parliament and proposing how it should be amended. There was a growing gap, as McGrath saw it, between what parliament and its members could do "and what the electorate thinks. . . can be done." Sure, backbenchers still had constituency work — for most of them, acting as unofficial ombudsmen to their communities formed the bulk of their parliamentary duties. But the voters did not seem to understand that parliamentarians had become as redundant as they themselves to the political process.

"Years ago, Parliament was the primary source of legislative initiatives," McGrath wrote in his 1985 report. "Today, the legislative role of Parliament and its members is not to formulate, but, at best, to refine policy." Even at that McGrath was being optimistic. Far from refining anything, the legislative role of most members is to be in their seats when told, to jump to their feet when called, and to keep their mouths shut in between.

"The member that disagrees consistently with the party is often dismissed as a maverick," McGrath said, adding, "the country would be better served if members had more freedom to play an active role in the debate of public policy. . . ."

McGrath sought to turn back the clock, to create a parliament in which private members once again became "instruments through which citizens can contribute to shaping the laws under which they live." To McGrath's mind, "the formulation of legislation used to be a central task for members of parliament, and it must become so once again." In the wake of his report, committees were beefed up; they could be struck to report on specific legislation; they were given increased powers to call witnesses, conduct research, and set off on their own initiatives. All this was intended, in McGrath's words, to "hold the executive accountable."

Fine and ringing sentiments, and they were backed in the report by seventy-eight recommendations. In theory, parliamentary reform was going to bring about a new era: MPs would once again count. In practice, private members were still washed aside by the great issues of the day. If it suited the prime minister on a controversial issue such as hanging or abortion — if the executive did not wish to be accountable for the law — he allowed the private members a "free vote" in the Commons. Otherwise, party discipline was maintained.

Committees that dared instruct the executive on the will

of the House were regarded with suspicion and alarm — the finance committee, for instance, that took the government to task on issues ranging from the tax system to bank service fees. During the 1988 campaign, the committee's independent-minded chairman, Donald Blenkarn, embarrassed the Tories by wondering aloud how much his government was going to increase taxes. The gall!

NO SUCH ROOM for error was allowed the House of Commons Standing Committee on External Affairs and International Trade in its examination of free trade. For one thing, the committee did not even have the full text of the free-trade agreement. It had something called the "elements" of the deal. Witnesses who appeared before the committee, lacking the text, "tended to describe their expectations and worries, rather than take a firm position for or against the agreement," the committee members noted in their report. "Members of all parties found this frustrating at times." Committee members were unanimous in complaining that their function of holding the executive accountable had been stripped.

Nobody had the text of the agreement, but in a way it didn't matter. By the time the committee began its deliberations, the free-trade deal had already been negotiated. Or, in the words of the Conservative committee chairman, William Winegard, "The elements were there and we could not change the elements. Perhaps in the early stages we could have made some recommendations, but by the time we were into cross-country hearings the agreement was pretty well locked up."

Suppose a witness had come forward to object that clause 2014 (a) meant that the Americans had the right to finance anti-government terrorists in Canada in the event of an NDP electoral victory — a sort of Contra Accord. At the outset, there were officials from External Affairs in attendance to note such objections. By the time the hearings began in earnest, however, there was nothing the officials could have done. And even if the committee had included this objection in its report, there was nothing the cabinet could have done. The committee was reduced to preparing a largely meaningless report and putting it on the library shelf.

Winegard said the real purpose of the hearings was to "get the concepts out as quickly as we could"; to "get the debate started, if there was going to be a debate." This role of parliament reduces it to the status of a debating club and is referred to by academics as "manufacturing consent." As a way of accommodating and co-opting special-interest groups affected by legislation, parliament can invite them to speak. This presents the veneer of consultation; if no consensus emerges, the process at least lends a patina of sincerity to the government's avowed concern for the people's opinion.

"The burden of mobilizing consent is placed on post-decision processes," wrote C.E.S. Franks, in his scholarly review, *The Parliament of Canada.* "Here, the government is in the unenviable situation of having to gain support from an uninformed public for policies created in private, in the face of particular interests which stand to lose, and a hostile opposition in parliament. One way of winning consent is to use the techniques of mass communication. . . . But the main forum for mobilizing consent is parliament."

Franks, I think, underestimates the role of mass communications, but he is talking here about routine business rather than an election campaign. He describes the parliamentary process as little more than ceremonial combat. "At the end of the war, bloodied but triumphant, the government has its legislation and the opposition, although it has lost, has fought the good fight. . . . The government victory is acceptable because the game was fought well and hard. The government's willingness to suffer and endure the combat is proof of its sincerity." He adds: "Most times, when a battle is over and the dust settles, an advance has been made towards clarifying and defining national identity and values."

A MONTH AFTER trade representatives of Canada and the United States signed the free-trade agreement, a pale, thin woman strode up the steps of the parliament buildings in Ottawa. She was one of the most influential polemicists Canada had ever produced. Through her writings and her speeches she had doggedly pursued a number of objectives. Primarily, her doctrine concerned itself with the advancement of feminism, the most significant political movement in her country during her lifetime. Because this movement lacked its own political party, she was non-aligned — her influence had been achieved outside the caucus chamber. If forced to sit in a caucus, she would probably have settled most comfortably on the middle left fringe of the NDP. Besides advancing feminism, she had also worked to defeat the enemies of feminism. Her most popular tract to date — a novel called *The Handmaid's Tale* — was a political manifesto attacking the theocratic ambitions of conservative Christians. Her name was Margaret Atwood, and she was a phenomenally successful writer of fiction and poetry.

Atwood had been invited to appear before the Standing Committee on External Affairs and International Trade, and Winegard, the chairman, looked forward to her appearance. "Margaret Atwood is, of course, a very bright gal," he said, adding, rather unnecessarily, that he disagreed with some of her opinions.

Atwood's appearance was part of the committee's deliberations on the free-trade agreement. Free trade had been placed on the committee's agenda as a form of "consultation with Canadians." It was the first of several such exercises — later, another parliamentary committee on free trade would call more witnesses, and the Canadian Senate would have its own deliberations.

Atwood was helping to "define national identity and values." Some of her words would be used by propagandists against the free-trade pact in the coming election; some of her words would be used by those in favour of the agreement. But calling her to testify was no proof of the government's, or anyone's, sincerity. Nothing she said was going to change or in any way affect the agreement. In any case, no one who was listening could change it. Atwood personified the powerless speaking to the helpless.

Still, her appearance did matter, to the country and, more specifically, to the 1988 election campaign. It was the beginning of the process whereby a neutral object — free trade — would be identified with a meaningful one — Margaret Atwood — and so become a symbol for something else. It was the beginning of the marketing of the free-trade debate.

MARGARET ATWOOD'S smile, like a hawk's wing, is polyhedral. It turns sharply up from the centre, up again at the edges. You might be tempted to call it a smirk, but it's too self-aware to convey silly conceit. The smirk part, which is what most people notice, is wrapping paper; the smile underneath is sage, although mildly embarrassed by its wearer. Atwood has the sort of smile that started out awkward but got superior along the way.

She began by refusing to take her seat. "I will stand up," she said, "because I am short." She then equated her appearance before the committee to an earlier experience. "This is about as bad as grade thirteen exams," she said, "because I know I am talking to a group of people whose wives just love my books."

A clever put-down? Maybe Atwood had noticed that most of her audience were Conservative males, and presumably Conservative males don't read, but their wives do, because they are trapped in such awful marriages, and so forth. That would have been a bitter sort of joke, but nothing out of character. Not long after making this appearance, Atwood was the featured attraction at an evening of political theatre known as the Night of Defiance. The evening was held in, of course, Toronto, and featured Canadian writers, singers, actors, and Bob White. The evening started with a staged sword fight between a five-metre-tall Uncle Sam puppet and a little boy waving a sword with "Canada" written on it. (The little boy, of course, won.) Atwood's contribution was to characterize the United States as "Uncle Sam the Rambo Man." According to a Canadian Press report, the audience "erupted into laughter and thunderous applause" when Atwood turned her withering acumen on the prime minister. "He's the kid known as Brian," she said, "a name as we know that's 'brain' with the letters scrambled." Ah, the wit of the Toronto intelligentsia.

Perhaps, though, she didn't mean any of that. Perhaps she was just being light-hearted, because she added: "I also have to tell you that you are getting a speech at the Canadian rate. The English rate is a couple of hundred pounds of British Rail tickets and a very nasty sandwich. The American rate is $5,000 U.S. and airfare and a hotel. The Canadian rate is I pay myself, and you get it for nothing. If this goes through, we are all going to world rates."

Atwood's voice does not rise easily to jest, or to drama, or to emotion of any kind. It is the flat grinding of bones against washboard. Many people confuse her elocution with her smile, and regard her speaking style as a verbal smirk. Her delivery strips the words of adornment. The word is laid, naked and vulnerable, before the audience. Here are the words, the voice says. Listen to the words, because words matter. I'm not going to dance a fandango or kiss your ass. I'm just going to give you these words.

"I am very honoured to have been invited here this evening to engage in a dialogue with you on the extremely important subject of the proposed trade agreement between Canada and the United States," Atwood said. "At the same time, I am puzzled.

From among all the possible people who ought to be given a hearing, why me? I am not an economics expert. . . I am neither a trade-union official, nor a big business executive, nor do I represent farmers or consumer groups. I am one of those unlikely folks, an artist. So what is a nice artist like me doing in a place like this?"

If the question was not rhetorical, Atwood was suffering from the same delusion as the committee: that her words were important to a "dialogue" on free trade. She may, however, have been using the term in its literary sense — in the tradition of Plato's dialogues, or Walter Savage Landor's *Imaginary Conversations*, or André Gide's *Imaginary Interviews*. As a literary device, dialogue is a contrived conversation intended to demonstrate a philosophical or intellectual attitude. In that sense, a nice artist like her was in a place like Ottawa to engage in a totally fanciful conversation intended to give meaning to free trade.

Atwood listed her credentials — "I stand neither to gain nor to lose financially by this agreement. . . I belong to no political party. . . I am pan-Canadian. . . I know what it is like to be poor." (Like most people who say that, she also knows what it is like to be rich.) When she turned her attention to free trade and culture, she had two specific objections: the loss of preferential postal rates for Canadian magazines, and her advocacy of an independent Canadian film-distribution policy. The substance of those two concerns could be found in the text of the agreement, but they were obviously of less interest to Atwood than the panoply of other issues she raised — issues that could be found nowhere in the text of the agreement. Take, for instance, her discourse on the subject of xenophobia.

"As for xenophobia, Canada wrote the book on it," Atwood said. "I do not mean fear of the big bad eagle; I mean fear of each other. I believe this issue has the potential to fragment and destroy the country in a way that nothing else has succeeded in doing — not conscription; not the expansion of the NHL, though that has come close; and not free trade the last two times we considered it.

"If the one million jobs to be lost are lost in Ontario, you are going to see something you have not seen in a long time; an Ontario separatist party that will make the FLQ look like a birthday party. That is not a threat, just a prediction."

INTERESTING IDEA, an Ontario separatist party. This would represent the first oxymoronic revolution since the Great Leap Forward. To most Canadians, it sounds rather like Victorian London becoming swept up in a self-rule movement against the British Empire. From what, one wonders, would Ontario separate? The Orange Lodge? Which representative of colonial rule would the separatists kidnap? Michael Wilson? Which symbols of economic domination would they bomb? The Toronto Dominion Bank?

"I lived on potatoes and hot dogs for sixteen years," Atwood went on, "holding down jobs and writing in left-over time, before I became self-sufficient as a writer. Being poor is no joke. Are the spread-the-wealth social programs we now have going to remain in place, or not? How about medical services? Are we too going to go in for a bleed-to-death-if-you-cannot-pay policy? [This was translated into French by the Commons interpreter as "la politique américaine," but let that pass.] If this agreement makes rich people richer, are we going to rely on the so-called trickle-down effect, which has been such a signal failure south of the border? We don't even have a Guggenheim-and-Rockefeller tradition of philanthropic millionaires, so don't count on it."

In a few sentences, Atwood had based her argument on premises peculiar to the populous manufacturing heartland of southern Ontario. The first premise is that the federal government has an obligation to pass no laws that benefit other regions more than Ontario. Since the government's macroeconomic policies ensure prosperity in Ontario, but not necessarily elsewhere, there is a need for the second premise: that the government has an obligation to help the disadvantaged regions outside Ontario. This logic, while escaping the inhabitants of the outer regions, has a certain pleasing symmetry; it forms the headwaters of the currents of nationalism and social justice that flow so strongly through Canadian public life. Atwood had other worries. She told the committee about her dreams, in which "Dief the Chief . . . appears to me . . . jowls quivering in outrage, and asks me what is going on . . . while Sir John A. Macdonald revolves rapidly in his grave." Perhaps artists have dreams more vivid than those of the ordinary person — it's the price they pay for their art. But Atwood invited the committee members to share in her nightmares of jowl and bone: "Don't ask me, ask them, I say. But ghosts have a way of visiting only those who remember them."

Atwood provided her opinion on the "great star-spangled

Them." John Lennon once said, "Woman is the nigger of the world," and Atwood extended the metaphor: Canada as defenceless woman, the nigger of the north. "Canada as a separate but dominated country has done about as well under the U.S. as women world-wide have done under men. About the only position they have ever adopted toward us, country to country, has been the missionary position, and we were not on the top. I guess that is why the national wisdom vis-à-vis Them has so often taken the form of lying still, keeping your mouth shut, and pretending you like it."

She held out the distinct possibility that, under the free-trade agreement, Canada would end up joining the United States. "If it is Washington making the decisions anyway, why do we not just join them?" But even without formal union, she wondered who would get the better of the deal. "We would like to think we are about to get the best of both worlds, Canadian stability and a more caring society, and American markets; but what if instead we get their crime rate, health programs, and gun laws, and they get our markets — or what is left of them?" Presciently anticipating one possible response to these remarks, she declared, "It is no use saying that this is mere anti-Yank paranoia.

"I would like to close," Atwood said, "with a few hints drawn from folklore, which is the accumulated wisdom of human societies expressed in story form. First, in the folklore of the schoolyard there are big boys and smaller boys. The big boys beat up the smaller ones. No equal exchange is possible, because of the nature of reality. The big boys are big. The smaller boys are smaller. But sometimes a deal is made. The deal usually is give me your marbles and I will not beat you up. Such deals are binding only upon the smaller boys, who lose their marbles."

She reminded the committee that Mercury, the god of exchange and money, is not the god of gifts. "He doesn't make something-for-nothing deals." The other deal-maker is the devil: "He never offers give-aways either. His usual deal is your soul in exchange for the promise of future wealth. But he is even trickier to deal with than Mercury is, because in a typical devil's bargain you end up with neither."

Finally, Atwood turned to a bit of folklore about Canada's national symbol. She could have said that the beaver is industrious, hard-working, and peaceful — but nearly became extinct because of its highly prized fur, which is, well, something like Canada's energy resources. She could have said that beavers make little fortresses of sticks and mud, and the only way to overcome natural beaver protectionism is by breaking up the ice, which is somewhat analogous to the Canadian spirit. She could have said that beavers are of placid disposition and work co-operatively, whereas eagles are aggressive and hunt alone. Any of these beaver facts could have been marshalled in her argument against free trade. The one she chose, however, was a stunner:

"In medieval bestiaries [the beaver] is noted for its habit, when frightened, of biting off its own testicles and offering them to its pursuer. I hope we are not succumbing to some form of that impulse."

As cultural symbols go, this one lacked the resonance to reach deeply into the public consciousness. It was, however, undeniably memorable. It made for great politics. Atwood did not have to wait until it appeared, along with a photo of her polyhedrous smile, in the "People" section of *Maclean's*. Her achievement in lending meaning to the free-trade agreement was confirmed immediately, when Liberal committee member Lloyd Axworthy declared: "If you put this between covers, you would have another best-seller on your hands!"

They waltzed around awhile, each nibbling the other's ear. Axworthy asked her what the American version of the deal meant, the section that said the U.S. "retains the right to redress any adverse commercial effects of any future cultural measures enacted by Canada." Atwood provided the substantive answer: "It could mean if we wear different clothes it is some kind of violation."

Axworthy asked what Canadians thought of the deal, and Atwood replied that she had done some polling of her own. When she asked people if they were in favour of free trade ("which is a positive word, as in free gift, free lunch, free world and free speech"), some people said yes. But when she asked in terms of what it "means" — "if it means you have to give up your health insurance, unemployment benefits and regional development aid. . . if you also have to give up Canada's foreign affairs autonomy and our visibility in arts and entertainment, and if it means the loss of a million jobs with only a vague notion of how they will be replaced, and if it also means we are committed to playing only by the other guy's rules. . . and if it means the disintegration of Canada" — then, gosh, a lot of people said no.

DURING ALL THIS, Clément Côté, the Conservative member for Lac-Saint-Jean, had been quietly boiling in his chair. Côté was a party loyalist — he was soon to relinquish his Commons seat so that a personal friend of the prime minister, Lucien Bouchard, could run for office in a by-election. To sew up the seat, the prime minister of Canada had, in effect, ordered the Royal Canadian Mint to increase production and the Armed Forces fleet of Hercules aircraft to crisscross the riding, spilling fresh $100 bills out the cargo doors. Côté became the instrument of the single most enormous flood of public funds to hit a federal riding in history. The people of Lac-Saint-Jean should erect a statue in his honour.

Côté had strong feelings about the free-trade deal. He liked it. He didn't like some fancy Anglo writer lecturing the Quebec people about what was good for their culture. When he moved in for the kill, though, he crept up on delicate little feet, purring, waving a scented cuff in her direction. "What a pleasant way to end such a long day," he said, "with as charming and competent a witness as you, Madame."

"Thank you, sir."

"You spoke, Madame, of George Bernard Shaw. One day, a very charming actress who wanted a child by him told him: What a child this would be, with your brains and my looks. And Shaw answered: What a terrible monster it would be, with my looks and your brains. I say: What a pity for Canadians and the world that your looks and your brains — both unquestionable, and, I daresay, I hope never questioned — are not put to their best use, in politics.

"This being said, dear Madame, I would find it terribly difficult to imitate your style. As a matter of fact, I would never dare do so . . . . Your brief shows excellent style and content, and yet I can hardly imagine that it comes from you. If I closed my eyes," he said, closing his eyes, "I would feel I was hearing Shirley Carr." At the mention of the strident trade-union leader, Côté shivered slightly. "I would rather not even think of it."

He clicked open the stiletto. "You have read the agreement, of course?"

"We do not have the complete document," Atwood replied. "The agreement is not complete."

"What do you mean by 'not complete'?"

"Is it not true that the lawyers are working on the fine print at this very moment?"

"Yes."

"Well, then, this is not a complete document. . . . Furthermore, there is one version in the U.S. and another in Canada."

"Which version," Côté asked, barely able to contain his delight, "did you use to write this superb brief? The American one or the Canadian one? You certainly used one or the other, if not both, versions."

"Like everyone else in Canada," said Atwood, who lives in downtown Toronto, "I read *The Globe and Mail*. Its editorialists are very much in favour of the agreement. Those of the *Toronto Star* are very much opposed. From time to time, I also read the *Sun* to see what it has to say."

"When you speak of the fine print," Côté persisted, "what are you referring to — *The Globe and Mail*, the *Toronto Star*, or the *Sun*?"

Atwood stirred to object, but Côté continued: "This did not prevent you from saying, 'If the one million jobs to be lost are lost in Ontario, you are going to see something you have not seen in a long time.' I do not know if you have your black cat and your black dress, because we are being. . . ."

"No, no," Atwood interrupted. "I said 'if.' The employment studies are not over yet. There is no way of knowing where the job losses will occur and how many there will be. I got those numbers from *The Globe and Mail*."

"The fine print," said Côté.

He then began to read, slowly and with relish, the section of the abstract that defined a "cultural industry." Even in the abbreviated version, the definition took some time to read. He had just got to the part describing radio communications — "in which the transmissions are intended for direct reception by the general public, including all — " when a Liberal member, Sheila Copps, shouted across the floor: "She does know how to read, Mr. Côté!"

"Yes," Côté replied. "But she did *not* read. That is why I read it for her. Artists who speak to our committee do not do so only for monetary reasons, but also for intellectual ones."

"We know that," Atwood said, exasperated. "I might also point out that I got the telephone call to appear before this committee on Friday evening. That was a little late for me to memorize the accord. I rearranged my life. I sacrificed my five working days between then and now to appear in front of this committee. I don't need a lecture. If I had not come, you would have said I didn't care. You have to realize that it was on Friday evening that I was asked to come here. Nobody sent me this," she added, waving the abstract.

"I think we all realize that," said Bill Blaikie, the New Democrat, "except the idiot across the way."

"The idiots are not always those you think," Côté grunted.

"I don't particularly like being compared with Shirley Carr," Atwood sniffed, a bit later. "I am not affiliated in that way, and I don't really need that. I think it is necessary for artists to keep their consciences unaffiliated in those ways."

She may have been rattled, though, because she turned to Blaikie, a lunch-bucket social democrat from a working-class Winnipeg riding, and said: "Continuez, monsieur, je vous en prie."

Blaikie and Atwood then discussed the question of Quebec culture, over the odd muttered objection from Côté. Atwood dismissed the unqualified support given free trade by Premier Robert Bourassa: "Mr. Bourassa is not the only person in Quebec."

"Mr. Bourassa is not just sort of anybody in Quebec," Blaikie gently pointed out. "Mr. Bourassa is the premier of Quebec."

"Any premier of any province," said Atwood, "is going to try to do the thing that is most likely to get him re-elected."

With that, her appearance was pretty much over. It was left to William Winegard to close the meeting. "I might end by saying I must go home and pick up my marbles," he said, with a glance in Atwood's direction. "I am not sure how I am going to do it with my legs crossed."

NOW THAT was a dirty trick for Côté to pull — referring to the agreement. Any debate about free trade ground to a rapid halt when confined to the actual terms of the agreement. One of the seminal ideas in the agreement was a passage that considered whether closer economic union with the United States would necessarily lead to closer cultural union — whether, in trading with the Americans, we would grow to resemble them more closely. Atwood's brief was largely concerned with that issue. Here is the crux, as set forth in the agreement:

1. Cultural industries. . . are exempt from the provisions of this Agreement.

2. Notwithstanding any other provision of this Agreement, a Party may take measures of equivalent commercial effect in response to actions that would have been inconsistent with this Agreement but for paragraph 1.

As an animating political concept, this passage lacks impact; it is not nearly so gripping, for instance, as the beaver tale. One could not imagine members of the Toronto cultural bourgeoisie taking to the streets with placards, marching and shouting, "No measures of equivalent commercial effect!" Or, "No buts for paragraph one!" After months of deliberations, the best the Conservative majority on the committee could say about the passage was that it changed nothing. "In essence [it] simply preserves the status quo," the committee report said. "Canada can defend and promote its culture and the United States may object to the trade-distorting impact of such activities from time to time."

This reassurance — which grew directly out of the agreement — was neither more nor less credible than Atwood's alarm. It painted the retaliatory action of the United States in terms of a gentle cough from behind the curtain. The U.S. "may object," the committee said, while ignoring the real penalties allowed by the clause, for "measures of equivalent commercial effect." The committee did not surmise what form these measures might take; nor did it imagine whether such measures, over time, could crumble a government's resolve to continue defending its cultural institutions. The committee clung to the belief that the status quo could be maintained while the surrounding environment changed: that the captain's table would remain neatly arranged while the ship sailed into a storm. In other words, the committee did not speculate.

And speculation was necessary to any discussion about free trade: the agreement could not be reasonably discussed on any other terms. It was rather the reverse of the fable about the elephant. In that fable, a group of blind men approach an elephant — one feels the animal's mighty legs, and concludes it is like a tree; another feels its sinewy trunk, and insists it is like a snake; and so on. A sighted man comes on the scene, hears the blind men describe the animal, and laughs at them all: "You silly fools," he says, "it is neither a snake nor a tree — it is an elephant."

"An elephant?" the blind men reply. "What is an elephant?"

"Well," the sighted man explains, "it is something like a snake, except that parts of it are like a tree. . . ."

Unlike the elephant, the Canada-U.S. Free Trade Agreement had no tangible existence. It consisted of words denoting a set of trading principles. Whether the tariff on softwood lumber would be settled was neither here nor there to most people. Such details were merely the bits and pieces of the beast. What people wanted to see was the whole elephant.

But there was no whole elephant.

The elephant wouldn't come into existence unless free trade actually took effect; everyone was describing an imaginary beast from the pieces in their hands. Atwood and Côté were looking at the same pieces, but their imaginations led them to very different constructs of the animal.

This pattern was being repeated across the country, and at exactly the right time. Just as political campaigners were mastering the ability to impose meaning on an issue, along came an issue that could mean anything at all. What better foundation on which to build the manufactured campaign?

SOMETIMES free trade was a pocketbook issue — whether people would benefit from a higher standard of living. Other times it was an environmental issue, or a health-care issue, or a social-program issue. At times, it was just a fun issue, at least for hecklers. Very rarely, though, was free trade a trade issue.

When we look for evidence that the 1988 election was about free trade, and the issues it engenders, we first take in hand the agreement. In the section on defence, which has to do with purchases of defence matériel, we find that much of military procurement is exempted from the deal. One exception is clearly spelled out — Canada and the U.S. will compete freely in defence purchases of pins, needles, sewing kits, flagstaffs, and flagpoles.

This was hardly even mentioned during the campaign.

One prominent critic of the agreement, an Edmonton publisher named Mel Hurtig, said that the free-trade agreement meant the United States could instal nuclear-warhead-tipped intercontinental ballistic missiles on Banks Island, in the Arctic

Ocean. Hurtig also suggested the agreement would lead to the placement of Star Wars launch sites on Baffin Island. I have personally searched through the entire agreement for such a clause, and found it lacking.

This is not to ridicule Hurtig, who was well intentioned. He had long complained that the United States regarded the Canadian north as an extension of its defence perimeter, and he had previously protested assertions of U.S. military strength in the north. When the U.S. navy sent its icebreaker *Polar Sea* through the Northwest Passage, for instance, Hurtig's Council of Canadians demonstrated against the exercise. The U.S. regarded the disputed passage as international waters, and had not sought Canadian permission for the voyage. Hurtig retaliated by having nationalist propaganda and Canadian flags dropped on the icebreaker from an airplane.

This publicity stunt helped arouse Canadian concern about Arctic sovereignty, which led in turn to the government's decision to build a $500-million icebreaker to patrol the surface of northern waters and an $8-billion fleet of nuclear-powered submarines to prowl beneath the ice. Hurtig didn't like the subs, either, but the government saw them as a marked improvement over Canada's existing method of northern defence and assertion of sovereignty — patrols by rifle-toting Inuit on snowmobiles.

This Inuit patrol was sometimes mocked by members of the defence establishment, but the Inuit had advantages. Like the rather more expensive Stealth bomber, they could not be picked up by radar. Admittedly they were no match for a frontal assault by the Americans, or by Canada's northern neighbour, the Soviet Union. To begin with, the 640 members of the patrol were armed with Second World War .303-calibre Lee-Enfield rifles, equipped with bolt action and five-round magazines; 200 rounds of ammunition; and blue baseball caps indicating that they were working for the Canadian government on official sovereignty and defence business. In a firefight, they might expect to meet a Soviet nuclear-powered attack submarine armed with torpedoes and missiles.

An uneven match, but then it's not likely ever to take place. According to defence department scenarios, Soviet submarines would be unwilling to tackle the Inuit directly. Instead, they would probably offload platoons of soldiers from the Soviet Special Assignment Force, or Spetsnaz. Deployed to attack forward air

61

bases, these trained commandos (comparable to the U.S. Delta Force) specialize in guerilla and sabotage work and would be armed with Kalashnikov automatic rifles, Strela 2-M anti-aircraft rocket launchers, 7.62 mm PKTM machine guns, explosives, and the Bic lighter of grenade launchers, the Mukha single-shot (which you use once and throw away). This may seem to weigh heavily against the defenders. Then again, Inuit hunters are crack shots.

There wasn't a word about the Inuit defence force in the free-trade deal, of course, but that didn't exclude the force as a potential subject of debate. Nor was there anything about repro-ductive technologies, but that didn't stop Liberal MP Sheila Copps from suggesting that the deal would turn Canada into a womb reservoir for the United States. Copps said it could reduce Cana-dian women to the degradation of becoming bearers of bastards for rich Americans. Sharpy American lawyers would come north to seduce Canadian women — some poor, some little more than girls — into becoming surrogate mothers for childless American cou-ples. The Canadian "hostess" would then take advantage of Canada's medicare system to deliver the child cheaply in Canada, then send it, duty-free, across the border. An enterprising notion, but entirely outside the terms of the agreement as signed.

Nor was there anything in the agreement to back wide-spread fears that Canada would adopt American gun laws. This was a persistent notion — Jeff Rose, president of the Canadian Union of Public Employees, said the Canadian government had sold out to "carpetbaggers with profits in their nostrils and guns on their hips." I don't know about that. I once threw a softball to Peter Murphy, the U.S. negotiator. He reached up to catch the ball, and I had a clear view of his hips. There were no guns on them. There were love handles, but they weren't in the agreement, either.

Not to say that guns, wombs, and Star Wars are not valid topics in any debate about what sort of country Canada would become under free trade, or that Copps, Rose, and Hurtig were being alarmist in raising them. The remarkable thing is that three such disparate issues could be raised in the name of free trade. Because the agreement had a quality that might be described as talismanic, anything could be raised in the name of free trade.

TALISMANS are neutral objects — a carved piece of wood, a lion's tail, a mask. None possesses, on its own, the power to alter the course of an illness, to ward off evil, or to ensure fertility. But in the minds of superstitious folk who cannot otherwise explain the onset of disease or the failure of crops, these objects become charged agents of good or evil. Vested with these powers, talismans bring order and reason to the chaos of life.

Take, for example, the tiger and the Koran. Tigers represent a real threat in Asia, where the number of human victims of tigers over the past four centuries has averaged about 2,500 a year. This is not in primitive cultures of long ago — tigers pounce on people in rural Asia even today. Police in Riau Province, Sumatra, reported in 1979 that more people were killed by tigers than by other people: Tigers 30, Humans 25. Vietnam veterans reported that tigers scavenged bodies on Indochinese battlefields; some became so emboldened by contact with man that they attacked live soldiers. In a quiet village in the Hpanma Bum region of Burma in 1974, one tiger killed twenty-four people in three days, pouncing from the bushes. Remember this when complaining about the stress of urban life, or of election campaigns.

As a way of coping with tigers, many cultures understood them as "Avengers of the Forest," agents of the supreme being in the punishment of sinners. As Jeffrey McNeely and Paul Spencer Wachtel reported in their book *Soul of the Tiger:* "When one hundred people were killed by tigers near Bengkulu on the southwest coast of Sumatra in 1951, this was seen as the revenge of Allah and not something to blame on the tigers."

Not surprisingly, the same Islam that brought an explanation of the tiger killings also provided a talismanic means of protection. According to a British colonial officer, Lieutenant Colonel A. Locke, if you ask a Malay guide why a tiger always pounces on his human prey from behind, "he will tell you that this is inevitable, because on the forehead of every person is inscribed a verse from the Koran, proclaiming man's superiority over all other creatures. It is this inscription that the tiger cannot face."

This little illustration demonstrates two things: first, that Malay guides should have inscribed verses from the Koran on the backs of their necks, their thighs, places that tigers can get at. And second, that talismans, which usually take the form of natural objects in the pre-literate world, easily adapt to the form of text in the literate world. In the post-literate world, such as ours, they adopt a hybrid nature. Though textually based, the talismans derive their meaning from identification with a non-textual symbol — such as a personality, or an event, or a document.

So it was in the early 1980s that the National Energy Program became, for those in the oil-producing provinces who had never actually read the document, a talisman explaining their sense of alienation. The NEP was almost always identified with "the Trudeau gang and the Ottawa bureaucrats," and viewed as the explanation for the economic recession. Westerners were actually angry with Trudeau, the federal bureaucracy, and the recession — the NEP, which few understood and fewer had read, merely became the talisman of their anger.

So it was in 1982 that the Constitution Act became, for residents of Quebec, a talisman of their frustration with the rest of Canada. And so it was during the 1988 campaign that the Mulroney-Reagan Trade Deal came to represent so much of the public's anxiety and fear — it became a talisman of such monumental proportions — that a great many people actually believed the election amounted to a referendum on the subject.

The talismanic quality of free trade was a source of confusion to those who felt the election really was about free trade, rather than public anxiety. The more churlish opponents of the deal argued after the election that the results gave the government no moral mandate to proceed with the agreement. The government had seized a commanding majority of the elected members, all right, but had done so with slightly less than half the popular vote. More people had voted against free trade, they argued, than had voted for it.

This argument not only betrayed a widespread misconception about the true nature of the campaign, it also displayed a naïveté about the fairness of the Canadian electoral system. Canada elects its legislative members on a first-past-the-post system: votes cast for a losing candidate are worthless. Only two governments since the Second World War have had any "moral right" to govern, those of Diefenbaker in 1958 and Mulroney in 1984. Every other government received less than half the popular vote.

Because the first-past-the-post system discriminates against national third parties (where the protest vote is spread thin), while encouraging regional ones (where the protest vote is concentrated), the New Democratic Party has always "deserved" far more seats than it has won. For most of the twentieth century, the Conservatives have had a "moral right" to about a fifth of the seats from Quebec, where they consistently polled about twenty per cent of the vote — yet in 1984, when they swept the province, only two of their Quebec members had any parliamentary experience.

As a representation of popular will, in other words, the Canadian electoral system is about as fair as a shooting gallery at a carnival. One of those who refrained from arguing that the election result denied the Tories a "moral right" to a mandate was John Turner. Under the "fairer" system, his party would never have formed a post-war majority government.

Turner did say that the election results amounted to a popular vote on free trade, that "the people have decided," and that he would bow to the popular will. In doing so, he was maintaining the myth that the election was about free trade.

In and of itself, the free-trade deal was neutral: a schedule for the removal of tariffs on goods and services traded between sovereign nations. It provided a mechanism, however faulty, to deal with trade disputes. It extended the principle of national treatment — meaning that American firms operating in Canada would be given the same rights and obligations as Canadian firms; and Canadian firms operating in the U.S. would be treated effectively as American firms. These concepts are benign; stripped of speculative inference, they provide neither for the destruction of this nation nor for its guaranteed access to a golden age of prosperity.

Still, during the campaign both Turner and Mulroney repeatedly played the game of inviting critics to read the document. Turner told hecklers, "Read it for yourselves," as if they would find in it the basis for his fears. Mulroney insisted that, if people read it, they would find nothing about social programs, culture, regional development, or language.

Neither leader expected anyone to read the agreement, of course. The invitation was pure demagoguery. The few voters who did read it were disappointed that it had so little to say.

CHAPTER 4

# MILLENNIAL ANXIETY

*Now is the time when the
mid-twentieth-century takes pride
Pompously in its civilization
But what an ominous omen is this?*

YU CH'I-HWAN

T HE VOICE OF COMMERCIAL
radio will be the final comfort in the days of doom. When the
seventh seal is broken and the trumpet sounds, when infinity
cracks and thunder rumbles off the mountains, the moment will
be heralded by the imbecilic chirpiness of a radio announcer:
"Skies rolling up *all over town.* . . . Voice of God, next! Stay tuned
to the Big Nine-Five!"

It's summer, 1988, and Canada's "world-class" city is hot.
Damn hot. Hot and humid. Heat that swells ankles and chafes
necks and drenches waistbands. People breathe in short gulps, like
landed fish. In the ethnic quarters — Toronto's cosy ghettos — the
vegetables droop in defeat; women sit, splay-legged and unashamed, on doorsteps. Shoppers linger in the air-conditioned malls
and stay away from the blistering sidewalks and suffocating closeness of the tiny boutiques along Yorkville. On Bay Street, workers
stay indoors — summer has become as uninviting as winter. The
afternoon transit home is the worst, making enemies of clothes.
Bloated feet are sliced like steamed hot dogs on the uppers of shoes;
men twitch under their shirt collars, which feel like horsehair; and
the women, the wretched women, bound in an iron maiden of

66

nylon from waist to toe, festering, boiling, pray for bare legs and cotton. Headache hot, nausea hot, heat that chained bodies in irons of apathy and clutched thoughts in a vise of indolence. In Toronto the summer heat was inescapable. It was a heat of resentment, a heat of entombment, a heat of fear.

"It's official," said the radio. "Metro's heat wave is the *worst* in history. . . Environment Canada saying today's high beats the old record, set in nineteen twenty-three. . . meanwhile, Metro hospitals reporting *two* dead and another in a coma. . . heat wave continues. . . ."

Out west it was hotter still, loco hot — a dry, windy, dusty heat that made men see visions: sylphs dancing on heads of grain, rocket ships coming out of grain silos — that sort of heat you can climb into and ride to Jerusalem.

"Farmers on the prairies finally getting rain. . . after the worst drought in *fifty* years. . . and it's coming at the *worst possible time*. . . Agriculture Canada reporting thunderstorms coming *right* in the middle of harvest. . . wiping out what *few* crops are left."

"Nearly three thousand Ford workers getting an unexpected holiday today. . . the workers are going home early because it was just *too hot*. . . company spokesmen say they tried *everything*. . . ice, soft drinks, and cold towels. . . before sending people home. . . ."

"That heat wave has most of North America *sweltering*... but it's not the long-awaited *Greenhouse Effect*. . . weather experts say its just a *very* unusual weather pattern. . . but environmentalists warn it's a taste of things to come, unless we clean up that ozone layer. . . ."

"Hot and bothered at Queen's Park. . . the Ontario government's dusting off an emergency plan to deal with the record high temperatures. . . heat wave causing some *very* high pollution ratings. . . the plan *could* force Ontario industries to *shut down*. . . ."

"This just out from Environment Canada. . . and it's bad news for *skiers*. . . higher temperatures will wipe out the Ontario ski industry within fifty years. . . well, who could afford *lift tickets*, anyway. . . ."

"Record-breaking weather also hitting Manitoba. . . seems even the *fish* can't cool off. . . government there saying low water levels and high temperatures are *killing the fish*. . . ." "That drought is going to be expensive. . . figures just out show eight hundred *million* dollars of crops lost in Saskatchewan *alone*. . . that's *twice* as much as the previous record. . . set in the drought of eighty-five. . . ."

"A Washington think-tank saying droughts and high temperatures causing a potential *food shortage*. . . the WorldWatch Institute says the global warming trend will just make things *worse*. . . the institute says the world has a *thin* cushion of food supplies. . . about fifty-four days' worth. . . the think-tank calling it 'the bottom of the bin'. . . ."

It could have been worse. We could have had Chernobyl. As it was, we had Saint-Basile-le-Grand. A fire broke out in a warehouse storing PCBs, and nearly 4,000 people were evacuated from their homes. Images of coiling black clouds — not the quick death of chemical wars, but late-twentieth-century environmental death, slow, undetectable, random — were on the nightly news. Editors across the country had the same demand — get the reaction story, find out if it could happen here. A legion of reporters came back with the answer:

"That PCB scare in Saint-Basile-le-Grand still keeping people out of their homes. . . officials in Metro admit it *could* happen here. . . not to worry though. . . officials add it's *highly* unlikely. . . ."

THERE WAS a dislocated feeling to it all — Toronto was in the midst of an unparalleled economic boom. The market for homes, land, office space, and luxury goods was so overheated it had prompted the Bank of Canada into fears of another round of inflation. The entire country was being forced to pay higher interest rates to curb the material lusts of Toronto.

At the same time, the street people had returned with a vengeance. Bag ladies, teenaged runaways, men sleeping on benches — there seemed more of them than ever before. One hot night on Yonge Street, where respectable citizens of Toronto the Good once walked and shopped, people were jostling and pushing for a decent view. Against a storefront, writhing on the sidewalk, two young women were fighting. They fouled each other in short, breathless curses, pulled hair, punched faces.

But they were not the main attraction. A young man was. He was dressed in a fashion that might be called landfill chic: faded blue jeans torn open in a stepladder pattern, painted black leather jacket, bare midriff, chest covered by a pale blue T-shirt. His bare arms were set off by studded bracelets. Wrapped around one brace-let, and passing through his fist, was a metal chain. At the end of the chain was a pit bull terrier.

The terrier, encouraged by the young man, was tormenting the fighting women. The dog lunged in to bite a thigh, or a heel, and the victim screamed and lashed out at the dog; her attention diverted, she then got the worst of it from the other woman. There was blood — not the quick twelve-pump blood that pools, signal-ling death, but casual blood. The dog divided his attention between the two women. Both were driven to hysteria. The young man could have been a boyfriend, a dealer, a pimp; he gave the impres-sion of being merely a passer-by. He didn't call the women by name or shout invective at them. He just made cussing noises to the dog.

"Another *pit bull* attack. . . police report two women in hospital. . . ."

Torontonians talked incessantly — at catered dinner par-ties, over expense-account lunches, on cellular phones while stuck in the shimmering traffic — about flipping houses, cashing in, getting out. The Canadian Broadcasting Corporation's top-rated radio show, *Morningside*, devoted an hour to the question of whether Toronto was in decay. *Toronto* magazine carried a prom-inent article about the city's malaise, entitling the story "High Anxiety." *Toronto Life* devoted an entire issue to the subject; the cover read, "Are We Screwing Up? — Is the city that works still working?"

If this sense of creeping dread had established itself in, say, Vancouver, the country might have been none the wiser. But Toronto had become the hypothalamus of Canada, its emotions imposed on the country by the limbic system of the CBC, which had stubbornly resisted repeated calls of government commissions to extend its operations outside the Toronto region.

Ninety per cent of the state broadcaster's English-language television programming originated in Toronto. Eleven years ear-lier, a federal commission of inquiry had concluded that the CBC had "failed in its very important responsibility to contribute to the development of national unity." It referred to "cultural apartheid," and noted: "The regions of English Canada, from sea to sea, exist chiefly during the summer vacation." Ten years after that, another federal commission on broadcasting concluded that the CBC "re-

flects reality largely as it is understood in Toronto and Montreal...
[and by] the mainstream élites of Central Canada. As a result,
Westerners, Easterners, Northerners, women, natives, ethnic
groups and minority groups in general feel that Canadian broadcasting neither belongs to them nor reflects them."

But that, in the ubiquitous jargon of Bay Street, was the
downside. The upside is that a Toronto heat wave becomes a
national crisis. Without the Toronto heat wave, everything else —
the prairie drought, the dying fish, the gaping hole in the ozone
layer — would have lost significance. With the heat wave, these
other horrors took on a significance greater than the sum of their
parts.

"WE CALL IT millennial anxiety," said Allan Gregg, the Tory
pollster, in the Toronto offices of Decima Research. "We pick it up
in questions like, 'By 2001, do you think you'll be able to drink
water out of the tap? Will the average family be able to afford a
home? Will we be able to afford medicare? Will you be safe walking
the streets?' The answers are: 'No. No. No. No.'

"People think there's something out there, but they don't
know what it is. They just know there was more change in the last
ten years than in the last fifty, and there's going to be more change
in the next ten years than in the last century."

With a fluid gesture, Gregg bounded from behind his desk
and crashed into a nearby settee. The visitor noticed he was not
wearing trousers. He was wearing shorts.

Allan Gregg can wear anything he likes. Television and
magazine photographs have made many Canadians familiar with
his unconventional appearance — his long hair, which straddles
the border between flowing mane and unkempt scraggle; his ear-
rings, just large enough to be noticed. Successive visits to his office
reveal an equally unorthodox approach to personal attire. One day
he was outfitted in jeans with cowboy boots — by the looks of
them, hand-tooled Tony Lamas in reptile skin with a riding heel,
a genuine dress boot, unlike the silver-toe-capped multi-coloured
eagle-on-the-side poseur boot favoured by Tokyo cowboys. Another time, surprisingly, he wore a business suit.

Gregg can dress any way he likes because he is a genius;
for the same reason, he does not have to work in a regular office.
To most people, a personalized office means one with a picture

70

calendar showing an ape with its head in its hands, captioned: "I hate Mondays." In Gregg's case, a personalized office means that, once you have stepped out of the elevator and through the glass-and-marble lobby, spoken with the attentive and intelligent receptionist, admired the corporate art and the brass lettering, been asked for your preference in coffee and unburdened of your coat — once you have undergone the ritual of entering a big-city big-shot office — you're ushered into a playpen.

Gregg has pictures of professional wrestlers on the walls, a statue of Hulk Hogan on the coffee table, Hulk-O-Mania knick-knacks scattered about. A sound system occupies the better part of one wall. He sits facing it, which may be responsible for the hair loss on his forehead. There are comfy chairs and lots of room for pacing about. Some offices speak of labour, duty, and honour. Gregg's speaks of directed play.

On this day, he was wearing a Hawaiian print short-sleeved shirt in a floral motif, with red shorts. It was hot outside, though he didn't offer the weather as an explanation. If an explanation were required, it was surely the visitor who needed to explain why a suit and tie were considered necessary on such a hot day. Besides, it would have been out of character for Gregg to explain. If he were to show up, dressed in the style of Louis XIV, at a convention of defence contractors, his audience would assume that no one had told them it was a costume party. They, not he, would spend the rest of the evening mumbling embarrassed excuses.

In one of those statistical indexes that magazines nowadays favour as a means of filling their back pages — it may have been *Harper's*, which started the trend — readers were informed that seventy per cent of people who are successes in their chosen careers believe inwardly that they are frauds, and will be found out. Gregg makes his living from this seventy per cent, though he himself belongs to the other thirty. So self-assured is he, so natural in his unnaturalness, that it is never questioned; instead, it causes those in his presence to question themselves. Gregg's appearance is loaded with cultural values and, for an instant, when he meets with a client, the client can't help but reflect.

If the client is young enough to have once dressed like Gregg, he spends a silent moment considering whether he has copped out, compromised his values — whether lack of talent or commitment caused him to stop dressing that way. If the client is old enough to have automatically distrusted people who dressed like Gregg, he must spend a moment deciding whether he is open-minded enough to accept Gregg unconditionally (particularly if he is paying Gregg $25,000 a year for four issues of a public-opinion quarterly).

In either case, a crack of self-doubt has opened in the client which Gregg, by taking on all comers with understanding and acceptance, immediately fills. In this way, the visitor has, within moments of meeting Gregg, undergone a minor catharsis of self-inspection and reconciliation. It is something like the process we go through on finding a police officer or a priest on the doorstep. We end up so relieved, we buy the tickets to the charity ball.

IN MACHINE-GUN fashion, Gregg began to rattle off his assessment of Conservative strengths on the eve of the election call. Overall, the three national parties were close enough to be considered neck-and-neck. The Tories had lost the urban core — the rot there had advanced so far that they would never get it back. Primarily, they had lost the ethnic population of so-called Mediterranean Catholics who had voted Conservative for the first time in 1984. Two other groups were salvageable — the urban blue-collar vote and the well-educated urban/suburban professionals, who tended to be conservative in outlook but regarded the Conservative Party as hicks. The government's bumbling first two years in office had eroded their support. But there was a distinction to be drawn between yuppie men and yuppie women. The women's vote had become polarized in the past four years, with working women and homemakers coming to constitute adversarial groups.

"The difference between the two is stunning, when it comes to so-called women's issues such as abortion and day care," said Gregg. "Basically, women's issues break down by generation and ignorance, with the better-educated and younger population considering themselves as more 'pro-women,' regardless of sex." But the reasons for professional women's distrust of the Conservatives had less to do with ideology than with circumstances. "It is stunning how much working women identify with oppressed groups and minorities," he said. "The reason they don't like the Tories is because Tories court people with money and power, and they don't have money and power. They want credentialization, because they want the system to stop fucking with them. They can't see how that can be done in the absence of credentials."

Gregg was reciting lists, his first step in ordering the universe. The popularity of the list — *The Book of Lists*, the *ROB Magazine* list, the David Letterman list — is further proof that the geometric growth of information requires, in an inverse relationship, its dismemberment from context. The full range of information now accessible to the average person is a feast once reserved for the gods. Unlike the gods, we lack the capacity to digest it; so we absorb what we can, in bits and pieces, and reconstruct our reality in a manner more epidermal, more cross-referenced, more horizontal than our forebears'.

This is called post-modernism, and its voice is ironic. Not only television but the print and audio media, the visual arts, architecture, and literature are all headed willy-nilly down this path of eclectic self-derision. Reflective, internally braced thoughts create in their holders a sense of understanding, assurance, and conceit; which is the way most of us used to think. This tissue of conceit was challenged by the great shocks to Western (read American) culture — the student revolts of 1968, Vietnam, Watergate, Iran, the rise of moral equivalence. The subsequent way of thinking was tentative and externally propped; it reflected a sense of hesitance, paradox, and scepticism. The information bit — one obvious form of presentation is the list — was ideally suited to this way of thinking.

Many recent writers blame the decline in deductive discourse on television, and call for a return to a more "thoughtful" age. These writers are misguided on two counts. First, television did indeed make us accustomed to hearing in sound bites and seeing in sight bites; but it was the computer that made it convenient to think in thought bites. Second, there is no prima facie case that deductive, linear thought is innately superior to the alternatives; indeed, in present circumstances, the inductive reasoning of the post-modernist may be the way to go. It is certainly the way of the intuitive pollster.

IN HIS ESSAY "Hip Deep in Post-Modernism," the Berkeley university professor Todd Gitlin notes that "Post-modern currents run especially strong among [those] born in the 1950s and 1960s. [Gregg was born in 1952.] To grow up post-1960s is an experience of aftermath, privatization, weightlessness; everything has appar-

ently been done. Therefore culture is a process of recycling; everything is juxtaposable to everything else because nothing matters...
Perhaps the ultimate post-modern experience is to shift information bits and computer bytes around the world at will and high speed. . . ."

Little wonder the pollster rose to influence in the age of reconnection; he deals in information bits, which are generated and tabulated by computer. Polling is counting, and computers are counting machines; but poll analysis is thinking, and computers are inept at thinking. They are particularly bad at deductive reasoning. At a conference on artificial intelligence in Rome in 1987, the world's leading cyberneticists gathered to discuss their latest exciting discovery — a computer able to "reason," on its own, that if it were raining, and a newspaper were on the doorstep, and an umbrella were in the foyer, it would make sense to grab the umbrella before going out to get the newspaper. The Italian press, which has a way with such things, heralded the discovery in a banner headline: "Behold! The Million-Dollar Cretin!"

Affordable access to computer technologies made possible routine, extensive national polling, but provided no way of placing the lode of data in a suggestive context. Without an interpreter to make sense of polling data, clients would be left wondering whether the marvellous polling machine were merely a variation on the million-dollar cretin.

What television did for political leadership, then, computers did for polling leadership. In both instances, the technology created a cult of personality. And just as television influenced the way politicians thought, making them less parochial, less tendentious, and more impatient, so the computer affected the way pollsters thought, rendering their analysis less conventional and more spontaneous.

Polling is conducted at its most primitive level in the sort of "voter intent" polls newspapers publish during an election campaign. These polls are of little strategic value to politicians, and no genius is needed to interpret the results. Any harried editor or reporter with a basic grasp of the political situation can expound on the findings. Usually, these "interpretations" are based on nothing more than instinct. A reporter may write that declining Conservative support in Manitoba "follows on the heels of the unpopular federal-government decision to award a jet-fighter maintenance contract to Quebec, even though a Winnipeg contractor submitted a cheaper and technically superior bid."

That may be a perfectly good explanation, or it may be bunkum. Who knows? The poll's findings may simply express, say, rising Liberal sentiment in the province, growing out of, say, the personal popularity of Sharon Carstairs, the provincial leader. Then again, Conservative support may not have dropped at all — these polls, though reasonably accurate at a national level, have a margin of error at the regional level wider than the Canadian Shield. In his effort to pursue sound, deductive reasoning, the reporter has backed up the "scientific" findings of the poll with guesswork. The result is neither fish nor fowl, but it still stinks.

THE WELL-FUNDED pollster avoids such sequential reasoning altogether. He is presented each morning with the overnight "traffic," a pile of paper several inches thick. The pages bear densely typed calculations which reveal underlying sentiments, expressed concerns, and seemingly irrelevant variables. Computer technology, which made this raft of numbers possible, also attempts to provide a path through the maze — formulae for the cross-tabulation of results. Once more than two variables are introduced, however, the exercise becomes rather like trying to view commercial real estate through an electron microscope.

A device called the Kendall formula can tell you, for instance, what a Mediterranean ethnic middle-class woman with no unemployment in the family for the past year (F, ME,M/C,U-N) will think about free trade, compared to the attitude of a "non-ethnic" woman (F, W,M/C,U-N) in similar circumstances. This may be helpful in designing a message to address her concerns. What, though, if Mediterranean ethnics as a bloc view free trade differently from women as a bloc? What if support for free trade increases with income, but remains low among women? What if your numbers include not three but forty such sub-groups, and your client needs to speak to all these constituencies at once?

Because of the manner in which computers present information to the pollster, the pollster must be a non-linear thinker. He must graze on his results, draw cross-inferences, pinpoint the comprehensive thought bite. This thought bite must cover the major overlapping pools of sentiment, must speak to the wide variety of ephemeral and sometimes irrational explanations for events which underlie public opinion. This ability to process the results is what gives the pollster his reputation as part-scientist, part-alchemist; it is what bestows on the pollster his mystique; it is also what allows a pollster his leaps of logic and unlikely juxtapositions.

Gregg was asked who would win the 1988 U.S. presidential election on the basis of voters' architectural preference. That is, if Michael Dukakis looked most at home in the pink-marble lobby of an office tower designed by Michael Graves, and if George Bush were more suited to the Palladian revival of Thomas Jefferson's Monticello, could you predict by that who would win the election?

The question would be laughed at by almost all voters and most political pundits. Gregg, though, snapped open a package of Player Lights, flicked his lighter distractedly with his thumb, and thought it over at length. "I'm not sure," he said, finally. "But it's fascinating."

THE TOP HIT single of the summer of 1988 was Bobby McFerrin's "Don't Worry, Be Happy." Implicit in the song's appeal was not only its optimistic message but its optimism in spite of circumstances: "Into each life must come some trouble; when you worry you make it double; don't worry, be happy." A mantra of cheerfulness recited in the face of foreboding, the lyrics spoke to a broad cultural undercurrent. Again, to quote Todd Gitlin: "The culture [in] favour is a passive adaptation to feeling historically stranded — after the 1960s but before what? Perhaps the Bomb, the void hanging over the horizon, threatening to pulverize everything of value. So be cool. In this light, post-modernism is anticipatory shell shock. It's as if the Bomb has already fallen."

The anxiety of Canadians before the election reflected a curious double-mindedness. They thought their economic circumstances had improved and would continue to improve, yet they looked to the future with grave misgivings. Gregg called their fears millennial because for the first time in a generation people could look forward with some certainty to making it to century's end. The year had seen a thawing of East-West relations, reductions of intermediate-range nuclear weapons, the withdrawal of the great powers from client-state conflicts, and the ousting of dictators in Asia and South-Central America.

Canadians, like the people of all western nations, had

confidence in the world's ability to muddle through another twelve years without a great war or nuclear holocaust. But while their future had been restored to them, it was a future they anticipated with anxiety. Life without the bomb still meant a rapidly deteriorating environment, decaying social structures, reduced economic expectations, and the loss of a sense of personal control over their own lives. They felt they could make it through the future, in other words, if they only had more time.

It was an ironic twist. In 1984, Gregg had helped to steer the Conservatives to victory by isolating the desire for change as the main influence on voting behaviour. The blow of the economic recession of the early 1980s had persuaded Canadians that the existing systems of resolving conflict and encouraging growth were not working, and the Conservative campaign was designed to demonstrate a new approach to government. "The genesis of the eighty-four win," Gregg said, "was in the summer of eighty-two." But the reversal of the recession that had so damaged the Liberals in 1982 would not help the Conservatives in 1988. The economic prosperity of the previous four years was not being credited to the Mulroney government. Instead, like many issues, it was seen as a factor beyond the government's control. It was something happening outside Canada, but something that would not leave Canada unaffected.

That lesson had been memorably learned in the stock market crash of October 1987. Unlike the 1981-82 economic recession, which Canadians had viewed as being at least partly under domestic control, the 1987 crash was clearly the result of world forces. These forces were neither benign nor rational. The world market of real goods and services had been supplanted by a market of future expectations, represented by information bits and computer bytes whizzing among London, New York, and Tokyo. The stock markets represent, theoretically, assets of fundamental worth; but the futures market, which precipitated the crash, represented nothing of intrinsic value; it had no bottom.

Every broker was suckled on the historic tales of the Dutch Tulip Bulb Craze or the South Sea Bubble, when overheated speculative markets drove the value of tulip bulbs or company shares to thousands of times their intrinsic value. No one had imagined the same mass hysteria could hold computers in their grip, but that is exactly what happened in October. The global crash was triggered by computer programs trading on the futures market.

Designed to hedge, or "bracket," the holdings of large portfolio investors, these programs were primed to dump options in a downward market — and so became self-fulfilling vehicles of their programmers' worst fears. No one who was there doubted their role. Peregrine Hodson, a London banker, described the sense of helplessness on the trading-room floor in his book *Crash*: "The screens are red — completely red. No one can get through on the screens. No trades. No one is talking. . . . It's different from how I thought it might be. The market is in free fall, but here in the dealing room there are no wild-eyed figures screaming into telephones, no men in waistcoats with watch-chains sobbing that they are ruined, none of the clichés of stock market catastrophe.

"The numbers flash and blink relentlessly. Minute by minute, tens of millions of pounds are vanishing. Silently. The market has become an alien entity with its own destiny and momentum. We are watching a titanic process which none of us understand; the numbers seem to have a life of their own. I am thinking of a line from a song by Bob Dylan: 'This is what infinity must be like after a while.'"

The sense that economic fortunes were out of the hands not only of the Canadian government but of all sentient life-forms made it difficult for the Tories to bask in Canada's economic recovery. "In the same way we're not getting credit," said Gregg, "we're not getting the blame, either. What people are willing to buy is the fairly traditional Conservative understanding that governments do not create wealth; that governments create deficits and higher taxes. The scandal and corruption issues had led to a sense of profligacy in government."

BEFORE THE prime minister abandoned the news conference as a means of communication (Brian Mulroney has not, at the time of writing, held a formal Ottawa news conference in two-and-a-half years), his claims of creating a thousand jobs a day, reducing interest rates to manageable levels, keeping inflation in check, and curbing the growth of the federal deficit were met with laughter. Literally. It was an unusual sight — the leader of a western industrialized nation reciting the economic indicators while members of the nation's press groaned and chuckled and waited for a chance to ask the important stuff, like the size of the leader's clothes closet and whether he was a liar. Between 1984 and 1988 Canadians had, according to Gregg's polls, come to fundamentally change their view of the government's role in their lives. On most "top-of-mind" issues — those that preoccupy the electorate — the government seemed unable to alter the course of events. "People now understand the international factors," Gregg said. "There's a growing cynicism about government, and a realization that there is no quick fix."

Because Gregg had picked up this cynicism, and because he found free trade less appealing among the so-called "protect-me" list of voters (women, the poor, youth), the decision was taken to portray Mulroney in the 1988 campaign as one who would protect citizens from the worst effects of change. Although change in itself could not be stopped, and millennial anxiety would not be put to rest, an effort would be made to tag the Conservative leader with the reassuring label of "manager of change."

This initial strategy turned out, in retrospect, to have been a colossal error. It cast the prime minister in a low-key, tech-nocratic role, completely unsuited to the election. It had the effect of reminding people of their own worst fear — change — rather than reassuring them about the security of management. Worst of all, it was an inappropriate response to what Gregg himself knew to be the crucial question of the campaign.

"We track many questions," he said, "and eventually you come across the key variable." In 1984, he had found that the key variable was the need for change — not change of policy, but change of process. This led to Gregg's inspired decision to alter the original 1984 campaign theme: "Together, we can be better." Canadians felt there was nothing wrong with who they were; and the idea of "being" different may have unsettled them. The slogan was changed to: "Together, we can do better." This one-word amend-ment was the underpinning of Mulroney's hugely successful 1984 campaign.

Gregg, who was already speaking on condition that none of what he said would appear until after the election, made his listener swear that what was to come was really serious, cross-your-heart, off-the-record stuff. Satisfied, he said: "The key vari-able in 1988 is the question, 'Do you believe there are major, minor, or no real differences between the three major political parties in Canada?'" The party that could claim distinction, he believed, was the party that could win. But the distinction was to be drawn on the lines not of policy but of personality.

"People are evaluating leadership on completely different criteria," he said. "They recognize that politicians aren't deities, and that there's no quick fix. So their evaluation has gone from performance to motive — never mind what he will do, *why* will he do it? This is what people found so difficult with Mulroney. His problem, particularly in the '84 to '86 period, was not so much that he was 'Lyin' Brian,' but that he was a caricature of the stereotypical politician. The problem wasn't that he wasn't telling the truth. The problem was that he was telling us what we wanted to hear."

In Gregg's work with focus groups — gatherings of a half-dozen to a dozen representative voters — he had uncovered a surprising depth of cynicism about political leadership. He had also found an unexpected sophistication. "We get them in here and show them videos, news clips, question period," he said. "Their universal reaction is, 'Oh, his pollster told him to say that,' or, 'His image-maker dressed him like that.' It's all phony to them. The only thing they like is Broadbent's brown rumpled suits — they say it shows he cares more about issues than image. Isn't that incredible? And they love the scrums, because they're spontaneous. They love to see the politician cornered, questioned, sweating. What they're looking for is what I call the glimpse of the soul."

Gregg then condensed all this into his thought bite for the campaign: "The watchwords for the politician of the nineteen-nineties," he said, "are spontaneity, emotion, and motive."

This, Gregg reasoned, should have dictated how Mulroney played the free-trade issue. "Free trade has been very important in turning around Tory fortunes, especially assessments about Mulroney. People still have no personal frame of reference for free trade. What free trade has done is, first, provide evidence that there is maybe a different vision of the country available — a dividing line between the parties.

"But for Mulroney, in particular, there's a notion that he is the proprietor of this vision and is prepared to be unpopular and suffer negative criticism for it. I've been telling the Tories for ten months that free trade is a peg on which to hang other stuff. Brian's problem is not that he's a bad man, but that they can't get any measure of the man. Well, they can measure him on this."

Mulroney's best friends feared the moments when, as they

put it, he "took the glasses off" — when he removed his bifocals and deviated from his prepared text to deliver a spirited and partisan attack on the opposition. His friends were urging him to keep the glasses on, to run a statesmanlike campaign, to avoid rhetoric and cheap shots. But with free trade providing the "motive," Gregg reasoned, Mulroney could take the glasses off "in a very compelling kind of way."

ON OCTOBER 1, 1988, Brian Mulroney stood on the steps of Rideau Hall to make an announcement. Rideau Hall is the residence of the governor general, who remains neutral during elections and who calls on the winner to form a government. By appropriating the Queen's Canadian residence for his campaign launch, Mulroney was setting a precedent. Still, it was not nearly so bad as people imagined — he did not ask the chief justice to stand over one shoulder, after all, and the chief of the Defence Staff to appear over the other, as is done in "democratic" elections in Central America. Mulroney stood behind a lectern adorned with the Canadian coat of arms and read from a prepared text. He left his glasses on.

"It has been the Canadian tradition to call an election after a government has completed four years of a mandate," he said. "More importantly, we are at a point where the differences between our political parties require the judgement and decision of Canadians. Those differences are clear and substantial. The decisions Canadians face on November twenty-first will make a difference."

Gregg's prescription for seizing the campaign momentum — by distinguishing the Tories through the statement of a clear motive — had just barely crept into the opening statement. What's more, the expression of motive had been undermined by Mulroney's reference to the four years, as if the election were as automatic and routine as a Yellowstone geyser. Mulroney had submerged his personality in a fog of reassuring manageableness; it was a mistake as costly as Ed Broadbent's failure, on opening day, to utter the words "free trade."

"The key question for the electorate will be who can best manage change in the years ahead," Mulroney went on. "We intend to run on our record of the past and our plan for the future."

Managing change 1, Motive 0.

"Four years ago we inherited a Canada scarred by economic

recession and divided by mistrust among the major partners of our federation. Today we have an economy that is a world leader in growth and in job creation — almost a thousand new jobs per day for every day we have served in government."

There was, mercifully, no laughter from members of the media.

"We see a country and a world changing before us and we are determined to respond positively and aggressively to that change. The last four years leave us with absolutely no doubt that Canadians can meet these changes. We stand for liberalized trade because it is the key to future growth and prosperity. The free-trade agreement with the United States will mean enlarged opportunity for our producers and businesses, more and better jobs for Canadians, especially our youth, and higher living standards for our people."

Oops. Mulroney had just linked free trade with the economy, rather than with Mulroney. The prime minister was in the process of neutering himself. He used the first person just once: "my colleagues and I." The rest was all the regal "we," the party "we," the "non-I."

Managing change 4, Motive 0.

"We know that people, not governments, create wealth. We stand for social economic management that will encourage Canadians to grow and prosper, not frustrate them through over-spending and over-regulation. . . ." This was followed by a few words about child care, the environment, and "collective action and security."

"Ours is, above all, an agenda of confidence for Canada. It builds on our successes of the past four years — and on the lessons and values of our history. It is a coherent plan for the future which says, first and foremost, that Canadians can shape change to their benefit and their prosperity."

Not exactly the glimpse of the soul that Allan Gregg knew Canadian voters wanted to see in their political leaders.

Managing change 8, Motive 0.

Meanwhile, at the news that Mulroney had seized the royal quarters and called the election, the other parties sprang into action. Both Turner and Broadbent rushed off to staged pseudo-events. Pseudo-events are things that seem to happen but don't. They are produced for the television cameras and the reporters, who treat the pseudo-event as if it actually occurred.

Ed Broadbent dropped his suit jacket, grabbed his wife, Lucille, and rushed over to Ottawa's open-air Byward Market. He shook hands with "ordinary" fruit and vegetable vendors. He wasn't really campaigning in the Byward Market, of course, he was campaigning on television. Actors playing the part of "ordinary" fruit and vegetable vendors would have been more reliable, since one vendor, having just shaken Broadbent's hand, announced he was going home to wash.

In Toronto, Turner had a similar idea. He grabbed his wife, Geills, and two of their four children, Elizabeth and David, and dashed off to the Cafe Manna in Kensington Market. Together they wandered through narrow streets and crowded Italian and Chinese groceterias, a charming family out among the people. For Geills, it was the finest pseudo-event since the day she arrived at a food bank and pulled her donations of tinned goods from a Creed's shopping bag.

Some glimpses. Some souls.

# CHAPTER 5

# A Bit of Cleaning Up

*The choice of his ministers is of no
slight importance to a prince; they are
either good or not, according as the
prince himself is sagacious or
otherwise; and upon the character of
the persons with whom a prince
surrounds himself depends the first
impression that is formed of his
own ability.*

NICCOLÒ MACHIAVELLI

O NE OF THE FIRST HURDLES
Brian Mulroney faced in seeking re-election was his immediate
past. He needed to divorce himself from it. During four years in
office, the prime minister had lost no fewer than eight cabinet
ministers to resignation. His government had gained the reputation of being scandal-ridden; while he could not eliminate the
scandal, he could eliminate the reputation.

The resignations were the culmination of follies one might
expect from a party long excluded from office: incompetence, poor
judgement, and greed. One casualty was a defence minister, Robert
Coates, who had travelled to West Germany on military business.
After a meal in his honour at the officers' mess, he had retired to
bed. Sometime later, his fifty-six-year-old juices prompted him to
visit a nearby establishment. His departure was brought to the
attention of the base commander by a sentry. The sentry had orders

to stop people from breaking into the defence minister's room; he had no idea what to do in the event the minister broke out. The base commander demanded his car and driver, but was told the minister had already borrowed them. The minister was tracked to a club called Tiffany's. There he watched a German national with purple hair and the unlikely name of Mickey O'Rourke perform her interpretation of "Fantasia in White." Afterwards they discussed certain matters.

Another scandal involved a fisheries minister, John Fraser, who, following a plea from a New Brunswick cannery, allowed rancid tuna to be sold to the public. At this point in Mulroney's first term in office, things were still reasonably light-hearted. A "Tunagate" game was produced, the objective being to become prime minister by not getting caught with tuna unless you had the "Queen of Excuses" in your hand. A Halifax reporter, covering the prime minister's 1986 tour of Asia, went the entire route wearing a gag baseball cap. The prime minister finally noticed, while scaling the Great Wall of China, that the reporter's cap had a sorry-looking cloth fish on top. Its fins, tail, and mouth poked from all sides; hanging from its mouth was a little sign that said, "Tuna." The reporter was told, as a practical joke, that the prime minister was furious with him for spoiling the Great Wall photo opportunity.

The highlight of the Mulroney Asia Tour, however, went unreported in the Canadian media. It came after the stroll along the Great Wall, when the Mulroneys were preparing to step into their black limousine. Owing to the inefficiency of their Chinese hosts, the prime minister and his wife were not as isolated from reporters as usual. Making conversation, one asked: "So, what did you think of the Great Wall, Mrs. Mulroney?"

Mila looked back at the wall. Dusk was gathering, and the buff-coloured stone picked up the sunlight. The wall stretched further than the eye could see, and reached back further than the mind could imagine. Mila crinkled her nose in disappointment. "I thought it was going to be bigger than that," she said. "I just assumed it was going to be larger."

She had a point. The portion of the wall she visited was narrow — in some places no wider than a chariot — and no higher than 24 Sussex Drive. In the popular mind, the wall *is* larger than in reality. Mila's husband, who had spent his time on the wall joking about what a great make-work project it must have been — and hey, could you imagine one of these across Saskatchewan? — cast a quick glance at the reporter's tape recorder. It was rolling. Mulroney realized that his wife had just insulted six hundred million Chinese. He placed a gentle hand over Mila's shoulder, gesturing toward the wall. His head remained cocked in the direction of the open mike. He said that, yes, it was smaller than imagined, but width wasn't everything. It went on ever so far, which made it special. "Look at it from down here, Mila. It's not the width, but the incredible length of it." He said several other nice things about the wall. And then, diving into the back of the limo, he turned to the reporters and said, "I'll see you tonight."

As the reporters strode back to the press bus, one said: "You realize what we've got here, don't you? The Mulroney Bedroom Tapes." He went to work flicking dials, deleting and editing, and by the time he boarded the press bus, he was ready. The edited exchange went something like this:

MILA: "I thought it was going to be bigger than that."

BRIAN: "Ahh. . ."

MILA: "I just assumed it was going to be larger."

BRIAN: "I suppose. . . the photographs do tend to make it appear larger. However, you get a different perspective standing right next to it. Look at it from down here, Mila. It's not the width, but the incredible length of it. . . The symmetry, the beauty of its construction. It's truly one of the wonders of the world."

MILA: "Oh. . ."

BRIAN: "I'll see you tonight."

ANOTHER OF MULRONEY'S ministers, Suzanne Blais-Grenier, quit after it was revealed that she had taken the grand tour of Europe at the taxpayers' expense, attending the odd official function to make it appear a working trip. A sad and spiteful figure, she later retaliated with allegations of widespread corruption. Another minister, Roch LaSalle, quit after stumbling on the discovery he could charge people to meet with him; at one meeting, businessmen who paid $5,000 to attend were told they would be "on the train" for government contracts. Another minister, André Bissonnette, resigned after being charged in a land-flip scheme so complicated few people understood it; he was later cleared, but the damage was done. Another, Marcel Masse, resigned and returned, this time after being exonerated of breaking the limits on election spending. Another, Sinclair Stevens, was found to have violated conflict-of-interest guidelines no fewer than fourteen times. Yet another, Michel Côté, was fired because he forgot to declare a personal loan. There was no evidence of impropriety surrounding the loan — he simply forgot.

Has a more melancholy group of underachievers in larceny been assembled since governments began?

Still, the prime minister, entering the election, had a problem with what was known as the sleaze factor. In truth, the problem had less to do with the behaviour of his ministers than with his own failure to deliver on promises to clean up patronage. Mulroney had campaigned in 1984 on a platform of changing not the government's policies but its management, process, and attitudes. "This country desperately wants genuine, profound, attitudinal change," Mulroney had said in 1984. When, just before the 1984 campaign, John Turner appointed a slate of Liberal MPs to lucrative patronage positions, Mulroney had seized on the blunder. He had used it as an illustration of Turner's weakness, of his obligations to the Liberal Party old guard; as his forfeit of any chance to distinguish himself from the practices of the Trudeau government. Mulroney did this brilliantly during an exchange in a nationally televised debate, and it became the seminal moment of the 1984 election campaign.

Within weeks of his own swearing-in, however, Mulroney began a patronage process as inevitable for a party long out of meaningful office as the bumbling of its cabinet. In six months he made a thousand order-in-council appointments to government boards and agencies, largely replacing Liberals with people who had faithfully served the Conservative Party. The task was undertaken with typical Conservative Party efficiency — a computer was installed in the appointments office, and the names of prospective nominees were kept on a data base. The computer kept track of the 3,800 jobs controlled by the prime minister and his cabinet; it gave ninety days' warning of pending vacancies and listed suitable nominees. A political advisory committee then chose names for the prime minister to pick from. This growth industry spawned another: in office towers around Ottawa, new businesses were established that sold the "service" of government relations — some of these lobbyists had few tangible assets other than their personal rapport and influence with ministers and their aides.

Mulroney's promise to abolish the "old ways" of the Liberal Party had been made in the heat of a campaign; it reflected the advice of his pollster rather than a genuine desire for change. His government soon became so identified with cronyism, however, that he was prompted to alter his own powers of patronage. Some changes were cosmetic, such as the appointment of meritorious non-Tories to positions in the Supreme Court, the Senate, and the United Nations. Others were institutional. The rules of parliamentary procedure were altered so that prospective order-in-council appointees could be reviewed by committee. Although the committee lacked the power, as in the United States, to turn down a nominee, its recommendation against an incompetent applicant could make the appointment embarrassing for the government. A bill was passed to require lobbyists to register their names, their clients' names, and the issues being lobbied. This information would not be made public, but would be available to parliament.

Finally, the Mulroney government had introduced regulations to limit conflict of interest. The bill would have obliged government members and their families to list their holdings with an independent commission. The commission would have had extensive powers to disclose those assets, launch an investigation or pronounce a member clean. This act, alas, had not passed when the election was called; the Liberal-dominated Senate could have cleared the way for its passage, say many senators, if it had had just one more day.

BRIAN MULRONEY had raised public expectations about bringing merit and open competition to government operations. There was truth in the assertion that he had dashed these expectations; there was also truth in the assertion that he had tried to meet them. What Mulroney had never done was explain his actions in a sensible, coherent manner. He never said: "Patronage is a fact of life in our political system. It motivates the party apparatus and rewards those who make genuine sacrifices, in career and income, by becoming involved in public life. It ensures that the philosophies and manifesto of a political party are reflected in the decisions of its government agencies. It is important to have competent people appointed to these posts, but there are many competent people within the Conservative Party. We have provided a mechanism for reviewing these people, and if any are found to be unfit, we will find better Conservatives to take their places."

Instead, Mulroney attempted to persuade the public that he had moved away from the notion of giving Conservatives any special privilege at all. At times he spoke as if he wielded his discretionary powers in the interests of pay equity and affirmative action. "We moved immediately to double the number of women who were appointed to agencies, boards and commissions," he said. "We doubled the number of multicultural representatives . . . we increased by seventy per cent the number of women in federal judicial positions." Doubtless true, but what about the woman who entered the Senate on the strength of being the widow of a former provincial Conservative leader? Or the woman appointed to Telefilm Canada on the strength of having been a hostess at Mulroney's favourite fishing lodge?

"I believe it is fair to say that I appointed more members of the NDP and more members of the Liberals, more members of the Parti Québécois, the Parti Créditiste, the Parti Libéral Provincial than any other prime minister in history," said Mulroney. "And I am proud of that." He did not mention that he also appointed more 1963 graduates of the Laval Law School — his alma mater — than any other prime minister in history. That class must have been an extraordinary lot, other things being equal, to have included one future principal secretary to the prime minister, two senators, one ambassador to Paris (later a cabinet minister), and a senior policy adviser. Mulroney was proud of the other appointments; was he ashamed of these, or merely forgetful?

The "old ways" Mulroney had railed against to such advantage in the 1984 campaign included the Liberal cabinet's decision to push through 225 appointments during its last month in power. Mulroney, in the words of a newspaper of the day, was "the soul of piety and affronted honour." He condemned this last cynical grasp at the few remaining spoils of power as yet more evidence of the cancer that had riddled the Liberal cabinet. But he himself had been unable to put the disease in remission. In the four weeks before the 1988 election, his cabinet authorized 352 cabinet appointments.

Not all these appointments went to Conservative supporters. Of the thirty-five diplomatic postings, only four were political appointments. A further two dozen were non-partisan senior public servants, whose appointments were routine. Fully a quarter were simple reappointments of earlier recipients whose terms were nearing completion. More than a hundred were made to boards that would decide the future of foreigners claiming to be legitimate refugees seeking haven in Canada. A large number of these — Mulroney himself claimed no more than half — were members of visible minorities with no political connections. Among the others, however, could be found a former Mulroney aide; the wife of another former aide; a party fundraiser; and an actress who was a close friend of the prime minister's wife.

HIS FINGERS still numb from signing this flood of appointments, Mulroney entered the campaign needing to persuade voters he had reformed his ways. He was being strongly urged by his pollster, Allan Gregg, and others, that such a posture would be credible only if he were contrite, admitting that mistakes had been made and seeking the forgiveness of the electorate. Gregg said an admission of error was a "bare minimum." Merely pointing to parliamentary reforms and non-partisan appointments would fail to convince the electorate. In other areas, such as stewardship of the economy and federal-provincial relations, the public was willing to be convinced by results. These areas did not impugn Mulroney's trustworthiness. But in the matter of clean government, people wanted a demonstration of changed motive.

Mulroney was given the opportunity to apologize by the CBC television correspondent David Halton during the national debate in October. "I would like to start, Mr. Mulroney, by taking you back to those electrifying moments in the 1984 debate when you demanded an apology from Mr. Turner for making what you called those horrible patronage appointments. You promised to clean up the sleazy patronage habits of the Liberals. But once in office, you proceeded very quickly to start naming hundreds and hundreds of Tories to plum positions across this country. Sure, you also appointed some very high-profile Canadians from other parties. We know the list. But, surely, you have misled Canadians in promising them a new political morality in Canada and practising very much the old one?"

It was as clean and pertinent a question as any asked of a politician, and it opened the way for Mulroney to demonstrate the glimpse of the soul that Gregg insisted was so important.

"Mr. Halton, you are right," Mulroney replied, and for a moment it appeared he was about to ask pardon. But all he meant was, you were right about my making a damn fine showing in the last debate. "It was an electrifying moment, and I think one whose impact in terms of patronage and conflict of interest, uh" — the response was taking him down a trail he did not want to venture on, so he ended with a non sequitur — "which is a new reality for all Canadians, all of us."

The prime minister seemed to argue that corruption was not a problem, but that the public discovery of corruption was. "Access to information in 1984-1985 has impacted on all governments." Finally, he attempted to whiten his own wash by pointing at the soiled laundry of others: "The Peterson government of Ontario lost a number of ministers through conflict of interest; even the Bourassa government in Quebec, and the government of British Columbia."

Hardly the stuff of which great souls are made, and not the sort of glimpse Allan Gregg was recommending. Finally, though, Mulroney did eat crow: "These were realities that intruded upon our lives and I acknowledge, uh, as I have in the past, that I, as prime minister, did not, in 1984, uh, do as well as I should have in terms of moving more swiftly to de-politicize the appointments of what are called governor in council appointments."

That crow was possibly the smallest and toughest bird that ever lived. Nonetheless, Mulroney succeeded in what he had set out to do — not apologize, but settle the problem squarely in the past, "in 1984," when a regrettable crush of other matters prevented him from moving "more swiftly" to deal with a complex issue.

But the problem was not in the past; it continued to exist, up to and after the dropping of the writ. Governor in council appointments had not been "de-politicized," and never would be, unless they were taken out of the prime minister's hands. He hadn't moved less "swiftly" than he should have — he hadn't moved at all. He had merely replaced Tories with non-Tories in the awarding of some lucrative patronage plums. The motive remained partisan. A certain number of jobs that might have contributed to party loyalty had been sacrificed; they were now in the service of restoring the prime minister's credibility. When that political need no longer existed, they would revert back to party loyalists.

The problem was less one of reality than of image. And it was in the interests of image, at the outset of his national campaign, that Mulroney killed Sinclair Stevens.

THE EXECUTION was swift and unexpected. Stevens and his wife, Noreen, were driving in the newer of their cars, an Oldsmobile Cutlass, to a constituent's home for lunch. The cellular phone in the car rang: it's the prime minister calling. Would you hold, please?

Stevens had no idea what the call was about. Mulroney had paid scant attention to his former cabinet minister since a judicial inquiry had found that Stevens had violated conflict-of-interest guidelines. Stevens had resigned his cabinet portfolio but decided to seek re-election as the representative of York-Simcoe, just north of Toronto. Once, the two men had met by chance in the government lobby; Mulroney had remarked that Stevens appeared headed for an "interesting" fight. Other than that, nothing. Stevens had defeated a challenger for the party's nomination, and the provincial executive had informed him his papers were in order. Now this phone call.

Mulroney said he would not, as party leader, sign Stevens' nomination papers. That meant Stevens could not run as a Conservative. Stevens felt a terrible blow. "I did not want to leave the impression that I had been so disgraced that I didn't have the courage to go back to the people and run again," he said. "The Liberal line in this campaign is 'Let the people decide.' Why couldn't they let the people decide on me?"

The two men spoke on the telephone for about twenty minutes. The tone of the conversation was not pleasant. Stevens attempted, in the few minutes available to him, to seek a reprieve — to have the prime minister see the entire affair from his point of view. Since his point of view was diametrically opposed to that of nearly everyone else in the country — Stevens believed he was the victim of a media conspiracy which had compromised even the justice system — the task was impossible. Still, he did make progress: "On all of the points I raised, there were two that he had never even considered." Stevens pleaded; Mulroney remained steadfast. Eventually they agreed that Stevens had to go, if only for the sake of appearance.

"It was a very complicated thing, yes," Stevens said later,

asked if he had received a fair hearing. "But I would think the prime minister would agree, and I would agree, the essence of the problem is perception."

Mulroney made the announcement to reporters later the same day. Saying it would be "inappropriate to endorse [Stevens'] candidacy," he added: "I believe that the interests of the country would best be served by the decision I've taken and announced."

No one challenged that curious statement. Mulroney had taken the action as leader of the Conservative Party. As prime minister, he had no authority to deny Stevens his bid for election. By saying he had served "the interests of the country," Mulroney seemed to be suggesting that what was good for the Conservative Party was good for Canada, or at least that he was using his powers as party leader for the good of the nation. Perhaps Mulroney meant there was some national interest in removing Stevens from the race. Perhaps he meant that the tone of the national campaign would have been debased by a prolonged debate about ethics, when there were more serious issues at hand. Probably he didn't really mean anything; it just sounded nice, and prime ministerial.

Stevens' first reaction was to retaliate — he drove back to his home near Aurora, Ontario, and pulled the party constitution from the shelves of his dark-stained oak study. He pored over the papers for hours, looking for some legal manoeuvre. It appeared he could run as an independent, and had some claim to the funds raised by the local riding association.

But he was more concerned with the principle; he felt he had a right to campaign on the Conservative ticket, regardless of the wishes of the party leader. He called a closed meeting of his party executive. At the conclusion, he walked into a news conference. The reporters were as expectant as his own riding executive — he had told no one of his decision. In a lengthy preamble, which most reports described as "rambling," Stevens set forth many of the reasons why he felt he was entitled to run.

Then, to the surprise of all, he withdrew from the race. He announced he would run neither as a Conservative nor as an independent. He said he would turn over all campaign funds to the new Conservative candidate and help in whatever capacity he could. The nasty saga of Sinclair Stevens, it seemed, was over.

"SAY, HEY, COME down here!" Sinc Stevens called, the day after his withdrawal. "I want to show you the pool. I got that pool fixed."

Stevens was proud that he had got the pool fixed; the vinyl liner had been torn, and he had complained of the difficulty in getting a little thing like that repaired these days. It was another small confirmation that when the big things are not going right, the little things also stubbornly resist. The pool liner had been torn just before Chief Justice Parker released his damning report.

"They did a pretty good job, eh?" Sinc looked at the patch of blue vinyl. "Well, whaddya say? Do you want to go inside? Or sit on the patio? It's up to you."

It was always up to you. Sinc never found it necessary to impose his wishes on anyone. If a guest wanted another log on the fire, that was all right with Sinc. If you'd prefer to sit on the patio, where the view was nice, that was fine, too. If you'd rather move inside, where it's warmer, it was up to you. Sinc always accommodated, Sinc never demurred, Sinc was the perfect host and the ideal follower. If the request were odd, or the question unexpected, a brief moment of anxiety played over Sinc's face. His brows creased. His mouth, usually composed in an attitude of pleasant attentiveness, slackened slightly around the bottom lip. You could see his mind struggle for the pleasing response. He was like a man who had momentarily forgotten how to breathe, and approbation was like breathing to Sinc.

In others, such deference might appear to be servile. In Stevens it only enhanced an impression of acute vulnerability. His skin was as white and delicate as a filet of sole. He had the plump cheeks and cherubic mouth of an innocent suckling — only his quick, expressive eyes gave him the aspect of a savant. He was full of ideas and observations, which he cast out in bursts, followed by an inquisitive "eh?" Even the darkest comments about the world were accompanied by a bright, cheerful smile and this "eh?" — as in, "They were out to get me, eh?" He delighted only that he had figured it out. If led to the electric chair, Sinc would be composed in an attitude of chipper reasoning — "So, this is what they're going to do, eh?" — until the straps were tightened, and he cast an anxious look of confusion and beseechment at the executioner — not for reprieve, but for a clue to the appropriate response before the switch was thrown.

It was a face that inspired fierce loyalty on the part of the women who surrounded him — his wife, his legislative aides, his executive secretary, and his constituency manager, Lissie Pedersen, who said, "He was a good man. People would come in here with their problems and be angry. They'd talk to him and never be angry after. He could calm them down. He had a way like that. There's no one more charismatic, if you were to meet him."

ON THE PATIO, Stevens began, as he invariably began, with a tribute to his leader. "Brian Mulroney will go down in history as one of our most brilliant leaders, as well as our most misunderstood." This became a regular little sermon about Mulroney's role as "the great conciliator," his particular "genius" for bringing the country's factions together, the "remarkable" manner in which he learned his job on the run. It was usually followed with an attack on the Opposition, for being unworthy of brushing the great man's coat.

Stevens said that the prime minister's actions, in refusing to sign the nomination papers, were understandable. "I know what the man's living with, eh? I don't think he could have stopped Broadbent or Turner. Once the mindset is there, it takes very little to re-ignite it. All you have to do is press the Stevens button and the public thinks: 'Yeah, Stevens, he was involved in sleaze or scandal.' Having spent sixteen years in politics, I think I can say that once the public starts thinking something, there's no way you can dissuade them."

But he could have fought for you, Sinc. You've maintained your innocence all along. He could have stood up for you.

"I know what you're thinking," he said. "The easiest thing in the world would have been for me to say, 'Leader, why don't you give me one hundred per cent?' But I think I'm close enough to him to know the reality of being leader."

Here Sinc lapsed into reminiscence, recalling political fights he and Mulroney had waged together, cabinet decisions, conventions and campaigns. He still couldn't admit Mulroney had cut him loose. "I know what you're sensing," he said. "The reason you're sensing I'm that way is not because what he had to say was done in any soothing way. But I've had the opportunity to work at his side. In cabinet I was always able to counsel with him in a very close way. Once, it really hit me. He turned to me and said, 'If I'm asked about this, what do I say?' It was that kind of relationship." Brian Mulroney had just declared Sinclair Stevens contrary to the national interest; Sinc's fondest memory remained the day the great man had asked his advice.

Stevens seemed to have convinced himself that Mulroney had remained loyal. "With his business connections, he would have understood. He would have given me the benefit of the doubt."

What if it were just the two of you, Sinc? Here now. What would Mulroney say?

"It would be fair to say. . ." Sinc looked up an instant, checking. "You mean, if you could divorce the prime minister from the campaign?" Sinc imagined it a moment, his eyes fixed in the mid-distance. "He would be the first to turn to me and say, 'Sinc, I know you're no rogue. But unfortunately, you're one of the nasty products that get produced under this political process.'" It was plainly comforting for Stevens to imagine the prime minister saying this: "Sinc, I know you're no rogue."

Stevens did not blame Mulroney for the decision, then, he blamed the problem of "perception." He was as blameless as the victim of a soured photo-op. He compared himself to the former Conservative leader Robert Stanfield. "I know what the fumbled football did to Stanfield. It's unforgivable the way that sort of thing was set up — he caught the football so many times, but they just used the picture when he fumbled. Frankly, it was used to confirm an image that he was a bungler.

"Or Joe Clark and the lost luggage. I know that was a fabrication. So now you have Turner and Broadbent blowing this up just like the fumbled football and the lost luggage were blown up. When there's nothing there, really, to hang it on. That's the seamy side of politics, eh? The Opposition realize they can create a sleaze factor when, in reality, there's nothing to build it around."

AFTER HEARING from more than 90 witnesses over 80 days of hearings that generated 13,000 pages of testimony and 200 exhibits, Chief Justice William Parker of the Ontario High Court had ruled that Stevens had violated conflict-of-interest guidelines fourteen times while in the cabinet. Stevens, in dismissing the judge's findings as "all wrong," had appeared oddly detached: "I was hoping for an objective appraisal."

Parker ruled that Stevens had continued to manage the affairs of a business interest that had been placed in a blind trust established precisely to prevent him from doing so. Sinc had approved a government grant to Magna, Frank Stronach's auto-parts company, while his wife was negotiating a $2.6-million sweetheart loan from a company consultant. Sinc had approved lucrative government contracts for Bay Street brokerage houses, when he knew his own company was meeting those firms in its search for financing. Sinc gave work to another firm that was involved in trying to help his company. He endeavoured to use his public office for personal gain, Parker ruled, on at least five occasions.

In one of his more celebrated schemes, to commemorate the two thousandth anniversary of the birth of Christ, Sinc and his wife hatched an idea to market gold coins through the Vatican. They discussed the plan with a New York bank that was seeking government of Canada business. Another time, he attempted to obtain financing for his own company during a meeting with a British merchant banker, a meeting called to discuss Canadian government business in Singapore. On other occasions he paved the way for his wife to meet financial houses seeking government work, so that she could apply for financing for his own companies.

In reaching his findings, Parker dismissed much of the testimony of Stevens, his wife, and his secretary. The judge, seemingly incredulous, observed that Stevens had "demonstrated a complete disregard for the requirements of the guidelines and code and the standard of conduct that is expected of public office holders."

Stevens could not accept the judge's reasoning. The guidelines were inappropriate; the violations were minor; the public inquiry was "Star Chamber stuff." On the patio he said, "I suppose, when I look back on it, I ask myself, 'When did you honestly feel you did anything wrong?' And there's nothing. Then how did I get into this kind of a jam?"

Stevens had spent many hours, on this patio, or in the dark study, reflecting on that question. Just before Parker had released his report, he believed he had found the answer. The wind whistled across the duck pond that day, through the boneyard of fence railings and bare trees, up the hill to the exposed hilltop of house, pool, and patio. Stevens' farm is remote, and quiet as a cloister. On a clear day he can see five counties. On darker days he could see the cause of his misfortune: the faces that stalked him, the conspiracy that hounded him, the voices that lied about him and drove him to these hills.

Stevens had explained, before Parker's decision, that he had come to understand the conspiracy to get him. Actually, he said, it was a campaign to get the prime minister and the cabinet. But, in the process, "I became their best target. They stalked me, eh? They stalked me from the moment I became a minister, eh?"

But why did they stalk you, Sinc?

"Primarily they wanted the prime minister and his cabinet ministers. I suppose, with my business connections, they thought they could turn up something. They did it because they dislike the government. For completely ulterior motives. I suppose because of the trade negotiations with the Americans, and because they have so much at stake with the Americans coming in."

"They" had meant primarily *The Globe and Mail*, the Toronto newspaper that disclosed the questionable Stevens business dealings. The newspaper's editorial support of free trade simply did not enter his reasoning. Stevens said that the then managing editor of the newspaper "hates my guts."

As for Chief Justice Parker: "The media have warped him, eh? How much has the press succeeded in intimidating him, and how much has the prosecutor influenced him? Those, I think, are two very interesting questions. If *The Globe and Mail* writes this kind of stuff, then he's got to find some substantiation for it, eh?

"I think what happened to me is a bit like what happened to Oliver North. The media in the U.S. thought they had what they wanted, eh? If they could get Ollie, high profile, under investigation and one thing or another, my God, how could it help but put Reagan in a bad light?"

Sinc added that he was not suggesting he "end up some kind of a hero," like Oliver North. But he held out hope that, one day, he would be seen as the victim. Already, he said, he had noticed a positive side: "What I think you'd be absolutely amazed at is how I'm now perceived publicly. I have never been as well known as I am today."

Stevens had even gone down to the parliamentary library to check. They had a computer that could tell you how many times your name had appeared in the newspapers. In 1986, he had three times as many references as Brian Mulroney. "The only guy that beat me was Rick Hansen." On one level, Stevens had used the point to illustrate what he saw as the hysteria around the case. On another, there had been a touch of pride in the discovery. Second only to the Man in Motion!

THE ENSUING MONTHS, from the Parker decision to the Mulroney execution, had not altered Stevens' outlook. To begin with, he remained innocent: "To my mind, the Parker commission came down to an analysis that blind trusts were not sufficiently blind, and I had consequently mixed my private and public things to an undue amount. Having said that, there was no criminality, nor any suggestion of benefits given by me, or none received."

In other words, Sinc was a victim of the system? Something like Ben Johnson, the sprinter?

"You would be absolutely amazed," Stevens replied, "how often I get that on the street. People say, 'You have been victimized. You've been put into a position that's patently, grossly unfair. You and Ben, you were heroes one day, and the next day a total outcast.'" In a way, it wasn't fair to raise such comparisons: Sinc lunged at each one. The faithful servant like Oliver North; hounded like Gary Hart; victimized like Big Ben. But Stevens enjoyed the comparisons, and he relished the conversations, imaginary or not, that they evoked. The voices of the "people on the street" said what he desperately wanted to hear. You're no rogue, Sinc.

"As one guy said to me, 'What I don't understand about your affair is, why were you a well-respected cabinet minister one day, and overnight, people don't want anything to do with you?'" Stevens, naturally, did not have the answer. "They say to me, 'You are having to suffer needlessly. People are being more than unkind.'"

But if Stevens was convinced of his innocence, why did he roll over and die? The argument that he couldn't battle public perception didn't make sense. He had planned to do precisely that. He thought the battle, at least in his own riding, could be won. The call from the prime minister hadn't persuaded him to withdraw: his first reaction had been to marshal his legal arguments. No, something had happened at the meeting with his riding executive, something that had changed his mind, something he didn't want to talk about. What?

"Before I went into the meeting, there were three possible

positions the executive could take, eh?" The executive could have been hostile, adopting the position that the leader had spoken and Sinc's wishes didn't matter. They could have ridden the fence: 'Look, Sinc,' they could have said, 'we'd like to support you but the party constitution won't allow it.' Or they could have supported Stevens, wholeheartedly, whatever decision he made.

The first order of business had been a vote of confidence in the candidate. The executive voted unanimously to support Stevens in any eventuality, with one exception — an executive member who expected to replace Stevens, if the candidate resigned, abstained from the vote. "They didn't turn their back on me," Stevens said. "I found that personally gratifying. It allowed me to face my decision."

Would Stevens have decided to run, against everyone's wishes, if the vote had gone the other way? "Oddly enough, I might have," he replied. "My reflex might have been, 'You, too, Brutus?'" Sinc's voice rose in pitch. "My reflex might have been, 'Surely to God, you don't have to do this to me now. Surely to God, I've been through enough. I've been maligned, condemned, in a way no man should be subjected to. Surely, I could expect more than to get the back of your hand, now!'"

Stevens took a moment to compose himself. He wiped his eyes; it may have been the wind, whistling up the hillside to the patio. "They put me at my *ease*," he explained. "At least I felt their support. They allowed me to look at the national scene, and say, well, I'm not number one. There's a national interest, a national campaign."

That was it, then. The only cabinet minister to resign under conditions of proved conflict of interest became a necessary sacrifice to the Conservative campaign for the sake of public opinion. He could not accept the reality of his transgressions, but could understand the impression they made. He wanted, more than anything, to clear his reputation; he wanted to be seen as an honourable man. He was, in the end, a saddened but still optimistic little man who could not understand the cause of his misfortune.

In the contest of perception, his desires had conflicted with the prime minister's. Mulroney wanted Stevens to be perceived as a villain; in having Sinc put down, Mulroney could enhance the public impression of his own integrity. Stevens wanted to be re-elected, for the same reason. The contest had been settled by the simple expedient of a vote. The vote had settled nothing, other than to reassure Stevens: "Sinc, I know you're no rogue."

"I think I did the right thing for the party and for the national campaign," Sinc said, bidding his visitor goodbye. "But in your heart, eh? I miss the opportunity to meet the people, to campaign, and hopefully, to win — to have them show their confidence in me. Ah, well."

THE DRIVE FROM the Stevens home to the town of Aurora is a few short miles. Aurora's main street has no pleasant corners and is showing the pressure, as are all the towns in the area, of proximity to Toronto. Strip malls have grown to serve the commuter traffic, light industry has moved onto agricultural land, and the highway is encroaching on the city limits.

A small group of New Democratic Party supporters were gathered around a municipal building. They carried placards with Ed Broadbent's face and the slogan, "This time, Ed." A tour bus pulled into the parking lot. Members of the media piled out, and the cameras took a few shots of the group.

The journalists were upbeat, energetic; it was still early in the campaign. They were wrangling over the name of the Ed Broadbent campaign plane. Some of the technical crew, who liked loud music, were pushing for "Ed Zeppelin"; the NDP staff liked the sound of "Air Apparent." The print media thought "J'espAir," given Broadbent's tortured French accent, was clever.

They had travelled to Aurora in the expectation that Sinc Stevens wouldn't let Ed Broadbent give this press conference on his front lawn. The NDP's intention was to come as close as possible to the home of Mulroney's most notorious cabinet minister. One of the journalists dubbed the trip, "returning to the scene of the slime." Broadbent had planned to make his major campaign statement on government ethics here, but had been upstaged by Mulroney's swift manoeuvring. A more responsive campaign organization would have switched the venue; instead, it was left to Broadbent to make the best of the situation.

"Very clearly," said Broadbent, "I planned in terms of the national campaign to make the issue of ethics in government very clear early in the campaign." When the Aurora visit was planned, he added, "the prime minister had not had, at that time, the decency to make the decision of removing Mr. Stevens."

Broadbent tried to make hay of the deathbed repentance of Mulroney. He said the prime minister had waited "right up to the election call, for electoral reasons, to make the announcement he did." The removal of Stevens "was a right decision for all the wrong reasons."

NDP staffers handed out a yellow sheet outlining the Broadbent plan for clean government. But the Stevens story was already dead; the journalists allowed Broadbent a few remarks about the "ethics in government" package before diving in with their own questions. This was about the time that Mulroney was starting to be accused of campaigning "in a bubble." What about the Mulroney campaign? Why won't the prime minister meet with reporters?

Broadbent was asked if he would list his own assets, since the guidelines he proposed called for full disclosure. He played a look of surprise, then amusement. He pulled out a matchbook and began writing down his assets for the television cameras, which moved in for a tight shot.

"Let's see," he said. "I have a reasonably acceptable home in Ottawa, five thousand dollars in government bonds, and an Oshawa-built 1984 Pontiac 6000. That's it, folks."

The event wound up, and the reporters were herded back to the bus. Doug Small, of Global Television, was quite excited about the matchbook footage.

"But, Doug," someone pointed out, "that was just for the cameras."

"I know, don't you love it?" Small replied, grinning maniacally. "Oh, we're all such whores."

And we're all such johns. Still, at least one person in Canada believed the campaign to choose a representative of the good voters of York-Simcoe was not a test of the Mulroney sleaze factor. To Sinclair Stevens, it was a test of another principle altogether: the right of the people to select their own representation. Stevens knew that the Liberal candidate in the riding, his friend and neighbour Frank Stronach, was a very wealthy man who would spare no expense to secure the voters' approval. "The issue in this campaign isn't scandal," Stevens insisted. "The issue is whether, in this day and age, you can still buy a pocket riding."

Stevens had studied the history of his riding and knew that, in its earlier days, it had been a pocket borough. The right to represent York had been traded, like a patronage position, between favourites of the region's élite. Had Stevens looked even farther back in history, he would have found another parliamentarian, in another country, whom life had treated no less cruelly, but to whom history had been kind. In 1774 Edmund Burke had been elected representative of the electors of Bristol, to whom he wrote a famous letter. Burke's declaration that a member of parliament is a representative, and not a delegate, has reverberated through history. "Your representative owes you, not his industry only, but his judgment; and he betrays, instead of serving you, if he sacrifices it to your opinion."

Sinc would perhaps have been comforted to know that, in the election after Burke wrote that letter, the electors of Bristol threw the bum out.

CHAPTER 6

# BEING THERE

*GLENDOWER: I can call spirits from the vasty deep.*
*HOTSPUR: Why so can I, or so can any man,*
          *But will they come when you do*
          *call for them?*

HENRY IV, PART I — WILLIAM SHAKESPEARE

**M**ANY ENTRANTS IN THE *CANA-dian Who's Who* list their university degrees, scholarly tracts, and honours received from a grateful nation. Frank Stronach has no university degrees or scholarly tracts, but he does have money coming out his ears. His is the only entry to list his company's annual sales. Stronach, of course, is an industrialist of humble origin who came to Canada in his youth, eventually to make his fortune as the head of Magna International. Wealth defined him, yet it did not satisfy him. So he decided to seek the Liberal nomination in York-Simcoe — Sinclair Stevens country — and run for office in the 1988 election.

"Do you have an eye for shirts?" the woman asked. "You won't believe Frank's shirts." She had been called for her impressions of Stronach, with whom she had an acquaintance. "If you want to meet him, you can catch him just about any Thursday night at Rooney's, his disco at Yonge and St. Clair. Frank's there, just like Travolta, *Saturday Night Fever*. He goes there with his daughter. He loves discos, he loves his daughter, and he loves horses. He's horse nuts. He even sold some stocks to cover his horsy debts. Those are the passions. But he hates, too. Hates losing.

Cannot stand to lose. He wins by neutralizing his opponents. That's why he's gone to Russia. He says he's building links for world peace. But on a grand scale, the Soviets are the opposition. He's neutralizing the opposition.

"That's why he hated the Sinclair Stevens thing so much. It was the first thing he couldn't manipulate. Hated it, absolutely every minute of it. He's a next-door neighbour of Sinc's. He used to sit in Sinc's living room and talk about his economic philosophy, and Sinc was the doting student. Sinc would just about sit on Frank's knee. Frank's a visionary, you know. Sinc idolized him. I don't think they're even talking now.

"If you find out where he gets his shirts, let me know. They're the whitest, crispest shirts I've ever seen. They're so white, they're almost blue. They're perfect. He must change them six times a day."

DRIVING INTO Beechwood Farm, Stronach's seven-hundred-acre spread just north of Toronto, you can entertain yourself by watching the odometer tick over. Stronach's driveway, winding through pastures set off by white picket fences, is a good kilometre long. After a while, the road comes across a man-made lake, with waterfowl and a stone trim. The verdure of shrubbery and trees is neatly manicured, pleasantly arranged: nature neutralized.

Past the administration office and beyond the house is the low, oblong dome of the covered half-mile training track, for Stronach's beloved thoroughbreds. Inside, grooms and trainers were busy working with the horses, clipping hooves, trimming manes, carrying oats. Two or three things would strike a horseman as being odd about the Stronach stable. The first was the spongy surface underfoot: the entire stable was carpeted in a synthetic, rubberized material, to protect hooves. The second was the temperature: the stables are climate-controlled, and on this sweltering day it was pleasantly cool inside. The third was the smell. The smell of a working stable is an unforgettable ambrosia to anyone who explored its mysteries as a child, a sharp ambergris of manure, sweat, saddle-soap, leather, and sweet clover hay. Stronach's stable smelled of Javex and green wood.

A young woman pulled a currycomb over the burgundy flank of a stallion, her hand undulating as it defined the muscle. She didn't mind being watched, and explained there was room for forty-four horses now, but they were building stables for a hundred.

After a while, she asked, "Who you looking for?"

"Frank."

"He's not here. Better ask Joe where you can find him. Joe's in a green Jimmy, somewhere."

The green Jimmy was parked up by the house. "Mansion" is a rather tired word, and in any case does not fully describe the colonial revival building in grey stone, white oak, and black marble that Stronach was building. It sprawled on two levels. The heating and air-conditioning systems seemed adequate for a skyscraper. Joe explained that the place had about twenty thousand square feet of living space, counting the white-marble indoor pool, and that it was a quality job from top to bottom. Stronach was later to describe it this way: "It's got three bedrooms. It's got one guest room because from time to time we have business wives, or international things. And there's a small apartment in case of live-in relatives. It looks larger than what it is."

"No, he's not here," Joe said. "You better go to his office. Get back on the main road. . . ."

Magna headquarters, on Apple Creek Boulevard in Markham, Ontario, is housed in a low red-brick building of understated efficiency. Long-legged secretaries in cool silks glide through doorways, young men work assiduously at desks. In the second-floor corner office is the Magna boardroom. Oil paintings of Frank's thoroughbred horses cover the walls; their varnished coats are as deep and rich as the black marble table.

Stronach appeared, his shirt indeed flawless, vestal, and nearly blue. It matched his azure eyes, which are momentarily arresting — Stronach has the wondering eyes of a child. His handshake was firm, but not invasive. He had trimmed his long, curling blond hair, but it still described a curlicue behind the ears. His lips were somewhat pursed; this, combined with his slight Austrian accent, gave his speech a perceptible lisp. He said "woid" instead of "void," and dropped the "-ly" ending from some adverbs. Trim and athletic, he was fifty-five but could easily have passed for ten years younger. His blend of youthfulness and experience, of carnal lip and innocent eye, of feminine curl and masculine hand, made him a figure of considerable magnetism. His opening words were: "This is what you see. This is what you get."

Stronach left Austria in 1954 as a penniless twenty-two-year-old tool-and-die maker. His father, a Communist, had been persecuted by the Nazis, and this left in Stronach a deep distrust of all political systems. He dedicated himself to making his fortune. By the 1980s, Magna parts were in every car produced in North America and the company's sales exceeded $1-billion a year. Stronach was the highest-paid executive in the country, and his company had enjoyed an eighty-three-fold increase in sales over fifteen years.

But success had not fully satisfied him. He dedicated himself to charitable work by becoming the national campaign chairman for the Big Brothers Organization. But that was also less than wholly satisfying — it was tackling the symptoms of oppression, rather than the oppression itself. He had lately hatched a magazine called *Vista*, which would indirectly project the Stronach vision of the world as a place of "opportunities, innovations, success, power, profit." He was also producing his vision in book form, under the title *Philosophical Overview: An Overview of Ideas and Philosophies and their Application to Improve the Social Structure of Society*.

These were slow ways to infiltrate a culture, however, and Stronach's vision carried a sense of urgency. And so he had decided to enter politics, to share his discovery with the country. His political ambition had no limit — he knew in his heart that, once the nation had learned of his discovery, it would want him to lead it to its fulfilment. "Ottawa will never be the same," he said, "if Frank Stronach is sent to Ottawa."

WHAT STRONACH had discovered, and the rest of the world had not yet learned, was the Magna Way. The Way is complex and self-made; it came to him while he was "sitting on rocks and stones, reflecting on the purpose in life." Stronach ran his company according to the Magna Way, and his company was a success. He ran his own life in accordance with the Magna Way, and his life was the very picture of fulfilled desire. Who was to say, then, whether the Magna Way was potholed? Stronach was the Chauncey Gardiner of politics, and he believed that politics was ready for Chauncey Gardiner. Stronach was asked to explain the Way.

"First of all, I've never been the member for any party," he said. "For a number of reasons, because I believe the economic fabric is the dominant fabric in a society. . . . The economic fabric

107

and the political fabric, though, are closely interwoven. Together that will determine the social fabric.

"Even though I said the economic fabric is the more dominant one, in the political fabric you can fix things quicker or screw it up quicker. Most of the times you screw it up quick."

Stronach produced a yellow legal pad and began the Lecture. It filled three ninety-minute cassettes, and what follows is a condensed version. Stronach began, as he always does, by drawing a circle, and inside the circle, writing "The World." Beyond the world, two satellites are drawn. One satellite is labelled "Capitalism," the other "Communism."

"Communism is very noble in its basic ideas and I have always said if I were to have lived in Russia around 1917, if I would have been a peasant or a worker, I would have participated in the revolution. And if, I guess, people read history books most people would have. This system is not very conducive to great wealth. The little wealth they create the state does the distribution, that leads to more and more bureaucracy, and the build-up of bureaucracy is to such an extent it is choking the productive juices of society."

Stronach turned his attention to capitalism.

"So, now the free-enterprise system doesn't work too well either. It has a major flaw. Greed isn't checked. So when you look at the economic pyramid" — here he drew a pyramid — "you see, in an economic pyramid you got the capitalists at top, you got the masses at the bottom, somewhere in between you got the politicians."

Stronach wrote "capitalists" and "masses," and drew a squiggly line through the middle of the pyramid, representing politicians.

"Now, the free-enterprise system is based upon, on the great human charters of rights, which amongst many other things gives every person a wote. That is a must. That is not negotiable. But it also means that the system is constituency-driven. If the politicians don't cater to the masses they won't be elected. It's as simple as that. So the politicians have to constantly preach to the masses: 'If I am elected, this is what I can do for you, brothers and sisters.'

"So the law of gravity, the law of nature, is pulling this system over here."

Stronach drew an arrow from the capitalist pyramid to the Communist satellite, indicating the law of nature.

"When you have in nature a species which does not reproduce itself another species will take over," he explained. "The laws of nature are stronger than any man-made law."

Stronach interrupted his description of the Magna Way to give a narrative about his recent investment tour to the Soviet Union. "I was sitting down with the ministers and so on, we had some philosophical discussions," he recalled. Stronach told them he had two reasons for investing in the Soviet Union. One was to make money, both for himself and for the employees who are equity participants in his firm. The other reason, he said, was that "there are enormous differences between the Soviet Union and North America. If those differences will increase, it will lead unquestionable to war. And that would be devastating. Because the world is a relative small piece of real estate.

"So I said, differences come down by communicating, by doing things together, by ewolwing a better understanding for the needs to do things. So I do hope that I can make a small contribution to world peace. So those are the two reasons. And I told them, I said, there are very few things I agree with your philosophy, you know, with the exception, I said, very few things I agree even with Karl Marx, with the one exception. That would be that the capitalistic system, by itself, is self-destroying.

"They looked at me, and they thought it was very, very funny. They started to laugh. Yeah, coming from a supposed capitalist. So I said, 'Don't laugh, you guys. Your country's got a greater problem than the capitalistic system.' They said, 'What you mean?'"

Stronach returned his attention to the yellow legal pad. "Well, I said, in your system the pyramid's upside-down, you got the bureaucrats on top, you got the workers here." He labelled the upside-down pyramid. "I said I'm going to be kind to you, because I'm your guest here. I said you have regulated labour, but you also have some forced labour. If you didn't have regulated and forced labour, this pyramid would fall over." He drew in struts, labelled "forced labour," to prop up the pyramid. "See. That is the dilemma."

Stronach waved his pen between the two pyramids. "Basically what you have here, you add more and more bureaucrats. This system is not conducive to great wealth, and this system has one flaw, greed isn't checked. There's a certain amount of greed in every one of us, those are, I guess, our instincts for the survival of the human species. It's just that greed and stupidity is a bad combination, and there's just too much greed and stupidity here.

"So Magna really is a fourth system. A fourth system. Magna really is a whole new economic culture, we call it the fair-enterprise system."

Stronach wrote the words "fair enterprise" at the bottom of the pad. "Basically what that means is that we say — this is not conducive to great wealth, the totalitarian system is immoral, and this has a flaw. Greed isn't checked, and thereby greed is self-destroying.

"The basic philosophy in the fair-enterprise system is based upon that the human charter of rights around is not sufficient enough. It has to be fortified with an economic charter of rights. It is a right of workers to participate in capital building, that economic charters of rights will lead to economic democracies and economic democracies are the basis of democracy itself."

To illustrate this precept, Stronach drew a series of little pyramids across the centre of the pad.

"So thereby, there will be many pyramids, because in life, I guess the success of life can only be measured by the degree of happiness a person reaches. That means different people have different conceptions of happiness, right? And let that be, that is healthy, right? You might write, make a living, be totally happy, right? Money, and things, doesn't really let everybody be — some do social work, some paint, some make music, some do business, some do. . . . That's the great thing about it. Not every person is exactly the same, thereby you create a balance, thereby each is complementing each another. So, anyway, what you have here is, that you have many pyramids, but we know how deep the bottom is, how deep the valleys are."

Stronach left the little valleys for a minute to impress a thought upon his listener. "You see, what you have in here is, the history of mankind has always been dominated by the golden rule: 'The man which has the gold makes the rule.' I for one would not like to be ruled by somebody, thereby I cannot expect to rule somebody, either. I do not want to see my children ruled by somebody, thereby they cannot expect to rule somebody.

"So my mission, to a great extent, is really to dismantle the chains of domination."

Stronach returned his attention to the pyramids. "Here, to a great extent we have state domination, and here we have private domination. And unless we, in societies, can create economic democracies, we will really not have democracies. So, thereby, this has really dispersed the gold hoardings because conceivable all the gold could be in one peak and conceivable all the misery could be down in one valley. So here, you know you have different peaks of different heights but you know how deep the valleys are."

That was pretty well it. Stronach had finished describing the Magna Way. "I should give you this," he said, signing the legal pad. "It might have historical walue."

THERE'S A STORY about Frank Stronach that's popular in Ottawa. Stronach had been deeply moved when, in 1984, his friend Sinclair Stevens was named minister of regional industrial expansion. Stronach had appeared at Sinc's door the next day at 7 a.m., such was his excitement. He felt there was a chance to impose some form of the Magna Way upon the federal bureaucracy. So Stevens pulled some strings and had Stronach appointed to the Canada Development Investment Corporation, a federal holding agency for Crown corporations destined for privatization. At the first board meeting, Stronach sat uncomfortably while CDIC executives outlined plans and priorities for the coming year. Finally, he could take it no longer.

"You got it all wrong," Stronach said. Taking to his feet, he demanded a blackboard. He drew a circle on the blackboard, and inside the circle wrote "The World." He then proceeded, patiently and at length, to explain the Magna Way to the board. "He had these whirligigs all over the blackboard," recalled someone who was present. "There was chalk and hair flying everywhere."

When he finished, some time later, Stronach placed his chalk down on the boardroom table. He was met with absolute silence. Other board members stared at their briefing papers, or seemed to be gazing at something that had caught their attention, just outside the window. With a gentle cough, the agency's president finally broke the silence.

"Well, will you look at that," he said. "It's almost noon. What does everybody say to some lunch?"

A shame the agency did not hear the rest of the plan, for Stronach had not left his philosophy a cold, sterile thing. He had made it a reality in his own company, instituting an employee charter of rights. One of its provisions limited Stronach's salary to two per cent of profits, "give or take, you know." Other owners took more, he said, "and that disturbs the balance of nature. And therein lies the problem."

Stronach was asked exactly which natural balance he was referring to.

"The balance of nature is, in that case, society, right? Because in order for society to function you need teachers, you need writers, you need lawyers, you need accountants, you need machinists, you need bakers, carpenters. . . . They're all creative, make things, right? Now if certain sectors just pull out too much, right, there's not enough left over, for them. Thereby you disturb, you upset the thing, thereby people become unhappy, unhappiness leads to all sorts of things, right?"

And how exactly would the Way apply to the federal government?

"I will say there are two things you can do which influences a society. Two things which have the greatest impact. But the two greatest things are education and taxation. When education was introduced to society, to a great extent, and if we take a reference point the days of Charles Dickens, you seen in those days all the countries were ruled by kings. The kings recognized the need of education; the need of engineers to build better guns, chemists to create better gunpowder, for obvious reasons, to defend some country or conquer new countries. One thing a king did not want to do is teach his people how to be free, because if he teaches his people how to be free he's got to share his gold, right?

"So now education, that environment, has carried over to a great extent, not by design, but because people are a product of their environment, the environment has perpetuated itself. And I could give you many examples. . . . You see, when the kingdoms erode, and out of that, industrial empires emerged; industrial barons, to this day business do not teaches their workers how to be free. You see, if you teach the workers how to be free you cannot take all the profits. Therein lies the dilemma.

"So your specific question, what were I to do, how would I advance from that culture to a society, quite simple. And I'm coming back now to taxation. Now one of the first things I would do. First of all, have an income-tax form whereby a high-school kid could fill it out. Because if an income-tax form is very simple he can easily see, you know, is it fair? Because right now, it is so complex that the ones who create income-tax laws, even they need consultants to fill out their income-tax forms. So it's utterly amazing, it's utterly grey and thereby gives so much room to manoeuvre and loopholes and thereby the income-tax system is not a fair system.

"So the income tax would be very simple. And furthermore I would say to business, 'Lookit, you guys know better than the bureaucrat how to do things, where to invest and so on. If you want to invest in South America, fine. Go ahead. If you want to have it all here, that's fine. I'll tell you what. You pay the free-enterprise tax for it. Which is about fifty per cent. But I'll tell you what, Mr. Businessman. If you want to pay, let's say, approximately half, I'll tell you what you have to do, Mr. Businessman. First of all you got to have open books. Secondly, the employees got to be part-owners. Thirdly, you cannot rake the till. You got to do some research. And most of the monies you got to reinvest in this country.'"

Stronach was not in the least unsettled by the suggestion that it was not immediately clear exactly what impact these changes would have on the social, economic, and political systems. When it came to explaining the Way, he had the patience of a Jesuit.

"It would create a Canada which would be so far ahead of any country in the world, a Canada which would be a role model for nations in the world, for social and economic justice. We have never preoccupied ourselves as a nation what is economic justice."

Specifically, the Way, when applied to the country as a whole, would accomplish the following:

"We have advanced so much, that I say if a person in North America works for fifteen or twenty years that person should have enough accumulated that you own your own transportation, might only be a simple car; that person should have enough accumulated that you own your own shelter, might only be a simple house; that person should have enough in the bank that. . . in case you want to do something that nourishes your heart, mind or soul, in case you want to write, or music, paint or social work, that you could quit and live a modest life from your accumulated capital.

"Now," he asked, "how many people do you know which

own their car outright, their house outright, and have money in the bank? Those are the minimum standards of a civilized society.

"In essence, I am trying to get the message across: *fair* enterprise, co-existent with *free* enterprise, will prevent *state* enterprise."

Stronach's listener said, in all honesty, this was very interesting.

"It is," Stronach agreed. "You can throw the books away at Harvard. Use them only as a reference. You can throw the whole thing away, because present leaders have absolutely no vision about the kind of society, where do we want to go.

"I will say, one of these days I'm gonna be in Ottawa. One of these days I will have a say in Ottawa. I do believe that the most powerful energy in the world is people with good ideas. Providing you can prove they're not self-serving. If you have a great idea, provided you prove it's good for society, for people, it's the most powerful energy. So what that means is, I have great, great ideas.

"I know a few years down the road, if I were to look myself in the mirror, I would say to myself, 'You son of a gun, you had all the means, you had all the opportunity to bring about change to society. You didn't do anything.' So thereby I will try to have input to bring about change in a constructive way."

Did he have what it takes to become leader?

"I lead a very balanced life," he said. "Nobody could ever say Frank Stronach is drunkard. I'm very balanced, very much look after my health. Not too long ago, we had a ten-K up in Newmarket and I have never been much of what for jogging, and I just run it right through. I wasn't even puffing. I know of other political leaders which made a few steps and then walked away. So I have energies, like, and I am extremely healthy and I can't think of anybody who has an energy level like I have. I'm modest about that."

Stronach was asked whether, when he pointed out that he wasn't a drunkard, he was comparing himself to —

"Nonononewnonew! No. Absolutely. Make no thing, because I respect, I'm saying, when you said, energy, I strictly referred, I'm taking care of my body, make no . . . you mean, last thing — clarify that. I don't know John that well. I really don't deny, I do not, unless I really know a person, I will never make a comment, huh? I'm just saying people who know me, know I'm a very responsible, very balanced person. I don't smoke. I live a healthy life. Try to work out every day. I'm just in dynamite shape. I play tennis practically every day with young kids, huh, I'm in better shape, better stamina."

Stronach was asked his views on free trade.

"Free trade will have a devastating effect on Canada," he said. "There's two aspects to it, the economic aspect and the political aspect. The economic in a nutshell is, [this] would accelerate the selling of raw materials and resources at a relative low price; and we would accelerate the importing of finished products at a relative high price. Thereby we would lose thousands, hundreds of thousands of jobs, and that would lead us more and more to a nation of warehouse operators. We're already there to a great extent, a nation of warehouse operators.

"The political part is, under this free-trade agreement, Canada must adopt the American economic principles, and that means we will adopt the American way of life. And I believe it is just a question of time before we would lose our ability to shape and mould the kind of country Canadians would like to have.

"Now, I'm not anti-American. I'm all for trade. I think as a Canadian, if I would choose a nation as a neighbour I would choose the Americans. They are great people. But you cannot separate the economic fabric from the political fabric. Of course we will never lose the name 'Canada,' or the maple leaf, but we will be intertwined in the American economic fabric. And, I always said, I would hate to see if there is only one church. . . ."

THE LISTENER was transported, as Stronach spoke, to the place where he had heard those same sentiments about the interwoven economic and political fabric. It had been in Vancouver, some months earlier. Tex Enemark, a Liberal backroom boy, had just executed a passable swan dive into his pool. This late-afternoon swim was the sombrero on an afternoon of drinking beer, scoffing pizza, and bitching about the local Liberal scene, which was then dominated by the lack of a candidate in a crucial riding.

Vancouver Centre is the jewel of western ridings; it has traditionally meant a fast track to the cabinet, and always draws candidates of quality. At the time, the Conservatives were expected to run Pat Carney, the incumbent, and a three-to-two favourite, against the national president of the New Democratic

Party, Johanna Den Hertog. Den Hertog, a sort of David Peterson in drag who prefers the term "co-nurturer" to "husband," was expected to wage a spirited campaign on social issues.

This left a void on the Liberal side. Capable candidates had been found, but John Turner had decided to perform a laying-on of hands, giving his blessing to Sylvia Russell, director of the Vancouver food bank. The woman had dickered, and dallied, then finally decided not to run. "Unfortunately," Enemark had said, "this is a business where you have to fish or cut bait." At that point, Enemark had no idea where to find a candidate for Vancouver Centre. He did not know it then, but he would eventually take up the challenge himself.

Tex surfaced, spewing water like a baleen whale. "Hey, tell you what," he said. "Let's go see Turner tonight. It's his nomination night."

Enemark changed into a suit, then piled into the Volvo with his sixteen-year-old daughter Kirsten. They drove over to the Point Grey High School, which was being used for the nomination meeting. Enemark explained its forbidding grey exterior. "It used to be a prison," he said.

"It still is," said Kirsten.

The school theatre was packed and loud with excitement. John Turner was coming into town drugged with the amphetamine of renewed purpose, having just compelled the federal government to call an election on the free-trade issue. The way he did it was a stroke of political brilliance, which made it difficult, for those who knew him, to believe he had hatched the scheme himself. Turner had instructed his caucus members in the Senate to use a power they had not exercised in quite the same way for seventy-five years. The Senate had refused to pass the free-trade legislation until an election was called on the issue.

The Senate has the same powers as the Commons to propose, defeat, or amend legislation. It had the constitutional authority to do as it did. But a constitutional monarchy such as Canada's relies only partly on written constitutions to derive authority; the test of convention is equally important. The Queen's representative in Canada also has the constitutional power to defeat legislation, by refusing to grant royal assent to government bills. Had the governor general, Jeanne Sauvé, decided to force an election on the issue, however, it would have led to a constitutional crisis. Her position is appointed rather than elected; her role is more ceremonial than functional. The governor general, while lending stability to the machinery of government, is not expected to fire any of its cylinders. The role had been created at a time when popular democracy was of less importance than the need for stability. The governor general's powers had never been removed by writ, but they had been allowed to erode by convention. Sauvé was, in other words, in much the same position as the Senate.

Turner's decision to use the Senate as a blunt sword to remove the prime minister's prerogative of timing the election invited deep meditation. He defended the act on constitutional grounds, and reached back to the Senate's stalling of the 1913 naval bill as a precedent. It was an act of unashamed hypocrisy for Turner to refer to a seventy-five-year-old precedent when he had a three-year-old precedent at hand. In 1985, Turner had agreed to allow speedy passage of a money bill in exchange for other favours in the Commons. But when the bill reached the Senate, it was delayed by the Liberals. Faced with this unexpected recalcitrance, which made him appear duplicitous, Turner had defended his honour by distancing himself from the Senate.

Three years later he overturned that precedent and claimed that the Senate was a legitimate instrument of the party leader, a sort of government-in-exile. As the University of Guelph politics professor William Christian has pointed out, Turner's gambit transformed Canada into a single-party state. So long as there was a Liberal majority in an unreformed Senate, the Liberals would never really be out of power. When they held a majority in the Commons, they would be able to determine which legislation would proceed. When they were out of favour in the Commons, they could use the Senate to determine which legislation would not proceed. Elections would determine only whether they would be the engine or the brakes of legislation. It would not matter, in other words, which party the Canadian people had decided should form the government; the Liberals could not be removed from power.

Turner, who had written a university paper on Senate reform, knew that his gambit was profoundly anti-democratic, deeply cynical, and fiendishly callous. Because he had an innate grasp of politics in the post-literate age, he also knew how to make it acceptable, even heroic, to the Canadian people — he would give it a democratic-sounding name.

"Let the people decide!" Turner shouted, and because people like to decide, they decided they liked the gambit. It was simple, and it worked. The people had decided, four years earlier, to give the Mulroney Conservatives the largest majority in Canadian electoral history. The people had decided to reduce the Liberal ranks to a pile of ash. The people had admittedly not yet decided on free trade. The Conservative leader had been against the notion in 1983, but there was no precedent, in constitution or convention, to prevent a government from changing its mind in mid-term on major policy issues. The Trudeau Liberals had done exactly the same thing after the 1974 election, reversing their stand on wage-and-price controls. None of this mattered to Turner. The people hadn't taken away "his" Senate — perhaps only because they lacked the power to do so — and so now, champion of democracy that he was, he wanted the people to decide.

WHEN TURNER WALKED into the theatre of Point Grey High School, he was greeted with a banner carried aloft by supporters. It said: "Thanks for the courage, John!"

Turner's speech that night was a tour de force. There were minor blemishes — one man shouted "Boo!" and walked out, another youth rose to his feet on several occasions to shout, "What about peace?" Turner finally mentioned that he was committed to the North American alliance but also committed to peace. Overall, his first test of the election theme met with wild enthusiasm.

Turner's Quadra speech was misread by Conservative strategists in Toronto and Ottawa. Seen from afar, it looked like Turner's attempt to reclaim traditional Liberal support and base his attack on the Conservatives' patronage excesses. True, he did begin the speech with a paean: "We have built our party and policies in the way it should be — from the ground up," and, "We have moved from finding excuses for losing to finding reasons to win." And he did attack the Conservative patronage record: "The Conservatives did not end patronage — they raised it to an art form." He expressed concern for the disadvantaged: "I have seen the ugly face of poverty in the food banks of Vancouver, and I've met the street people of the East Side." He announced policies for national literacy and apprenticeship programs, for housing, and for child care.

But the heart of his speech was not contained in the prepared text distributed to the press. The heart of the speech, like the Gettysburg address, was not taken down by anyone in attendance. The audience watched spellbound as Turner, for the first time, outlined the elements of what he would later call "the fight of my life." Afterwards, an aide, asked for his copy of the speech, handed it over with the words: "I don't know what good it will do you." Until about page three, the aide had been making orderly marginal notes — which lines had gone over well, which needed brushing up, and so on. In mid-speech, the aide had begun to wander about the page. He drew arrows into margins, attempted to record impromptu phrases, bracketed paragraphs and surrounded them with question marks. Finally, in frustration, he had crossed out an entire page and written at the top, simply, "Winging it."

Out on stage, John Turner was winging it with lines like: "I'm not asking the Senate to kill the bill, I am asking the Senate to delay it — until the people decide!" That got a standing ovation. "Canadians are not anti-American," he said, "but we do happen to be pro-Canadian." Hooray, shouted the people. "This is the reversal of one hundred and twenty years of history. It is a monumental change for Canadians. This government had no authority from the people, no mandate from Canadians. What I have done is constitutionally correct, and well within the conventions of parliamentary tradition. I say, Let the people decide!"

The cheers still ringing in his ears, Turner turned deftly to the Big Hate. The deal, he said, "will force everyone in Ottawa," before making any decisions about anything, to ask, "What will they say and what will they think in Washington?" Boo, hooted the people. "This is not a trade deal which merely lowers tariffs," Turner said, "it goes beyond that. It's the Sale of Canada Act." Boo, boo, boomed the people. What's more, he said, the government had come within an ace of selling out your country when no one was looking. "They were hoping to take Canadians by surprise," he said. "They were hoping Canadians would be at the cottage and wouldn't care." Boo, boo, boo, shouted the people.

"This will really be an election that has something to do with history," Turner said, "because we'll be deciding as a people whether to recommit ourselves to Canada, or we'll be deciding to succumb, after one hundred and twenty courageous years of struggling against American continentalism and their spirit of manifest destiny."

One man could resist that continentalism. One man could turn back the tide of manifest destiny. One man could save Canada. "The question," said Turner, "is whether we have something worth fighting for. I believe we do. And I'm going to fight."

Turner lacked only four things in his battle to save Canada: a pike, a nag, a faithful sidekick, and a windmill. It was the beginning of the La Mancha campaign. At the end of it, much like the true-hearted Don Quixote, Turner would be convinced of the glory of his quest and the purity of his love. His only sorrow would be over an imperfect world which was not yet ready to receive him.

Along the way, Turner would be reviled and ridiculed, but this would only strengthen his determination. He was, after all, prepared to march into hell for a heavenly cause. If his armour were only tin, if his beloved Canada turned out to be no more than a barroom wench, well, all the more reason to embrace and to pity him. For he knew the world would be better for this. That one leader, scorned and covered with scars, still strove, with his final ounce of courage, to reach the unreachable star.

They raised the roof at Point Grey High School.

BACK IN MARKHAM, Ontario, the local Conservatives knew they had a fight on their hands the moment Frank Stronach sewed up the Liberal nomination. Stronach's equivalent of "Let the people decide" was "Let's be FRANK." This was his campaign slogan; it was succinct, and cute, and it served the underlying function of all campaign slogans in disguising, through reversal, the real issue.

Some remarkable coincidences had preceded Stronach's nomination as Liberal candidate for York-Simcoe. He had appeared several weeks before the nomination meeting at the Portuguese Community Centre in Bradford. In a fit of generosity, he presented the group with a cheque for $15,000. Locals said the cheque allowed the Portuguese to retire the debt on their community hall. When asked about the gift, Stronach said it was merely part of the philanthropic routine that had long characterized his role as patron of the area. Stronach's charitable acts are indeed many, and who could have foreseen the result? On nomination night, Portuguese by the hundreds bundled off buses at the hall, clutching paid-up membership slips and a grateful desire to vote Stronach.

The second coincidence took place at Magna itself. On nomination day, employees were given time off and allowed to reschedule shifts. Stronach hosted a barbecue, with free food and live music. In the warm afterglow, buses were provided — for those who felt so inclined — to shuttle people to the nomination meeting. Rare was the employee who could resist the mysterious urge to board the bus. Stronach said he was pleased and humbled by this demonstration of loyalty on the part of his staff.

Meanwhile, at the nomination hall, a local Liberal named Tom Taylor sat quietly awaiting the deluge. In twenty-five years of Liberal politics, as president of five different riding associations, and nominator of five candidates, including two cabinet ministers, Taylor had a pretty good idea how to nail down a Liberal nomination. But nothing had prepared him for Stronach.

Taylor had started his campaign slowly, relying on family and friends. Stronach had five full-time and ten part-time staff on the payroll for two months. Taylor spent $9,500 on his campaign. Stronach spent many times that figure. Taylor had signed up 900 Liberals — more than enough, he thought, to secure the toughest nomination fight. Stronach had signed up 2,800, an estimated 1,200 of them employees of his own company.

Taylor was expecting a tough fight on nomination night. Even so, the Stronach wave drew his breath away. People flooded off the buses, waving their "Let's be FRANK!" banners and donning their "Let's be FRANK!" T-shirts and chanting, to the music of Stronach's band, "Let's be FRANK!"

Taylor, as his fanfare, had arranged for two bagpipers.

Taylor challenged the legitimacy of 600 of the memberships taken out by Stronach supporters, arguing that they didn't meet certain technical requirements. It wouldn't have made any difference. Stronach won the nomination by 1,510 votes to 406. That's when the Conservatives knew they were up against a formidable and determined opponent.

THERE ARE TWO WAYS a candidate can approach political office. The first is to make his ideas and plans perfectly clear. This is antiquated and not very helpful; indeed, it's often harmful. The second approach is summed up by the American political consultant Hal Evry, who has batted .920 in more than five hundred campaigns. All a candidate needs to win, says Evry, is money, an I.Q. in three figures, and the ability to keep his mouth shut. Actually, all he really needs is to keep his mouth shut. Money is a defensive weapon: it will not guarantee a win, but lack of it will virtually guarantee a loss. To candidates who ask, "What can I do on a limited budget?" Evry replies: "If it's very limited, donate it to charity." The minimum I.Q. is needed, he says, simply to ensure that the candidate is able to realize the value of keeping his mouth shut.

"According to Evry, all candidates talk too much," said the writer of a *Life* magazine profile in 1966. "From the magic moment when first they feel that shaft of light from heaven, that ghostly finger touching their shoulder and summoning them to a life of public service, they also feel a compulsion to get out and bend the ears of their fellow-citizens — with messages, with arguments, with Issues; and their fellow-citizens couldn't care less."

Evry was an early master of the publicity stunt, or what is now called the pseudo-event. Too many candidates, he said, "are out giving speeches when they should be bowling." As early as 1966 he was encouraging candidates to toss coins across rivers to show that "a dollar doesn't go as far it used to." Newspapers were keen to run such photographs then. Nowadays, of course, the media are far more sophisticated, and would not dream of being manipulated in such an obvious manner. If Ed Broadbent, for instance, were to knock his opponents on Bay Street, and then greet his supporters on Main Street, why, the media wouldn't even mention such a transparent attempt at cheap symbolism.

Evry's favourite story is about managing the campaign of a candidate running for the board of the San Bernardino Municipal Water District. The candidate, a lawyer and a Stanford graduate, had no political experience, no machine, and was unknown in the area. Evry took control of the campaign. He encouraged the candidate to work off his energies in the bowling alley. He then saturated San Bernardino with a simple, repetitive message: "Three cheers for Pat Milligan." According to *Life*: "The voters saw those five winged words on billboards, they saw them on full-page ads in the papers, they saw them on facsimile telegrams sent through the mails. They saw them for days, they saw them for months; and by the time the election came round, they knew Pat Milligan as well as they knew Winstons or Buicks. When the ballots were counted, Milligan's name led all the rest."

Frank Stronach had adopted Milligan's techniques in Markham. The roadsides were littered with "Let's be FRANK" posters, telephone poles in towns were adorned like Christmas trees with "Bring FRANKness to Ottawa" hoardings. The area newspapers — Stronach was the co-owner of one of them — were saturated with colourful ads encouraging the voter: "Let's be FRANK."

The Conservatives were at a distinct disadvantage. They had changed candidates in mid-campaign — John Cole having secured the nomination after Mulroney's refusal to endorse Sinc Stevens — and they lacked Stronach's organizational ability to bring in such a saturation campaign within election spending limits.

They realized, however, that Stronach's Milligan-like campaign was based on a marketing theory at least twenty years old. It was simple name recognition, the principle behind door-knocking and lawn signs. It lacked the virtue of imposed meaning, the real secret of a modern campaign. So, in a masterly stroke, the Tory organizers allowed Stronach himself to impose meaning on the campaign.

"What we did was this," said one Conservative strategist. "We attended all the public all-candidates' meetings, which encouraged Stronach to do the same. We always made sure we had a blackboard with chalk, up on the stage. Then, in the course of the meeting, we'd have someone planted in the audience. That person's job was to get Stronach going. The person would get up and ask: 'Mr. Stronach, you have some interesting thoughts on how the government should be run. I wonder if you would elaborate.'

"Stronach always rose to the bait, and started in with his lecture. There was absolutely no doubt: the more we could expose him, and keep him talking, the more votes we had."

JOHN TURNER, MEANWHILE, had launched his La Mancha campaign across the country, losing no opportunity to remind voters this election was about the sale of Canada, the loss of sovereignty; this fight was the fight of his life. In the early going he demonstrated the very things Allan Gregg was urging on the prime minister — spontaneity, emotion, and motive. All in all, he was putting up a spectacular effort.

Only later — only after Turner had bravely resisted another

challenge to his leadership, only after he had defined the terms of the campaign, only after he had bared his chest during the televised debate — only then, when the Conservatives appeared headed for certain electoral defeat, would they decide to give Turner, too, a blackboard and chalk.

# CHAPTER 7

# LORD OF THE RING

*A good will is good not because of
what it performs or effects, not by its
aptness for the attainment of some
proposed end, but simply by
virtue of the volition, that is, it is
good in itself . . . .*
IMMANUEL KANT

T HE BUTCHER COULD HAVE SET-
tled it right away. Had he decided to stop at nothing in his bid to
become the member of parliament for Brome-Missisquoi, he could
have simply delivered his Conservative opponent, Gabrielle
Bertrand — the incumbent, and the frail, elderly widow of a former
Quebec premier — a coco-bonk to the forehead. But no. Paul "The
Butcher" Vachon was past that now. The former wrestler had
discovered respectability, and he wore it like a world-champion-
ship tag-team belt.

Vachon was one of the fighting Vachon brothers, and the
star candidate recruited by the New Democratic Party in Quebec.
He still lives with his mother in the log cabin in which he, along
with thirteen brothers and sisters, grew up. Vachon believes that's
how his mother lost the use of her knees, running after so many
kids. They had no money. To entertain themselves, the kids used
to fight.

The Vachon home was three and a half miles from the
schoolhouse, to which the children walked barefoot in summer.

The school taught grades one through seven in a single room. All the Vachon kids took their education there. Paul's elder brother Maurice was the first to leave home and join the wrestling circuit. They called him Mad Dog. He was a real wrestler, not like what you have today. He fought for Canada in the Olympics in 1948 and won the gold medal in the 1950 Commonwealth Games. That was something, all right.

Paul joined him a few years later. At seventeen, he walked out to the dirt road that led past the farmhouse and stuck out his thumb. He had seventy dollars in his pocket, which his father had borrowed from a neighbour. Vachon had placed second in a provincial wrestling match and would represent Quebec at the Dominion Championships in Regina. It was 1954. He'd never been farther than Montreal. He didn't know where Regina was.

Vachon bought a bus ticket in Montreal. It cost sixty-four dollars. The Trans-Canada Highway wasn't built, so the bus went through Detroit, Chicago, Minneapolis, then back across the border to Winnipeg. He slept the first night on the bus, but the second night it was in the station and he had to find a room, which he couldn't afford. By this time, he was also getting hungry. He went to the police station and asked for sanctuary. They put him in the drunk tank, where he slept on a bare pallet and avoided the sick on the floor. The next day he arrived in Regina, and fought that night. He placed second, winning a silver medal for his province, and got on the next bus home.

"I enjoyed that trip," he recalled, many years later. "It was kind of dull for a young man to always be on the farm."

Vachon joined his brother on the professional wrestling circuit. They became famous, the fighting Vachon brothers, and, though not rich, at least richer than if they had stayed in the cabin in the shadow of Mount Sutton. And they got to see the world. Paul was fighting in England one year — he was then a fresh-faced youth of 360 pounds who delighted in squeezing the juice out of his opponents — and a promoter was shocked at his technique. "You," he said, "are just like a bloody butcher in there." The name stuck. On the next night's card he was Paul "The Butcher" Vachon.

He fought under that name for most of his career, with one exception. Once, when a promoter needed a bad guy, Paul shaved his head and grew a beard; he fought under the name Nikolai Zolotoff. This was during the Cold War. Nikolai would climb into

126

the ring and shout gibberish, supposedly Russian, at the crowd. People hated him. One night, a group of Doukhobor farmers came into town. They spoke Russian, and knew Nikolai didn't. Angry and disappointed, they ended up climbing into the ring. Vachon had to flee for his life. The next night he was The Butcher again.

Oh, a lifetime of stories. He was a famous actor in the movies, in India, in the early 1960s. Someone saw him wrestling and asked him to try out for a role opposite Dara Singh, the Arnold Schwarzenegger of Indian cinema. They needed a heavy for a string of gladiator movies, and Vachon filled the bill. The plot was always the same: into the ring, fight the good fight, wind up with a trident in the bowels. . . .

ONLY ONCE did Vachon go to a movie theatre to watch his own work. He sat at the back, where he wouldn't be noticed, during a première in Bombay. When the big fight scene came up, the audience was visibly partisan on the side of Singh. The emotion built gradually. Singh would land a blow — hooray! Vachon would counter — hiss! There was always a point, just before the finish, at which it looked as if Vachon would win. Singh would be bloodied, his weapon lost, his legs tangled in a gladiator's net, helpless. The audience went nearly hysterical with grief — people were actually wailing and jumping from their seats. But then Singh rallied. He recovered his trusty trident. He speared Vachon's bowels. The crowd went wild with excitement and relief, tearing around the cinema in a satisfied bloodlust. Vachon tried to sneak out quietly.

"There he is, the son-of-a-bitch!" someone shouted. "He's not dead!" Vachon was rescued by police, and didn't go back to see his movies again.

But the movies also saved his life. He was wrestling in Dhaka, the capital of Bangladesh, then East Pakistan. There had been a border clash with India. Hundreds of people were dead; thousands more were trying to flee the country. Vachon couldn't even bribe his way onto a flight to Calcutta, so he hired a motorized rickshaw and drove to the border. He had to walk the last few miles; the driver wouldn't go any farther. "There were dead bodies everywhere, throats slit," Vachon said, with typical understatement. When he got to the border station, the guard looked at his passport and said: "Ah, Vachon — wrestler." He knew him from the movies and allowed him to pass through unmolested.

The highlight of his wrestling career was the period between 1968 and 1971, when he and Mad Dog were the world tag-team champions of the American Wrestling Association. He fought as long as his knees would allow it. They wouldn't allow it after 1986, and he retired at forty-nine. "I loved every minute of it," he says today. "I'd start over again tomorrow, but the body" — here he slugs a knee with the heel of his hand, and his gruff voice takes on a tone of deep regret — "just won't take it."

It was a year later, after the wrestling was over, that the Vachon brothers showed their true colours. Mad Dog had gone for an early-morning walk near Des Moines, Iowa, where he lived, when he was struck by a car. At first, the Montreal *Gazette* treated the incident lightly: "Mad Dog hits the mat in a hit-and-run attack." Before long, however, the gravity of Mad Dog's condition became known. "Mad Dog could lose leg," the paper reported, a few days later. The Butcher, who had rushed to his brother's bedside, was philosophical: "They're not going to amputate his heart," he said, "and that's what's kept him going all these years."

Soon the *Gazette*, like every paper in Quebec, was running daily reports on Mad Dog's condition: "Surgeons amputate Mad Dog's leg," "Mad Dog sore but looking up after losing leg," "Get-well wishes for Mad Dog." Then, after the amputation had not gone well, and the wrestler was fighting an infection: "Mad Dog faces toughest fight," "Condition serious, but Mad Dog feels better," "Mad Dog back in serious condition."

Mad Dog was in terrible pain, but he refused to succumb to blackness. While still in his hospital bed and in much distress, he said he'd like to play a pirate in a children's television program. "I told the producers, 'What good's a pirate without a leg missing?'" He also refused, despite the thousands of get-well cards and sympathy telegrams, to consider himself a charity case. "When I fell down, the whole nation helped me get up," he said. "When people help you like that, you have to help back." From his hospital bed in Iowa, he agreed to participate in a telethon for the Lucie Bruneau Foundation, which helps the disabled adjust back into society. He had only enough strength to stay on the air for fifteen minutes, via telephone, but his appearance generated $250,000 in donations.

The driver who had struck Mad Dog Vachon, then fled, was eventually fined $114. In Iowa, it seems, justice is neither as swift nor as certain as in the ring.

128

Paul Vachon, meanwhile, was acting as his brother's personal secretary, recording messages and keeping lists of all who had written. "When you're well again," The Butcher told his brother, "we're going to have to answer all of these." "You're god-damn right," Mad Dog replied. But then the cards began to arrive by the truck load. Mad Dog received more than 40,000 pieces of mail. He went on television to apologize he could not answer them all.

The first federal politician to call offering condolences was Ed Broadbent. "The prime minister, Mr. Mulroney, he called too," The Butcher recalled. "But Mr. Broadbent, he called first."

Mad Dog Vachon returned to Montreal to begin a lengthy rehabilitation. A supporter had arranged for a private jet to make the journey. Mad Dog was met by about a hundred relatives and well-wishers at the airport. For a moment, he was overcome with emotion. His voice choked as he thanked his friends with the tenderest, most poetic sentiment he could muster. "This," he said, "is like getting out of a penitentiary."

The Vachon brothers launched a fast-food chain selling Mad Dog Burgers, and settled into life as small businessmen. But when election time came near, The Butcher decided to enter politics. His reasons were simple. "Mad Dog had eight operations that would have cost us $125,000 without medicare," he said. "I've spent thirty-two years in sixty-five countries, and I have realized through the years that the country where you have the best chance of a good-quality life is Canada. And that is in great part due to our social programs that exist, again in great part, to pressure the NDP has put on minority governments. It's not written in stone we're going to keep those programs. I don't trust the old parties to keep them."

IT'S A SAFE bet that, when The Butcher decided to run for office, he didn't know the detailed origins of the NDP and of Canada's social programs. His life had been spent head-butting people with names like Junkyard Dog, not studying Canadian political history. But he felt the NDP was different from the "old parties" which had ruled Brome-Missisquoi for as long as he could remember, without much benefiting families like the Vachons; and he remembered that Ed Broadbent had called first. Maybe the NDP would help him run for office.

The first thing the NDP told him was that he had to form

a riding association. The New Democrats were not exactly thick on the ground in Quebec. In the 1984 election, they had boasted only about four thousand paid members in the province, one dedicated campaign worker, and a budget of fifty thousand dollars. No one was very surprised when the party failed to make a historic breakthrough. The New Democrats had never elected anyone from Quebec; why should it bother with organization?

Vachon was told he had to sign up 150 people to form a legitimate riding association. He licked his lips and wrote down the number. It seemed like a lot of people, but he would try. First, he went home and signed up his mother, Marguerite. Then he signed up Mad Dog. Then he ran out of prospects.

Phil Edmonston, a consumer advocate with a flair for organization and himself an NDP candidate in a neighbouring riding, came to Brome-Missisquoi to lend a hand. Vachon soon got the remaining 148 signatures, informed a surprised national executive, and was duly nominated as the party's candidate.

The nomination caused a sensation in the Quebec media, and The Butcher was invited the following day to appear on an open-line radio talk show in Montreal. He accepted the invitation, but immediately regretted having done so. He was paralysed with fear. "What did I know about New Democrat policy?" he asked himself. So he picked up the telephone and called the people who had told him how to get nominated. He explained his anxiety; party headquarters told him to wait by the telephone, someone would call him back shortly to explain policy. Vachon waited, and half an hour later a policy expert was on the line — Ed Broadbent.

Broadbent understood the stage fright, and put The Butcher at ease. New Democrat policy wasn't complicated, Broadbent said. Just be yourself and tell the truth as you see it. Then Broadbent gave him a little confidence. "He told me he was a college professor when he went into politics," Vachon recalled, "and he didn't know anything, either." Broadbent passed on another piece of advice. When he himself was first elected to parliament, he told Vachon, he had won by only fifteen votes out of 40,000 votes cast. Broadbent believed the secret of his victory lay in his having visited eighty per cent of the homes in his riding in the six months before the election.

The NDP's professional advisers had told Vachon that the victory formula combined a high-profile local candidate with money, organization, and platform. Vachon had little money. He had a laughable organization. He had a shaky grasp of the platform. But high profile? This was something he understood.

Vachon posed for a camera, for perhaps the first time in his life, without a snarl on his face. He still had his trademark shaved head and thick underbrush black goatee. Even in retirement he is a fearsome-looking man; but he has kind eyes and a hesitant, self-conscious smile. He used the photograph on a brochure with the party colours. Part of the brochure was devoted to Ed Broadbent and the New Democrat message, the other half to Vachon and the issues as he saw them. He was proud of the result.

Vachon worked late into the night signing each brochure with a little message, then putting it in one of two piles. In one pile, the message thanked the voter for meeting with him; in the other, Vachon said he was sorry the voter had been out when he'd called. It took time — his penmanship was laborious — but he thought people would like the personal touch. Then he stuffed the brochures into the pockets of his good suit and wobbled like a drunken sailor from door to door, his bad knees creaking.

David Johnston, a reporter with the Montreal *Gazette*, was with Vachon one day and recorded this moment:

"He always says the same thing. He shakes hands and says: 'My name is Vachon. Paul Vachon. Candidate for the New Democratic Party.' Then he raises his voice for emphasis. 'The party of Ed Broadbent.' He lowers his voice again. 'On November twenty-first, I ask that you keep me in mind. That's Paul Vachon. NDP.'

"But at the next door there is trouble. An old woman answers. When she sees Vachon's menacing demeanour before her, she gasps and retreats a step.

"She's looking at the floor. You can tell by her eyes she can't see properly. Vachon takes a step into her home. The woman gasps again. What is he, crazy?

"'Can you see me?' asks Vachon.

"'Not well,' says the woman.

"'I give you my hand, madame,' Vachon says in his gruff voice.

"The woman extends her hand reluctantly. Vachon takes it and shakes it gently. Then he makes his pitch, altering it slightly, delivering his words more gently.

"The woman raises her head and turns one ear so she can

hear him better. When he's finished, Vachon says, 'I give you my hand again, madame.'

"They shake.

"'Thank you, madame,' says Vachon.

"'It's me who thanks you, Monsieur Vachon,' says the woman.

"This," wrote Johnston, "is where you first get to like Paul Vachon."

By the end of the campaign, working alone, Vachon had visited more than twenty thousand homes. No one ever accused the Vachon boys of lacking desire — which, as it turned out, is more than could be said for the New Democratic Party.

IN THE PERIOD leading up to the election, the New Democrats confronted a troubling development. They were popular in the polls. It was terrible, unprecedented, and they could not agree on how to deal with it. For a year Ed Broadbent had been the national leader most esteemed by Canadians — he was consistently seen as the one who would do the best job as prime minister, who was most trustworthy and honest, and who was most inspiring. His leadership ratings had climbed steadily since 1984. The New Democrats were accustomed to this view of their leader, and to their repeated failure to translate it into support at election time.

In mid-summer of 1987, however, something dramatic seemed to be developing. The NDP, according to the Gallup survey conducted August 3-5, led the other two parties. The New Democrats had 37 per cent of the decided vote (if an election were held immediately), compared with 36 per cent for the Liberals and 25 for the Conservatives. Of course, it could have been a bad poll — the "one poll out of twenty" that falls outside the predicted margin of error. But the lead held through September, and in October the New Democrats reached 38 per cent in the polls. The lead was to fall through early 1988, but the New Democrats still held about a third of the decided vote during the election-planning period.

The NDP had broken through a number of traditional obstacles to widespread support. By the fall of 1988, the party was as popular in Quebec as it was nationally. Its support was stronger among the *thirtysomething* age group than among its traditional bastions, the young and the elderly. It enjoyed balanced support from all education and income groups, fading only slightly among people earning more than $40,000 a year. It had also broadened its support beyond urban manufacturing centres, posting as high a backing in small towns as in major cities.

Much of this new support came from voters "rented" from the other two parties, people disenchanted with the failure of the Conservatives and the Liberals to demonstrate significant differences between themselves. Three out of five New Democrat supporters said they were motivated by disgust with the other parties, not by attraction to the NDP. This was a source of nagging concern for NDP election planners, though not nearly so ominous as a polling result that drew even less attention.

The one really dark spot in the polling data was a blip as easily overlooked as a shadow on the lung. Respondents were asked which party they thought would win the next election, regardless of their own preference: 51 per cent said the Conservatives; only 5 per cent said the New Democrats. When Tory supporters were asked which party was going to win, 87 per cent predicted, why, of course, the Conservatives. When New Democrats were asked the same question, however, only 13 per cent said the NDP. In a survey conducted a fortnight before the election was called, nearly half the New Democrat supporters were conceding a Conservative victory.

The New Democrats were motivated, in their survey and election practices, by two qualities which are anathema to the conduct of the modern campaign — democracy and thrift. True, their $250,000 polling operation was the largest they had ever undertaken and allowed them to track between 200 and 500 respondents a night, and to pay some attention to specific ridings. And they cut their costs by half in farming out the intensive labour of polling, known as fieldwork, to private telephone-survey operators. But raw survey results were fed into party headquarters for analysis.

The New Democrats had established, for the first time, an in-house polling-analysis branch. It was similar to the one established by Allan Gregg for the Conservatives in the early 1970s, before he set up Decima Research. Like the Tories and the Liberals, the New Democrats turned to an American pollster for advice. They looked to the expertise of a Democrat from Washington, Vic Fingerhut. But the NDP lacked the resources to conduct the deep, cross-referenced polling used by Gregg. And in their effort to save money by conducting their analysis in-house, they exposed themselves to the chill hand of survey analysis — the committee.

In the NDP, the process of translating poll results into election strategy went like this. The party developed the "instrument" — or questionnaire — which was sent to the field for responses. The fieldwork, once completed, was returned to a polling working group for analysis and recommendations. The working group consisted of a handful of party staff and external advisers such as Fingerhut. They generated a report, and shipped it up to the working group of the strategy and elections planning committee, or SEPC.

The working group, during the pre-writ period, met every week. It in turn was responsible to the steering committee of the SEPC, which met bi-weekly and was supported by a party secretariat to the steering committee. The steering committee in turn reported to the full SEPC, a pre-campaign offshoot of the standing elections planning committee, or EPC, and which met every six weeks or so. The SEPC, as the final arbiter, attempted to decide election strategy through an overall consensus of its forty-odd members, drawn from elected party ranks nation-wide. Once the findings of the field workers were fully digested by the SEPC, a follow-up instrument was developed.

This process was accelerated during the campaign itself, and not all instruments had to work their way entirely up and down the ladder. But many did. And — most tellingly — the campaign strategy position paper, which the polling was meant to influence, worked its way through this process not once but more than ten times between the summer of 1987 and the fall of 1988. Democratic? Very. Efficacious? The NDP's internal structure was not, to put it kindly, designed to bring out the intuitive flash of insight that can transform reams of polling data into an incisive election message.

The New Democrats had, in short, adopted the polling mechanism without accepting its influence on other party mechanisms, particularly strategy formulation. The New Democrats built national data on electoral attitudes and sentiments, information well suited to a national electronic campaign. But these data, once collected, were thrust back into the hands of regional, sectoral, and factional interests, which were supposed to decide exactly how they were to be transformed into an election platform.

A national finding of significance — say, the previous party affiliation of new NDP supporters — would be debated by New Democrats from both British Columbia and Ontario. Such a finding supposedly would help identify the "enemy" in the campaign. A B.C. New Democrat wouldn't even mention the Liberals, while his Ontario brother would consider them the natural enemy. Yet the two were expected to reach a consensus on which opponent was the "default" party in the campaign, and this consensus was supposed to be reflected by the national leader. It was a hellishly bad campaign road paved with the best of intentions.

MODERN CAMPAIGNING had shifted the strategic role of the party from conception to execution. The New Democrats, through their painful adherence to high-sounding but counterproductive principles, had stubbornly resisted this fundamental change. They were like the primitive tribe that's presented with a television set by a missionary. The missionary finds on a return visit that the machine has been placed among the audience; the villagers are still listening to their own story-teller. "But," the missionary protests, "the television knows many more stories than your story-teller." "Yes," the villagers reply, "but the story-teller knows us."

The New Democrats had not decided whether to campaign to win, or to continue their approach, as the Conservative strategist Nancy Jamieson described it, of "strategic losing." They had not decided whether to campaign against the Liberals or the Conservatives. They had not decided whether the overriding theme of the campaign was to be fairness, the "average Canadian," or integrity of government. They had not decided whether to relate free trade to the overriding theme, or to treat it as a separate issue. They had difficulty agreeing on what resources to devote to Quebec. Most damaging of all, the party — unlike The Butcher — was not singlemindedly determined to win.

The New Democrats were a little like some of the Canadian athletes who, that September, headed off to the Olympic Games in Seoul. They were prepared to give their best, and hoped it might win a bronze, maybe even a silver. Bronze-medal attitudes virtually guarantee, at best, bronze-medal performances, but the New Democrats seemed concerned that a more ambitious posture might ultimately cause more harm than good. When Ed Broadbent, three weeks into the campaign, mused during an open-line program that Canada might be on a path toward a two-party system, with the New Democrats on the left and the Conservatives on the right, his own prospects of success seemed to chill him. He began back-pedalling within moments of leaving the studio. His statement had contradicted the democratic consensus of the SEPC: that he was to campaign without appearing to threaten the political status quo.

It was because of this bronze-medal approach that Broadbent didn't bother to mention the words "free trade" in his opening speech. It was because of the bronze-medal approach that he waited until the fourth week of an eight-week campaign to predict that the Conservatives would not win, that they were "finished, as of right now." Not until November 2 — less than three weeks before the election — did he dare announce what the voters had known from the beginning: that, to defeat free trade, they had to choose between the New Democrats and the Liberals.

"Canadians want to say 'no' to the Mulroney trade deal but 'yes' to a fairer Canada," Broadbent said, without uttering the dreaded V-word. The Liberals by now were first in the polls, the New Democrats a distant third; the obvious conclusion for voters who agreed with Broadbent was, ironically, that they should cast their lot with the Liberals. Another leader, perhaps, would have campaigned with optimism. Ed Broadbent appeared to be campaigning for his own retirement. Like the party of under-achievers he led, he did not want to spoil his popularity with success.

NEVER BEFORE HAD the New Democratic Party been offered such an ideal platform. Handing the free-trade issue to the NDP was rather like giving His Holiness the rebuttal in a debate on canon law, so naturally did the issue dovetail with traditional social-democratic policies. Contrary to popular belief, the thrust of the NDP polls and the advice of Vic Fingerhut was not that the New Democrats were incapable of sustaining a credible campaign on the free-trade issue. It was that they could not sustain a free-trade campaign on economic terms. They could, however, sustain it in the social-policy area, their natural turf.

Why, then, did the New Democrats enter the campaign treating free trade as a tariffs issue — particularly when their polling data showed they were the most trustworthy party to point out the deal's potential threat to social programs? Why? Because

136

those polls had fallen into the hands of dunces, in the literal sense
— "dunce" deriving from the writings of John Duns Scotus, a
thirteenth-century theologian regarded by sixteenth-century hu-
manists as a hairsplitter. By failing to do what John Turner had
done by instinct and the Tories had done by design — imbue free
trade with a transcendent meaning — the New Democrats had, in
effect, been served a gourmet lunch and allowed the Liberals to eat
it.

One senior party strategist, Robin Sears, put it precisely.
As campaign director, he was involved in all stages of policy
formulation and maintained close proximity to the leader during
the campaign. After the election, at the end of half a day's soul-
searching over the party's disappointing performance, while refusing to point the finger elsewhere and accepting his own share of
the blame, he summed up as follows:

"If we had known that we were all in agreement on
whether we were going for government or not, whether the Liberals
were the enemy or not, whether we were going for fairness or
honesty, what we would have said about the trade deal, as part of
that larger message, was: 'This is a right-wing agenda to destroy
the social fabric of everything that makes Canada the country it is
— and if you don't believe me, listen to this.' Then run through
the five or six best metaphors, and say that again and again and
again, from October 1987 to November 21, 1988.

"And if we'd had the confidence to do that, based on a
conviction about our competitiveness, things would have turned
out very differently. Now, we did say some of that. That's what the
nurses was all about. ['Nurses' was a television advertisement in
which an operating-theatre nurse — actually, an actress representing a nurse — said that she wouldn't want free trade to destroy
medicare.] That's what going to Tommy's [Tommy Douglas's]
church in Weyburn was all about. That's what the pensions [Broad-
bent had argued old-age pensions were threatened by free trade]
was all about. But it wasn't done with enough coherence and focus
that it could compete with the flag-waving that Turner was doing.

"To some extent, you cannot confess to ambiguities in a
campaign, you know. As I said to a Republican friend of mine in
the States: 'Doesn't it make you a little bit unhappy that basically,
your campaign message was that Michael Dukakis wants to let
black men out of jail to rape white women?' He laughed and said,

'Yeah, but it sure the hell is effective.' Well, that's the level on which a lot of politics is fought.

"So the problem, I think, had less to do with alternative conceptions [about free trade] than with the confidence of our execution. And the lack of confidence about the execution stemmed from where we started off. You have to metaphor. You can't be a boy *and* a girl. You have to really choose."

The NDP strategist's use of the term "metaphor" is enlightening. A metaphor is, by standard definition, an implied comparison. It is subtler, yet often more memorable, than the explicit comparison of a simile. A metaphor derives its meaning by comparing one thing to another, suggesting a likeness or an analogy between them. A mixed metaphor can be especially arresting, as demonstrated by the great metaphor-mangler Robert Thompson, one-time leader of Social Credit, who warned a startled parliament: "If this catches fire, it'll snowball across the country."

But "metaphor," as used by the strategist, denoted an approach to politics which had come to distinguish campaigns in the post-literate age. It was a way of talking about things by describing what they were like, rather than what they were. In the modern campaign, a black rapist becomes the metaphor for the Dukakis record on law enforcement, just as a disgraced minister becomes the metaphor for Tory avarice. Metaphors are useful, of course, but the mere entry of the term into the political vernacular indicated the extent to which metaphor had come to animate political discussion. When something can be described only as what it's like, rather than as what it is, it no longer has intrinsic meaning; it is no more or less than what has been attributed to it by metaphor. In this environment, a politician is at a disadvantage if he refers to the free-trade agreement, for example, without using the metaphor of the Sale of Canada Act.

Among their other sins, the New Democrats refused to metaphor. As Robert Thompson might have put it, they threw the baby out with the bath water and missed the brass ring, which left them, yet again, crying over spilt milk.

ONE POLITICIAN who had no problem using metaphors was Paul Vachon. For The Butcher, the whole thing was straightforward. Free trade meant a system under which Mad Dog would have been forced to pay $125,000 for his operations. Free trade would mean that his mother, eighty-three years old and with artificial knees, wouldn't get her pension. Vachon's favourite metaphor, however, had nothing to do with free trade. It was about a tree.

"When I was a kid," he would say, "we had this great big maple tree in the front of the house. It was, oh, seventy-five feet to the west of the house, not far from the dirt road. On the south side, the branches would cover the road; but on the north side, it covered the yard.

"We used to spend a large amount of our family life under that tree. My dad built a swing from the tree, and us kids would swing there. It had a fire pit, and we'd cook out there two, three times a week. Afterwards we'd all sing together. And I'd wrestle my brothers under that tree, all the time. We used to play under that tree whenever we had spare time, which was not often.

"Then the roads department came along and said they were going to widen the road and straighten it out, and that the tree was in the way. It made us sad. Our dad, he thought of protesting, but anyway we cut it down. That big tree was so huge that it took the three big brothers, all hand in hand, to go around it. When we cut it down we found out it was 360 years old. It was standing when Jacques Cartier came to Canada. Think about that.

"Anyway, we were all sad about it, but my dad said: 'Don't worry, we'll go out to the sugar bush and transplant some trees.' The boys, we all took shovels. It took us half a day to transplant one tree, digging so's we wouldn't damage the roots. We transplanted four of them, about two inches thick, good and straight they were. Three survived. Now they're big enough for me to put a bear hug around.

"The thing is, though, now they're dying.

"When a tree's growing, you don't really notice it grow. But when it's dying, you know. They've stopped growing. And in the spring, when they used to reach up, now they're drooping. Anyway, the punch line is this: I can't tell my kids, 'Don't worry about it, we'll just go to the sugar bush and transplant some more.' Because the trees in the sugar bush are dying, too. It's the acid rain.

"You know," Vachon said, "that story strikes a chord with everybody I told it to."

And he told it to hundreds, maybe thousands of voters in Brome-Missisquoi. The campaign was going fine until some NDP nationalists in Montreal started saying that the English in Quebec didn't deserve rights, or something like that. The Butcher noticed that English-speaking people in his riding didn't have as much time for him after that. He wanted to talk to Mr. Broadbent about it but, try as he might, he was never able to get through.

# CHAPTER 8

# THE MO-JO MINI-BUBBLE

*When dealing and working with*
*people, things may not always run as*
*smoothly as this book will indicate ....*
READY, SET, GO! (1988 CAMPAIGN MANUAL)

C ANDIDATES ARE WONDERFULLY
available during elections. To get through to one in the middle of
a campaign, you simply pick up the phone. If the candidate isn't
around, someone will go check by the coffee machine, or look at
the map board to see if the candidate is out door-knocking. To meet
a candidate in the middle of a campaign, you simply drive over to
the campaign office, pour yourself a coffee, and stand around until
the candidate walks in. This technique did not work, however, in
the case of Maureen McTeer, who ran for the Tories in Carleton-
Gloucester. To get through to McTeer in mid-campaign, you had
to telephone her personal public-relations consultant and sweet-
talk awhile. This was but one more indication that Maureen
McTeer was not just the wife of the secretary of state for external
affairs, not just Mrs. Former Prime Minister Joe Clark. She was an
important candidate for public office, a woman in her own right.

Maureen McTeer was perhaps best known — as a woman
in her own right — for her monthly column in *Chatelaine*. The
magazine is a uniquely Canadian publication. It is of particular
interest to women, but unlike its American counterparts it does
not fall neatly into one of the many sub-categories of such magazines. Some women's magazines are clearly aimed at the tradi-

tional homemaker. Some of these, in turn, are wholly devoted to home decorating; others to cooking and child care; some offer the light escapism of romantic fiction; a fourth category comes heavily scented and encourages women to decorate themselves. On the other side of the market are those magazines aimed at the professional woman. These promote the notion that women should take charge of all aspects of their lives, from workplace to bedroom.

*Chatelaine* is not fully described by any one of these categories; instead, it borrows a little from each. The ideal *Chatelaine* reader is probably a career woman who juggles work and family life, and requires steady reassurance on both fronts. The magazine offers articles on food, fashion, beauty, health, child-rearing, decorating, and relationships. It does not ignore the larger world of politics and social issues, and it routinely dips into soft-core feminism with articles promoting the advancement of women.

This hybrid style is evidently satisfying to its readers — *Chatelaine* has a circulation of more than a million and makes pots of money for Maclean Hunter — but at times it leads to a certain confusion. When a *Chatelaine* headline reads "Smart! Sassy! Sexy!" the reader is unsure whether the article is about spring fashions or Barbara McDougall. The pages that trumpet "Brash. Bold. Blue!" could explore either the new summer colours or the new Quebec. In the layout department of *Chatelaine*, as elsewhere, words have become sound bites. Sad. True. Post-literate.

This clutter of roles renders *Chatelaine* capable of delivering, under the title "Beautiful Beastie," this assessment of a premier: "Bill Vander Zalm, 53, the upright macho square who runs British Columbia, has the hard-edged style of the self-made man. He's completely unselfconscious and a dazzling showman. 'The sexy singing sensation from Canada' wowed 1.4-million viewers when he performed a folk song on Dutch TV. To the humorless NDP, who jeer he is all style and no substance, Bill replies, 'Style *is* substance.'"

A sentiment that was surely met at *Chatelaine*'s offices with a rousing chorus of cheers. That Vander Zalm. Loud. Retro. Ethnic.

In the same magazine, a senior parliamentary correspondent for the state television broadcaster was described as "hugely huggable." "Huggable and reassuring" also applied to the leader of the country's socialist party. All these descriptions come from *Chatelaine*'s annual survey of Canada's sexiest men. It is difficult to gather what message *Chatelaine* is delivering to women by including articles about politics alongside articles about sex, and occasionally blending the two. The message seems to be that it's okay for women to be interested in politics, so long as their interest includes daydreaming about whether political figures are G.I.B.

MAUREEN McTEER was an ideal columnist for a magazine of trans-mutable qualities such as *Chatelaine*. She was identified with politics — the identification was, albeit, a bit awkward — and she was a feminist. But she was the *Chatelaine* kind of feminist, which means a feminist with a make-over. The Maureen McTeer who gazed from the pages of her monthly column was not the gawky woman in the frowzy printed frocks of her youth. She was dressed for success, her colours were done, her arms were crossed in a power pose. She was clearly her own woman.

But who, exactly, was that? *Chatelaine* did not list McTeer's credentials with the column. The luckless reader already knew everything about her or was destined to know nothing at all. If the magazine failed in identifying her, well, how could it have done otherwise? To say, in a little tag-line, that McTeer was "the wife of Joe Clark" would not have been in keeping with the spirit of the thing. It would not have shown her as a woman in her own right. It would have been downright degrading. The problem was that there was no other way to identify her. Her column was called "Ottawa Report," but Maureen McTeer's ticket to Ottawa expired, in the absence of her husband, some miles short of the station.

The magazine could have listed her other credentials, but what were they? McTeer had tried a brief fling at a legal practice with a high-ticket Ottawa firm, then left, citing potential conflict of interest with her husband's work. How else could she identify herself? "She has travelled the world extensively with her husband, a diplomat." "She has a deep and thorough understanding of Ottawa, where her husband has a political practice." "She is a well-connected member of the parliamentary spouses' association." It was fraught with difficulty. Best to drop it altogether.

*Chatelaine*'s editor, Mildred Istona (*Spy* magazine take note: Mildred Istona and Mila Mulroney were separated at birth), once finished a three-handkerchief editorial column on the role of

143

political wives with the conclusion: "What's a woman's role in politics in 1987? North American society seems to be as confused as ever." So, evidently, was *Chatelaine*.

It is, of course, quite possible that the magazine hired McTeer as a freelancer on the basis of her captivating style, her ability to present opinion in a readable fashion, her clear-eyed assessment of the Ottawa scene; in short, on her own merits. She wrote the column as her own person, and if her views appeared, once or twice, to coincide with those of the Conservative government, why, it was probably simple confusion arising from the fact that a member of Joe Clark's staff did research for her column. After this fact came to light, Clark's office announced that McTeer paid a third of the woman's salary. The researcher had not mentioned this arrangement when worked over by one of the more thorough and aggressive reporters, Robert Fife, then with Canadian Press.

Odd. Zany. Zaftig.

As a columnist in her own right, McTeer appears to have been dedicated to illuminating the role of women in Ottawa. Thus, the column was devoted to topics such as: "Women's Job Futures — How Can the Federal Government Help?" And "Disabled Women in Canada — The Federal Record on Improving Services." Occasionally she carried the firebrand in the tradition of Nellie McClung, dealing with such controversial topics as: "Pay-Equity Laws — Should the Federal Government Amend Them?" Her columns were unfailingly positive. More can be done, was her message, but do not forget how much has been done already. If some people described the column as a collection of warmed-over press releases for the government, well, such people were carpers. McTeer's column was an antidote to the prevailing cynicism of the day.

Oddly, for someone whose column was scrubbed clean of partisan taint, McTeer was careful to wave a warning flag before presenting an opinion. Was this to prevent *Chatelaine* or the Conservative Party — perhaps both — from being associated with her ideas? Of course, any other column is expected to be a collection of ideas, so no such warning is necessary. No one would suggest that McTeer was compelled to flag her ideas because she wasn't a columnist in her own right. That she had her own mind was an unquestioned assertion, made frequently by herself.

So McTeer's prose adopted a tone similar to that of a youth

parliament, with the most innocent premise prefaced by a hearty breath and a fierce scowl: "In my opinion," she wrote, "university students are still well served. . . ."

"I think," she ventured, "these [government] publications are excellent. . . ."

"Here are, in my opinion," she dared to say, "some of [the Mulroney government's] major accomplishments this past year in meeting its commitment to equality and greater opportunities for Canadian women." This was followed by: "Fifty-five per cent of Canadian women are in the paid labour force. Yet, women working full time earn, on average, only sixty-five per cent of what men earn." In McTeer's opinion.

Virtually every column told the reader where to write for more information. McTeer told Canadian women where to write for information on awards for women, on wife battering, on job futures, on what the federal government was going to do, exactly, to advance the cause of women this year. She even told readers where to write to get a list of places they could write to.

She never mentioned where women could write to find out why they got paid sixty-five cents on the dollar. Maybe men got thirty-five cents more because they wrote away for the right brochures.

IF THERE WAS one niggling complaint to be made about the *Chatelaine* column, it was that McTeer never told her sisters the Brownie secret of getting ahead. Certainly, this secret was not to marry an important politician — as can be seen, that did McTeer no good at all. But one can imagine the legions of loyal McTeer readers who followed her advice assiduously, who wrote away religiously, who meticulously studied the federal government projections of job opportunities for women, and still found themselves waiting tables at a diner in Kicking Horse Pass.

This is because they didn't know the Brownie secret.

The Brownie secret to getting ahead in Ottawa is to be no Brownie. Thus, to take one piddling example, McTeer wrote a column called "Women Diplomats — Ten Who Represent Canada Around the World." The column was a list of women who had risen, through dint of talent and experience, to the position of Canadian representative abroad. All ten were undoubtedly capable of the job; some had even worked in the diplomatic corps to get it.

Certainly, many women would be interested in which career path might lead to such an important job.

Pierrette Lucas was made consul general in Philadelphia, and then Boston. Before that, McTeer wrote, she "worked in the federal government and public relations." Yes, and those who know Lucas are adamant that she does a fine job "providing valuable feedback to Ottawa on political and economic developments in that part of the Eastern seaboard," as McTeer put it. But they also know her "public relations" included a stint as press aide to the then prime minister Joe Clark, who, as readers of *Chatelaine* might recall, is McTeer's husband. Lucas was also an active Conservative organizer, and a close friend of Mila Mulroney; which is something McTeer knew, but readers of *Chatelaine* might not.

Similarly, Joan Price Winser, the consul general in Los Angeles, had "a lifetime in the volunteer sector in Montreal (e.g., helping to raise funds for the Y.W.C.A.)." Those who know the capable Winser would add that her résumé includes, e.g., helping to raise funds for the Conservative Party. Another little Brownie secret mysteriously withheld from the readers of *Chatelaine*.

McTeer's column was something to add to her credits — something she had achieved on her own, something that set her apart from people like that silly ditz Mila, who never aspired to be anything but a prime minister's wife. McTeer, who has described herself as "having ideas of my own," of being, "like Panasonic, a little ahead of [my] time," and of having been, thank goodness, "born with a brain," apparently felt these qualities were lacking in the current prime minister's wife. According to a profile in *The Globe and Mail* in 1985, McTeer felt Mila "certainly presents a different image to Canadians. . . [one] more traditional and 'rigid' Conservatives were yearning for." While Mila may be the perfect wife "by some people's standards," McTeer allowed, "there are some people who brand my kind of life as the perfect wife, someone who can earn an income but also hold up her half of the world." Mila's influence on the women of Canada would be a "negative force," the article paraphrased her as saying, "if it appeared as the only option open to women."

But it was, thanks to McTeer, not the only option. Unlike Mila, who had risen to prominence by marrying a prime minister, McTeer had shown women another way. She had, for example, written a book. Two books, in fact. One was about Canada's official residences. She was particularly suited to write a book on official residences, having lived in several of them. The other book was called *Parliament: Canada's Democracy and How It Works*. She used the Parliamentary Library to research this volume, which contains the revolutionary premise that parliament works. The library is closed to the public, but "I never pretended and said I was calling for Joe Clark," she said. "I told them I was doing a book."

Back in the early days, McTeer was sometimes eviscerated by the press for her flinty manner, her independent ways, and, most of all, for keeping her maiden name. It seemed important then that she had kept her name. But times had changed; by 1988, her reviews were fawning, the natural result of her many accomplishments. A profile published by the *Toronto Star* bore the headline: "Maureen McTeer at 35; lawyer, author, columnist, and speaker." Her life, she reflected, allowed her "to be curious on an international scale, to stimulate myself and to learn."

Among those who witnessed McTeer stimulating herself abroad were Canadian aid workers in Nicaragua, which she visited with her husband in 1987. At a luncheon, Clark asked how Canada might improve the delivery of programs in the region. A member of Canada's Save the Children Fund replied that it was hard to deliver services when he had to keep attending funerals for Nicaraguan friends killed by Contra rebels. McTeer then took what, in diplomatic euphemism, is called an "active role" in the discussion. She suggested, among other things, that the Canadian aid workers tell president Daniel Ortega to "stop haranguing the U.S. government."

McTeer and Clark had just toured an aid project sponsored by Alberta farmers. The project was close to a village that had been attacked three times in a year, leaving eleven dead. The attackers were sponsored by the U.S. government. In the most recent attack, a fifteen-year-old altar boy had been dragged from the village church and executed in the public square. The boy had not wanted to join the rebel group. His execution was by way of example, to encourage the others to join.

McTeer's interventions — she also took an "active role" in a meeting between Clark and Cardinal Miguel Obando y Bravo, who was trying to negotiate a ceasefire in the region — led to the inevitable grumbling that she had no right to speak out. After all, she was just Joe Clark's wife. She hadn't been elected.

THERE ARE MANY reasons for running for public office, reasons as varied and complex as the people who seek it. Maureen McTeer was an exception: her ambition was as clear as the flint in her eyes. McTeer wanted a seat in the Commons the way orphans want to find their real parents. McTeer had been attached to politics, in one way or another, for most of her life. Her campaign literature credited her with twenty-five years' involvement in public life. But there is a vast difference between a rink rat and Mario Lemieux. McTeer had spent her career attempting to define herself as a person. A seat in the Commons would settle the matter once and for all.

In her book on parliament, McTeer said she wanted to protect children from the "cheap, gratuitous cynicism" of the day. Instead, she wanted to impart some of the emotion she had felt as a nine-year-old Brownie visiting Parliament for the first time. She rode the elevator to the observation deck on the Peace Tower. "I remember being small and everything being so overwhelmingly huge," she recalled. "I can remember. . . being terrified that the cold and howling wind would blow me away, like Dorothy in *The Wizard of Oz*." She recalled that, years later, working as a young aide to Joe Clark, she would walk home from work through a thick Ottawa snowstorm and hear the carillon from the same tower ringing the hour. The bells were muffled by the falling snow. "It was," she said, "the most peaceful feeling in the world." McTeer would forever feel that way about the Commons. She had known it long as a place occupied by both hobgoblin and faerie — a frightening place, but one that offered sanctuary.

The first step to getting into parliament is receiving the party nomination. McTeer's was contested, but she triumphed over the other two contenders. As one writer observed: "She had a top-flight campaign manager, a public relations firm and a milk-and-water, twelve-minute speech that frothed about her rural roots and her 'strict and traditional family' upbringing on a Cumberland farm." She also had a dozen members of Joe Clark's staff at External Affairs roaming the hall with walkie-talkies.

Carleton-Gloucester had been newly created by the redistribution of seats before the election. A suburban riding on the fringes of Ottawa, it included Rideau and Osgoode, rural Gloucester, Beacon Hill, Blackburn Hamlet, Orleans, and Hunt Club Park. To anyone else in the country, it was just Ottawa, but in Ottawa

148

— a city with more school boards than movie theatres, a place where the municipal governments resembled the warring city-states of fifteenth-century Italy — it was an unusually disparate riding.

The riding was the fourth most populous in Canada, and the second-fastest growing. Most of its residents worked, in one way or another, for the federal government. Eighty-five per cent of the residents in the riding owned their own homes; many of these homes had been built in the past five years. A large number of voters were raising young families. The sentiments of the riding were predominantly Liberal, which made it a tough slog for a Conservative candidate. The voters of the area had even defeated Jean Piggott, a high-profile and respected Conservative member of parliament.

Odd that McTeer would land in a difficult riding, given that her campaign manager was David Small, a former Clark aide who was known as "Mr. Mander, Gerry to his friends." A cartographer, Small had headed the Tory effort to influence the electoral redistribution. Riding boundaries in Canada are set by an independent commission, but an alert and active party worker can organize community groups, make representations on behalf of his party, and generally influence the process. Small was an unqualified success. In Toronto, for instance, he was instrumental in stripping the WASP vote from the riding of Eglinton-Lawrence — a predominantly ethnic riding the Tories could not hope to win — and placing those useful votes in St. Paul's, where Conservative cabinet minister Barbara McDougall needed all the help she could get. Small played margins like this across the country.

In Carleton-Gloucester, though, McTeer had a fight. "The issues here are free trade, child care, and defence," Small said. "The Conservative party is not seen as doing very well on social issues, softer issues. We're not going to win unless we bring around people who traditionally voted Liberal."

McTeer's campaign was organized by the book. Desktop computers hummed almost silently, guarding their electors' list, which was being cross-indexed with street address, telephone number, and voting preference. The phone bank was installed along one wall; the phones had been installed way back in July. Behind the offices was the direct-mail room, organized for envelope-stuffers. Inventories on the wall traced the installation of lawn signs and kept track of people who were willing to volunteer. A copy of the 1988 Progressive Conservative policy manual was on hand for ready reference. Morale in the office was buoyed (see Book Two, Campaign Management) by favourable press clippings posted to a notice board. Volunteers called themselves "Mo's Mob," and wore T-shirts bearing the slogan. Even the office bathroom was organized. "This facility is non-gender specific," said a notice, which went on to outline rules of use for male and female patrons. "I've been to party leadership conventions," said David Small, "that were less well organized."

Small reflected on the demographic blip which had been tagged the "new traditionalist." There were, he felt, more than a few new traditionalists in the riding. "The party does quite well with the male half of that crowd," he said. "Thankfully, we've got a candidate who can appeal to the female side of it, too."

At that, a van pulled into the parking lot. The side door rolled open, and the candidate stepped out. Maureen McTeer wore grey. Her escort wore brown. McTeer strode purposefully into campaign headquarters. She passed a knot of three reporters who had been permitted to accompany her on this day's canvass. She cast them a wary glance, as if she had just caught a whiff of grapeshot in the rigging. "Hello," she said, the last word she would exchange with members of the news media that day.

Joe Clark stopped, to exchange pleasantries with the reporters.

"Nice tie," someone remarked.

"Thank you," Clark said. He smiled and looked down at his tie, a green repp stripe. A clerk at Harry Rosen on Rideau would later explain: "It's a power tie, very popular with the politicians this year."

After a few moments' consultation with her workers, McTeer was ready to conduct her canvass. She sailed off with her husband, two campaign aides, and a family friend, who carried the lawn signs. Even the signs were first-class, printed in two colours on corrugated plastic at two dollars a pop. The reporters followed several paces behind. It had been made clear to them they were welcome only as a major courtesy; McTeer's job was to meet the people, not the press. With that, the Mo-Jo mini-bubble hit the road.

McTEER'S AIDES WORKED the homes in hopscotch fashion, as pre-scribed in the campaign manual, keeping one step ahead of the candidate: "Hello, I'm with the Maureen McTeer campaign. Ms. McTeer and the Right Honourable Joe Clark are in the neighbourhood. Would you like to meet them?" The worker would get the name of the resident, then Clark or McTeer, or both, would bound up the step. It is an old trick to walk smartly, or run — people like to see their candidate run. A few words of greeting, a few nods of commiseration, and on to the next. "Now, Mrs. Smith, can we be counting on your support on election day?"

The canvass began well enough. At the first house, an elderly woman invited the candidate to step inside a moment, out of the cold. So delighted to meet you. Oh yes, you can put up a sign, right there. Oh yes, you can count on *our* support. At the next home, more of the same. Would you like me to pose for a photo-graph? Certainly, it would be an honour. We'll stand right here, while that nice man puts in a lawn sign.

At the third house, paydirt again. But something was odd — McTeer had passed nine doors but knocked at only three. After the entourage left, the homeowner at Lawn Sign No. 3 was inter-rupted again. Her name was Ethel Pharoah, a woman in her late seventies, and she had lived in the neighbourhood a long time. She planned to vote Conservative. "I'm not wild about that Mulroney, but I like some of the things he's done."

Had Mrs. Pharoah been surprised to find the local high-pro-file candidate and the secretary of state for external affairs on her doorstep? "Oh, no," she replied. "These people came along this morning and said, 'Do you want to see them?' I said sure, you can even put a lawn sign up if you want." Down the street, another lawn sign was being hammered in. Mrs. Pharoah explained that, even though she let them put up a sign, she still didn't care a lot for politics. "I think image makes the whole thing, these days."

It was a set-up. Candidates do not, as a matter of course, pre-canvass a riding — unless perhaps members of the press have been invited along to take pictures and note the reactions of voters. The bubble-blowers around McTeer didn't miss a trick.

The Mo-Jo mini-bubble continued its charmed course for another few blocks. At one intersection, a teenager expressed his desire to work at External Affairs, telling Clark, somewhat ambig-uously, "You're the damnedest." While crossing a parking lot,

Clark and McTeer ran into Gilbert Leclerc, a retired public servant. A small man, Leclerc emphasized his smallness by bowing slightly as he shook hands. "Oh, Monsieur Clark, enchanted," he cooed. "Madame, enchanted." He smiled and gooed, and, after the entourage had left, he remained transfixed.

"Monsieur Turner, when he was finance minister, he came through here, oh, many years ago," Leclerc recalled. "And Monsieur Pepin, and Madame Piggott. But Monsieur Clark. He was a prime minister, you know. That's really something, prime minister. That's history."

Leclerc was asked whether McTeer's pro-choice stance on abortion was in keeping with his own way of thinking. Abortion was brewing as an issue in the riding. McTeer had allowed her name to stand as a director of the Canadian Abortion Rights Action League, and been criticized by her bishop. "You're tempted to ask them outright about that," Leclerc admitted. But he recoiled at the thought. "I wouldn't ask her outright about that, at this time, here."

And so the afternoon passed quickly, McTeer following carefully in the footsteps marked out by that morning's pre-canvass canvass. The trouble with walking in a bubble, though, is that you never know who might throw thumbtacks in your path.

"Oh, yes, I've been waiting to meet with *you*," said Bill McLoughlin. A realtor who had spent thirty-five years in the navy as a submariner, McLoughlin had a dignified presence. He stepped out on his porch to talk with the candidate and her husband. "What I want to know is, why is the Conservative Party giving Canada away to the United States?"

"We're not," Clark shot back. "That's absolutely false."

"The agreement specifically excludes all areas pertaining to national identity and sovereignty," McTeer chimed in. "We'll send you a package, if you like."

"You," McLoughlin sneered, "are nothing but a flag-waving feminist."

A radio reporter moved her microphone a bit closer. Shreds of mini-bubble could almost be seen floating away on the wind.

"Another thing," McLoughlin said. "I don't like to see people roughed up and kicked out of meetings, just because they heckle Mulroney. It's a free country, isn't it?"

"That happened once," Clark began. "That —"

McTeer, dander up, decided to handle it her way. "When you have a prime minister, when someone is trying to talk, as a courtesy you should let them finish their speech." Her voice had the patronizing tone of the schoolmarm. "Otherwise, it leads to anarchy, and I don't think anybody wants that."

"You," McLoughlin replied, "wrote a letter to women on women's issues. You wrote my wife a letter. You wrote my daughter a letter. You excluded me.

"Another thing," he continued, turning back to Clark. "I've been thirty-five years in submarines, but I'm against submarines now. We'd last a lot longer if we spent that money on the environment. We don't need nuclear submarines — "

"Nuclear-*powered* submarines," McTeer corrected.

McLoughlin snarled, and the entourage took the opportunity to move on. This fellow was a waste of time.

An aide rushed to McTeer's side. "I'm sorry, Mo," she said. "He was *much* friendlier this morning."

IN ITS OWN small way, Maureen McTeer's campaign foray had reflected the problems the Tories were encountering on the national hustings. Their national campaign also got off to a flying start and proceeded flawlessly. Too flawlessly. Within three days, it was axle-deep in mud.

It took three days for reporters to dub it the "bubble campaign," after a Paul Simon song. In another song, "You Can Call Me Al," Simon croons: "I want a photo opportunity, I need a shot at redemption, Don't want to end up a cartoon in a cartoon graveyard." You would think, after a year in which even a pop singer had conceived lyrics around the notion of political illusion, that the Tories might have striven for something less contrived.

Brian Mulroney's sixteen-hour days generally started with a factory tour, the venue selected to turn up workers who hoped to benefit from free trade. At noon, the service-club circuit would get a stock speech. After lunch, thirty reporters and as many aides would climb aboard Mulroney's chartered DC-9 jet and take their places two curtains behind the prime minister, flying, as they grumbled, "hostility class."

In the evening, it was another speech to another partisan crowd. Mulroney always gave a few lines in French, for the Quebec press. If he noticed the crowd shift uncomfortably, he would defuse the situation with humour:

In Wolseley, Saskatchewan: "I learned that French at Es-
terhazy High School."

In Georgetown, Ontario: "I learned that French in
Brampton High School."

It was close to the script, a safer, blander Mulroney. A
rather more inspired Mulroney method of handling anti-French
sentiment was demonstrated in 1986, during a speech to striking
meat packers at the Gainer's plant in Edmonton. Shortly after
Mulroney made some remarks in French, one of the workers had
shouted something that sounded very much like, "Mulroney,
you're a fraud!"

Mulroney hotly replied that nobody got away with calling
him a "frog," that he had fought separatists in Quebec and would
damn well fight them in Edmonton, too. It was one of his finer
moments. If in fact he knew the worker had actually shouted
"fraud" (Mulroney's inner-ear problem affects only his balance; he
has the hearing of a fox), well, then, it was finer still.

The problem with the scripted campaign was that it was
boring, predictable, not newsworthy. Strange that reporters would
grumble about this, since they tacitly accept such a deal the
moment they step on a leader's plane. "The parties are exploiting
the media by setting up a campaign tour complete with chartered
planes and buses and hotel stops," the Conservative strategist
Hugh Segal has said. "If nothing else, it is bad news judgement by
media editors to put the coverage of the campaign in the hands of
politically designed schedules. I think it's insane on their part."

In recognition of this insanity, several news organizations
— including the CBC and a number of newspapers — pulled their
more experienced staff from the plane. This left a predominant mix
of younger reporters, many of whom had never before covered a
federal election. They were still under the impression that the
exercise was designed to generate news.

By the end of the first week, many reporters were filing
stories complaining that they had no access to Mulroney. It was
not true. Mulroney answered questions for twenty-five minutes on
the Saturday he called the election. He had a twenty-minute
session with reporters the following day. He held another twenty-
minute news conference on the Tuesday. Nonetheless, his aides
were being quoted as "denying they are trying to wrap Mulroney

in a cocoon of silence to eliminate risky, unscripted encounters with the media, as numerous reports have suggested." And as that particular denial, carried by Southam News, also suggested.

When the gripes on the campaign plane were distilled to actual encounters, two or three objections emerged. Reporters didn't like being screened off from the prime minister on the plane — as if they expected him to saunter back and trade a few lines — "no whore like an old whore," perhaps, or, "until every living, breathing Tory has a job" — for old times' sake. They didn't like it that an RCMP dog named Straps sniffed their luggage. (Police wouldn't confirm whether the dog was checking for explosives or Mulroney biographer Claire Hoy.) They didn't like the rope or chain barriers that kept the cameras at a distance during photo opportunities. And they didn't like Marc Lortie, the prime minister's press aide, when he spoke the blunt truth in response to an interview request: "When he has something to say, he will talk to you."

Lortie has an aristocrat's nose, a smart haberdasher, and a patrician air. He could easily be taken for haughty. He is too honest for politics and this forthrightness hurt him — as when, for example, reporters asked why the prime minister wouldn't come down the aisle to answer a few questions on free trade.

"What is the purpose?" Lortie asked.

We were kind of hoping he'd say something controversial. Maybe even give us a glimpse of — you know — his soul?

The problem reporters had with Mulroney was not that they lacked time with him; but that they lacked what a character on *thirtysomething* might call "quality time." They had to make do with Mulroney's one-sentence explanation of the Sinclair Stevens decision, for instance, and his elegant dance around the abortion issue, and his two-word response to the latest Gallup poll, shouted above the jet engine's whine to the barricaded press: "C'est bon!"

Meanwhile, they flew all over the country together, 9,700 kilometres and fifteen cities in the first six days, listening to Mulroney's reassuring, endlessly repeated slogan: "This election is about choices." The reporters still thought that was supposed to mean something. They wanted it explained. They wanted to ask the prime minister questions, they wanted to analyse his answers, they wanted to be part of a process that would allow them to understand and help define what the exercise was all about.

"This election is about choices," Mulroney told one city. Fine, sir, but what does that mean exactly? "Canadians have real and profound choices to make," he reminded another crowd. "Choices that begin with a different view of Canada itself," he told Calgarians. But choices about what? Evidently not abortion, or the deficit, or taxes — these subjects he avoided in interviews.

"This election is about choices," Mulroney said one day, after yet another round of tour food. "Hawaiian pizza or cold burgers."

THE REPORTERS, meanwhile, continued their grumbling. They wanted to be part of the campaign, to know what it all meant, to tell the world what it all meant. They were even willing, in a balanced, objective sort of way, to help the leader explain what it all meant, if he, or they, or anyone else just knew what it meant any more.

They evidently didn't realize that, by boarding the plane, they had abandoned relevance. To the campaign handlers, the media advisers, and the wagon masters, the television reporter in 23D no longer existed. She had been reduced to scattered electrons — their electrons — which would fly into outer space that night and bounce back into living rooms, shouldering a backdrop she hadn't seen yet. That radio reporter, fiddling with his earphones and boom mike in 14A, was a wraith, disconnected sound — a voice clip he hadn't heard yet. That pompous ass from the *Star* was just a few lines of print that hadn't yet been written, a dash of colour not yet painted.

And after the DC-9 landed, the reporters would be bundled into buses and driven to the television studio, which was a pep rally at the Capri Centre in Red Deer, or a tour of the potash plant in Estevan — it really didn't matter a damn what or where the studio happened to be — and there they'd see supporters filling the seats, chanting the candidate's name, waving the candidate's picture. These crowds were simply extras on the set, the cast of millions, sign-wavers who had no idea what it all meant either.

Like the campaign reporters, however, the supporters liked to believe there was meaning in just being there. They would see the cameras rolling and figure surely this was what it all meant — to be here, to be on the news, Mabel, to be part of a process. And the cameramen on the set would see the crowds cheering and reckon this must be what it all meant — the emotion, the drama, and even, if there were hecklers, the confrontation. A snake pursuing itself presents a circle; through the middle of the circle leaps the politician; he must be the one who can say what it all means.

"This election is about choices," the prime minister explained, "between different views of the world. Ours is confident and outward-looking. Our opponents — and frankly I do not see much difference between them — would either ignore the changing world around us or hide from it."

And no one could contradict him, because no one knew what it could possibly mean. It is delicious to monopolize meaning, and if anyone tried to crack the monopoly, well, as Marc Lortie put it, what is the purpose?

"This year represents something close to a dismantling of the American presidential campaign," Lance Morrow lamented in *Time* magazine, speaking of the other post-literate election conducted in 1988. "The candidates perform simulations of encounters with the real world, but the exercise is principally a series of television visuals, of staged events created for TV cameras. The issues have become as weightless as clouds of electrons, and the candidates mere actors in commercials."

The Canadian Broadcasting Corporation, with its mandate for national unity, which is nothing less than national identity, which is, beneath the rhetoric and the empty choices and free trade and Meech Lake and abortion and the deficit, what the campaign of 1988 was all about — wasn't it? — the state broadcaster had the problem licked from the start. John Owen, head of television news at the CBC, announced at the outset: "The ropes, the way the media are excluded from events, these will become issues in themselves."

Now there's the way to cover an election. Turn the cameras back on themselves, show the media stymied by the barricade, and watch the snake — poof — disappear up its own asshole.

# CHAPTER 9

# THE DANCING
# TOPSPIN MASTERS

*Seek truth they said*
*All I find*
*The seed is lost*
*The ploughman — blind.*
SPIKE MILLIGAN

$\mathbf{S}$OMETHING WAS UP. SOMETHING big. Here it was, ten o'clock on a Wednesday night, time for the *National*, and Peter Mansbridge wasn't in the chair.

Mansbridge was always in the chair, five nights a week, pretending to read from papers on his desk while actually reading from a prompter. He delivered the news for the national English-language television service of the Canadian Broadcasting Corporation, which set him apart from news readers on private networks — it made him a trusted public servant. The public relied on him. If Mansbridge wasn't in his chair, it had to be for something important.

It was October 19. The biggest story of the election campaign was about to be broken. Mansbridge wasn't in his chair because he himself was about to break it. The fourth item into the broadcast, the replacement news reader, Sheldon Turcotte, set up Mansbridge's report:

"For the last several days there has been some astonishing manoeuvring at the highest levels of the [Liberal] party," said

Turcotte. "Some of the most senior people in the party thought the unthinkable. Deep into this election campaign they thought about putting pressure on John Turner to quit. But CBC News has learned they pulled back and are now prepared to work to salvage the campaign. Our chief correspondent, Peter Mansbridge, has the story of a party in crisis."

That should have been a tip-off right there. According to the introduction, Mansbridge's story would be about: a) what some people thought; b) what they didn't do; and c) what they didn't want to happen. They may have a name for that kind of story at the CBC; newspaper editors of yore would call it a piece that doesn't know whether to spit or cut wind.

Mansbridge appeared on the air, from Ottawa. Because of the light it sheds on television's role in the post-literate campaign, his report, unusually long for a broadcast item, is worth reproducing in its entirety:

"Last Thursday, four top Liberal strategists met at party headquarters in Ottawa. Michael Kirby, John Webster, Al Graham, and André Ouellet met to discuss just how poorly the Liberal campaign was going. They talked about a lot of things. The polls, the ridings where they couldn't get candidates, the poor image of the leader. Even the impact of an immediate change in leadership.

"The next day, all four men signed documents outlining the desperate situation the party was in, and sent them to John Turner at the Liberal leader's official residence, Stornoway. They did not include their thoughts about leadership, but they did ask to see Turner in a face-to-face meeting.

"At Stornoway, Turner read the briefing but remained resolute, convinced the campaign was still winnable even if he had to do it alone. He refused to meet the strategists.

"The next day, Saturday, Turner talked to some of them by phone, leaving them convinced he would not step down. The strategists decided a leadership change was not an option any longer. And others impressed upon them that the campaign must go on, the dissent must end.

"But then Sunday night, the CBC poll results. Especially the leadership questions, where Turner ranked dead last on every one of ten different qualities. A frenzied series of cross-country phone calls took place by strategists and senior Liberal candidates, trying to assess the damage and the options. Five of the candidates,

Turner's front bench in the House of Commons, called for a crisis meeting with Turner. Herb Gray from Windsor, Lloyd Axworthy from Winnipeg, Bob Kaplan from Toronto, André Ouellet, who'd been in the strategist meeting, and Raymond Garneau from Quebec.

"By late Monday, Gray put in the request by phone for a meeting with Turner. But he was blocked by principal secretary Peter Connolly. Connolly was determined not to allow Turner to get into these kind of discussions until he comes back to Ottawa later this week.

"It's not clear yet what the five MPs wanted to tell Turner. But it is known that asking Turner to step aside had been discussed by some of the group. But some also felt that if Turner was forced out, the party could be left in ruins by a very public bloodbath.

"For the next two days, right up until late this afternoon, there was confusion and chaos. The senior aides with Turner on the campaign trail would not talk to senior strategists and candidates on the ground. Connolly didn't know whom to trust any more. All this follows an incredible four-week period inside the most senior levels of the Liberal Party. Here's what we know has happened:

"Ten days before the election call, Michael Kirby went to see John Turner at his Parliament Hill office. Kirby told Turner that private polling showed the Tories with at least a hundred and fifty-five seats, a clear majority going into the campaign, and one of the Liberals' biggest problems was the image of their leader. Kirby did not ask Turner to quit, he just laid out the facts.

"Turner's next visitor was more blunt. During a meeting punctuated with shouting, Raymond Garneau, the party's Quebec lieutenant, told Turner he must quit, that the future of the Liberal Party was at stake. But Turner said no, this was his campaign.

"Only Martin Goldfarb, the Liberal pollster, had good news going into the campaign. Goldfarb told Turner the election was still up for grabs. But by day ten of the campaign, after a few campaign fumbles, even Goldfarb was telling Turner all was lost. The Tories were sweeping, and a halo of victory hovered over Brian Mulroney. A halo too firm to be knocked off.

"While all this was going on Turner was in agonizing physical pain, he pinched a nerve in his back, could barely walk, could barely stand up for speeches. In Toronto just hours before this huge Liberal fundraiser, Turner was with his doctor trying to find some relief for the pain. He told friends he was worried about simply making it through the campaign on physical grounds.

"It was the following night, last Thursday, that the four top Liberal strategists met to file their campaign assessment and talk about asking Turner to leave.

"But late this afternoon there were dramatic changes in this story. Liberals at all levels seemed to realize that they were heading towards a major confrontation. And that the party in the process was only destroying itself. The strategists with Turner, and those back in Ottawa, have decided to have a special meeting on Friday to try and sort out the differences between them. And the candidates have backed off on their request for a meeting with Turner, convinced that Turner has no intention of stepping down.

"But they are not happy. They're not happy with the treatment they've been getting, they're not happy with the lack of consultation on major new policies like abortion, but mostly they're not happy with the performance of their party or their leader, now, almost halfway through the election campaign.

"Peter Mansbridge, CBC News, Toronto."

HOW'S THAT FOR a bunch of unhappy campers? How's that for a party in crisis? More to the point, how's that for a snake performing its disappearing act?

The impact of the Mansbridge story was immediate. Viewers concluded that John Turner had faced a coup attempt from within party ranks. He had, after all, faced other such attacks. In 1986, after being sniped at by such notables as the former cabinet minister Marc Lalonde, he had quelled efforts to have him unseated at a scheduled leadership review. Earlier in 1988, he had put down an uprising led by his Senate wing, which had drafted twenty-two people from the Liberal caucus asking for his resignation. Easy enough for the public to believe that it had happened again.

Which it had, though not without the help of producers and reporters whose investigating skills had been honed by years of arriving at work in the morning, reading what the other guy has got, and rewriting it with that extra bit of spin. In Ottawa, there are only three possible reactions to a piece of news: match it, ignore it, or beat it. Thus, Southam News fired off a startling dispatch the next morning: ". . . key campaign strategists and five of Turner's

front-bench MPs met last week to plot a coup against their belea-
guered leader."

Now that was more attention-grabbing than the rather
limp CBC report. It put the strategists and the front-benchers in
the same room, for one thing, which is more than the CBC could
do. And it had them "plotting" a "coup," when the CBC could only
report that the supposed dissidents were not "happy." The only
source for the Southam report was the CBC report; the CBC
evidently didn't realize what a powerhouse story it was sitting on.

This interpretation of the Mansbridge story was so inescapable that it was also drawn almost immediately by the CBC
itself. Introducing the *Journal* item on the *National's* news story,
Bill Cameron summed up the Mansbridge report this way:

"Good evening. Our top story tonight — the disarray inside
the Liberal election campaign. As Peter Mansbridge reported earlier on the *National*, some key Liberal power brokers think John
Turner is losing the election and they've talked about forcing him
to resign."

No one even blinked. After all, wasn't that what everyone
had just seen on the *National*? Well, not exactly. What viewers had
seen was an illusion, the *National* having performed the media
equivalent of sawing a woman in half. A careful reading of the
transcript — difficult, of course, when the item is televised —
shows that the Liberal strategists "talked about a lot of things...
even the impact of an immediate change of leadership." That could
mean that they talked about forcing Turner to resign, or that
Turner himself had asked to resign, or that they were preparing for
the eventuality of an unwanted resignation — in the event, for
instance, that Turner's back gave out. The CBC report does not
describe the content of this talk; it may well have been just that,
idle talk.

One strategist was reported on the *National* to have demanded Turner's resignation — Raymond Garneau, his Quebec
lieutenant, "told him he must quit." But this fact was tucked away
in a confused chronology and had nothing to do — contrary to
Mansbridge's assertion — with a crisis in leadership "now, almost
halfway through the election campaign." The Garneau incident
had actually occurred ten days before the election was called,
nearly a month before the CBC report was broadcast.

According to the Mansbridge report, nothing about leadership was included in the four strategists' memo to the leader. Yet, when Turner received it, he "read the briefing but remained resolute; convinced the campaign was still winnable even if he had to do it alone." Resolute about what? About staying on, in the absence of any demand that he resign?

Mansbridge's report said Turner called some of the strategists the next day and left them "convinced he would not step down." Maybe Turner was the sort of person who woke up in the morning and told Geills, "I will not step down." The implication, though, was that the leadership question had been put to him directly, an implication unsupported by the story.

According to the Mansbridge report, the "coup" was quashed by Turner's telephone calls on Saturday, after which "the strategists decided a leadership change was not an option any longer." Thus, the conspiratorial thoughts, if that is what they were, had enjoyed a life of, at most, twenty-four hours — from the Friday meeting (not Thursday) to the Saturday telephone calls from Turner.

As for the CBC poll results released on the Sunday, it was a different group of unhappy campers who responded to these — only André Ouellet was both one of the four strategists and a member of the group of five. This group of five wanted a meeting with the leader about something, "it's not clear yet what." Mansbridge added: "It is known that asking Turner to step aside had been discussed by some of the group." Well, yes. Garneau had discussed it with Turner a month previously. But had the five, as a group, discussed it? The report was not entirely clear — what is clear is that the five were not unanimous: "Some also felt that if Turner was forced out, the party could be left in ruins by a very public bloodbath."

Which view had prevailed? The report did not say. In any event, the conspiratorial thoughts didn't father any deeds. According to the report, no meeting was held, and the five had "backed off on their request for a meeting with Turner, convinced that Turner has no intention of stepping down." So they "backed off," even though the story never had them stepping forward. Had the five resolved to ask Turner to resign? Had their insurrection been apprehended by the Liberal leader? Only God, and perhaps the CBC, knew for sure.

The CBC report had run to 856 words. It could have been

condensed — "Four key Liberal strategists met this week and discussed the leadership of the party during an overall campaign review. They did not see fit to relay any leadership observations to Turner, and have agreed that changing leaders in mid-campaign is not an option. Later this week, five candidates also discussed the progress of the campaign. One of these candidates had, a month ago, demanded that Turner step down in the interests of the party. But all five have now resolved to help Turner fight the election. A CBC poll on Sunday had shown Turner at the bottom of voter preference among all party leaders. The Liberals are determined to turn those polls around" — at a saving of 742 words of precious air time. Mark Twain's twelfth rule of literary style: eschew surplusage.

The story was criticized by many Liberals not for being long; it was criticized for being wrong. In fact, however, except for minor details such as the dates of certain meetings, the story was right. The damaging implication of a coup against Turner grew not from the facts of the story but from their implications. The trick is to present the facts in such a way that other "facts" will be inferred by the reader or the viewer. In the trade, inferred meaning is called "topspin," because it carries a story that little bit further than it might otherwise have gone. Topspin can be imparted by those being interviewed; subjects naturally like to put their side of events in the best light. This is called "spin doctoring." But no spin doctor can operate on an unwilling patient; and, as often as not, the spin is put on a story by the journalist.

Liberals eager to knock down the coup story faced a formidable problem: it's difficult to hit a sidearm curve, which is a pitch with a lot of spin. So they resorted to the most time-honoured political expedient. They lied.

THE ORIGINAL FOUR strategists issued a written denial, which read as follows: "The four of us meet weekly, as we have for many months, to discuss the state of the campaign and to review what the strategy should be for the remainder of the campaign. As usual, the results of this meeting were communicated to the leader in a memorandum. It is preposterous to conclude that because we meet we are plotting against the leader. In fact, we are plotting with the leader to win the election." Remember that word, "preposterous."

A similar stance was adopted by the gang of five, who

dismissed the report with varying degrees of outrage. "The only plot that I'm involved in," said Herb Gray, "is a very public plot, and that's a plot to defeat Brian Mulroney."

Over in the Turner camp, meanwhile, Peter Connolly, the principal secretary, also called the report "preposterous." "I have talked to Mr. Turner about this just now," Connolly said, "and he said no one — none of those mentioned — has approached him with any suggestion that he should step down."

Whatever they pay Connolly, it is not enough. Who else could knock down a story by quoting a fact contained in the story itself? The CBC had said that no one had met with Turner to suggest he resign. Like a master of three-card monte, Connolly held this up to show it wasn't there.

The Turner people's tactic was to dissemble without con-tradicting a single fact in the CBC report — the same tactic used by the four strategists in their denial, which was issued in the present tense even though the CBC report had clearly said that the machinations had taken place earlier in the week and had since expired. This tactic relied on the fact that the CBC, while implying a coup, could marshal no evidence to show that the barracks had indeed been stormed.

The Liberals did not for a moment consider simply telling the truth of what happened. Instead, they set out to alter percep-tions of a perception — topspin versus backspin, deception versus inference, neither side seeming to realize that, in the middle of it all, the ball had disappeared from the court. The masters of this game are so practised that they can perform it almost thought-lessly, as in the following exchange between Turner and a reporter in Vancouver, minutes after the original CBC report was broadcast:

TURNER: As I say it is a lot of nonsense, now I'm going to go back and meet some real people.

REPORTER: The perception of this happening cannot be helping you. . . .

TURNER: I want to tell you something, ah — Mr. Garneau, ah — I've been dealing with reality. People in here are dealing with reality — so am I.

REPORTER: How does it make you feel? How does it make you feel during this campaign, you must be getting pretty...?

TURNER: I would, ah, I would think the country as I said today was to start to deal with the issues.

Turner's effortless use of some of the bolder techniques of the game — notice the Trojan denial and the Big Lie — reveal him as a bold if incautious player. The questions of the reporter show him as a plodder, a careful student who does not stray far from the routine gambits. Notice that the reporter was not interested in whether the CBC report was true. The ball, as it were, was the furthest thing from his mind. The reporter was interested in reaction, feelings, and, most of all, perception. After Turner's sweeping denial, the reporter did not ask: "What part of the report is nonsense? Is there any truth to it at all? What is your version of events?" Instead, he asked about the "perception" created by the report, and about how it made Turner feel. Abandoning pursuit of the actual story, the reporter opted for a miasma of emotional impressionism — a tactic very much in keeping with the practice of the day.

A PHILOSOPHER MIGHT observe that perception flows from reality, but is not reality itself. A quantum physicist might disagree, and argue that the two are interchangeable. Sixty years ago, scientists realized they could not observe the velocity or direction of an electron without changing its position through the mere act of observation — anything used to "illuminate" the electron, whether light or x-rays, would be more substantial than the electron itself. There was no way of "looking" at the electron without bumping it off course. For the first time, perception was shown to be an integral part of reality.

"The barrier between man, peering dimly through the clouded windows of his senses, and whatever objective reality may exist has been rendered almost impassable," Lincoln Barnett wrote in *The Universe and Dr. Einstein*. "For whenever he attempts to penetrate and spy on the 'real' objective world, he changes and distorts its workings by the very process of his observation."

The theory scientists created to deal with this phenomenon was called the principle of uncertainty, and uncertainty is endemic to politics. This theory helped us to understand the photoelectric cell, and the photoelectric cell was integral to the invention of television. The principle of uncertainty is to television, then, what original sin is to mankind — a sort of genetic seed that helps explain all subsequent behaviour.

By 1988 the principle of uncertainty had crept into political discourse so pervasively that every player of the game realized instinctively that perceptions of the Turner "coup" were vastly more important than any coup itself. To the uninitiated it might seem that, if there were no coup, that would end the matter. Not so. Campaigns, like electrons, inevitably get bumped around by the act of observation. According to the CBC's own report, none of the conspirators had put his thoughts on leadership to Turner. None had taken any action, such as quitting, to indicate displeasure with the leadership. There was simply no demonstrable revolt. By putting the story to air, however, the public servants at the CBC created the perception of a coup. By creating the perception, they created the coup.

This manufactured picture of Liberal insurrection was enhanced by the structure of the CBC report. Consider the breathless urgency — Mansbridge dashing off to Ottawa, the use of phrases such as "party in crisis" and "bloodbath." The CBC also added visual "spin" to the story. In referring to the group of five, it used the squeeze-zoom technique first developed to enliven sports broadcasts. This technology permits photographs to be broken down into digitally recorded segments, then reconstructed elsewhere on the screen; it allows, for instance, a football field to be flipped on its axis and transformed into a scoreboard. The CBC's pictures of the group of five were drawn from file footage — that is, photographs taken earlier, in other contexts. These images were reduced and shuttled to different parts of the screen. "It gave the impression that the five had actually met somewhere, and the CBC filmed them going through the door," said Hugh Winsor, parliamentary correspondent of *The Globe and Mail.* "Of course, as you know, they never held a meeting."

This technique, though, was a mere feint compared with the CBC's next move. The producers used another special-effects technique to create a "graphic representation" of the memo the four strategists sent to Turner. A "graphic representation" is, in plain language, a fake — the $20 Rolex of television news, worn on special occasions to add cachet. Older, more hidebound players of the game frown on its use during actual competition, as when a reporter on the *Washington Post,* Janet Cooke, wrote an article about a youthful drug addict named Jimmy and won a Pulitzer Prize. Jimmy was what Cooke called a "composite" — a graphic representation of a real boy. Cooke was convinced of the existence of boys like Jimmy, just as the CBC was convinced of the existence of the Turner memos; she just hadn't managed to lay her hands on one. She lost her Pulitzer, and her job, but then she didn't work for the CBC.

The CBC had no such memo, nor had anyone at the CBC read such a memo. Yet the four strategists were squeeze-zoomed into the four corners of a fuzzy memo, which viewers couldn't quite make out. Admirers of the game might ask why the CBC stopped there. Why not produce a graphic representation of the Turner-Garneau confrontation? It would require only a photograph of a door, perhaps, with muffled screams and curses, the odd "Fuck that!" and "How about a Scotch?" thrown in for authenticity. Why not film an actor in darkened silhouette, disguise his voice, and have him confirm that he schemed to have Turner resign — a graphic representation of a conspirator?

Which leads to the next problem with this problematic story. Why were none of the conspirators filmed on camera? The story relied on unidentified sources. When an unidentified source is used, the viewer cannot judge the veracity of a report by its sources; he must rely on the integrity and reputation of the news organization. The CBC defends its reputation with references to its journalistic policy manual, which has two things to say of relevance to the Mansbridge report. First, it concedes that unidentified sources are sometimes necessary to obtain information. But the source must be "known to the journalist and have a prima facie credibility," and the journalist "must carefully check the reliability of the source and must obtain corroborative evidence from other pertinent sources." Second, the manual rules that the CBC should be a balanced observer, but not a participant, in the news. "Particular care must be given. . . . during elections and referendum campaigns," the policy states, "so that imbalance does not occur through the manipulation of events."

The CBC had double-checked and, in some cases, triple-checked the items in its story. So said the CBC's chief news editor, John Owen, appearing on the CBC Radio show *Media File*. Owen said he wrestled with the question of whether the story would be an intrusion on the electoral process, and "the side we came down on was the side of basically free flow of information.

"We decided it would be wrong to withhold information we knew to be true and said something about a political campaign in progress," Owen continued. "We would have been deceiving the public to report on a leadership campaign, and on a political party's campaign, and at the same time know we were not telling the public a great deal about the conduct of the campaign."

But Owen also revealed what the public could not have known from the report itself — that the very sources who had fed the CBC the story would deny its truth. "We were satisfied. . . of all those people we talked to, if we went back to them, they might in fact end up denying something they told us about." Owen added: "It's a concern if in fact you did a story in which everybody you went to denied what you knew to be true."

This explains why the CBC did not seek out the reaction of the Liberal "insurgents" named in the Mansbridge report. It would have been downright hypocritical to take a story from a source, check it out, believe it to be true, then film the same source denying its veracity.

Why, though, did the CBC not confess to this dilemma in its report? "The CBC has cross-checked this story and will stand behind it," Mansbridge could have said. "But our sources are the very people who now want to bury the hatchet — and who will thus deny this ever happened." Such an admission would have cleared the air without identifying the sources — after all, even Turner wanted the hatchet buried.

But if — and this is the final layer of the onion — if, as John Owen put it, "everybody you went to denied what you knew to be true," then would what you knew to be true continue to be true? Perhaps, in this case, yes and no. True as a description of what had recently transpired in the inner chambers of the Liberal Party, but inaccurate as a representation of the current state of affairs. Who knows how brilliantly these masters play the game? Who knows when the topspin has been enriched by sidespin? It's possible that at least one of the CBC's sources confirmed the story in hopes that its broadcast would douse any smouldering embers of disloyalty to Turner — in which case the very act of broadcasting the true story would, in a sense, have rendered it untrue.

SO THE MATTER rested, until a post-election conference in Kingston, sponsored by the CBC and Queen's University, some months after the campaign. During the conference, Peter Connolly not only confirmed the CBC report but said the corporation had been "gentle" in the way it handled the conspirators. This drew the curiosity of Hugh Winsor of *The Globe and Mail*. Winsor recalled that Connolly had specifically denied the report during the campaign. On a coffee break, Winsor called him on it.

Connolly explained that he and Turner had discussed their response carefully. They chose the word "preposterous" to dismiss the report. (Turner, who often screws up little things like this, went with "nonsense.") Preposterous doesn't have quite the same meaning as wrong, Connolly explained. Look the record over, we never said the CBC report was wrong, we said the whole idea was preposterous. When we said that, we meant the idea of Turner's resignation was preposterous, which it was. We never commented on the facts in the piece.

Connolly imagined he had maintained his integrity with this subterfuge. He had not been lying, merely creating the atmosphere in which his words would be properly misunderstood. In retrospect, this tactic was widely used by others named in the story. According to a CBC staff member who kept a careful log of the sources' denials, "only one came out with a bald-faced lie. All the rest hid behind tangential explanations, denials of things we'd never alleged, that sort of thing." Members of the news media, too busy asking the sappy questions — "How do you feel?" and "What about the perception?" — never got around to noticing they were swallowing lies.

Michael Kirby, meanwhile, in a book he co-authored on the election, admitted that a discussion of leadership had indeed taken place. Kirby threw an entirely different light on the meeting, saying Turner's leadership was raised only in the context of what the party would do if Turner wanted to quit, or was forced out by his back trouble. "Only a few statements [in the Mansbridge report] were factually false," Kirby wrote, "and many of the statements, as written, were true."

That's not what Kirby said during the campaign. On the CTV network he said the CBC story was based on "all kinds of fabrications." He had signed a joint document using the same word Connolly had hidden behind: "preposterous." In a sense, Kirby wasn't lying. He was creating a perception to counter another perception with which he disagreed.

Asked later to explain the discrepancy between what he said during the campaign and what he wrote afterwards, Kirby

170

cheerfully admitted he too was merely seeking to be properly misunderstood. "It might have saved my neck if I had answered the facts of the story," he said. "But there were people [fellow strategists] who were categorically denying that any such discussion took place. Caught between telling an out-and-out falsehood and killing a perception, I chose the perception, and not reality."

# CHAPTER 10

# A New Way of
# Talking

*Media change does not necessarily
result in equilibrium. It sometimes
creates more than it destroys.*
NEIL POSTMAN

T HE CBC REPORT OF THE "COUP"
against John Turner altered the very events it was portraying. The
corporation's role in the story simply showed that the messenger
had become part of the message — that the snake, once again, was
showing a pathological interest in the higher reaches of its own
colon.

If the CBC report represented the death of useful discourse
through the medium of television, the demise of the heckler during
the 1988 campaign represented a similar defeat for one of the oldest
forms of grassroots political expression — open contempt. Contempt is the healthiest emotion to bring to bear upon politics; it
ensures a succession of players, it deflates pomposity, it establishes
the proper relationship between master and servant. The most
treasured right in a democracy is the right to hold one's leaders in
contempt — it is the very foundation of the concept of a loyal
opposition.

Contempt was once expressed at political rallies by genuine citizens who offered their opinions of the performer on the
stage. In the age of television, however, the stage was not just the
raised dais at the end of the hall; it was the hall itself. The people
in the hall were no longer an audience, they were extras. In the

172

post-literate campaign, the freedom to express contempt had to be curtailed, and in such a way that no one noticed.

In the early phase of the 1988 campaign, the Mulroney camp dealt harshly with extras who failed to exhibit fitting reverence for the prime minister. The Tories used security forces to hustle rabble from the hall, before shrewder heads realized such brute tactics were not only unnecessary but also damaging when televised. The Conservatives replaced force with fantasy; the battlefield of image is best taken with the artillery of deception.

By the late weeks of the campaign, the Tories had simply replaced genuine — and unpredictable — people with their own flying squad of wildly cheering sycophants. Wherever the prime minister landed, he was met by a fleet of signatured buses. The entourage consisted of three media buses, the leader's bus, half a dozen police escorts, and the spontaneous-demonstration bus. At each event, the spontaneous-demonstration bus arrived first. About fifty Conservative youths, dressed in matching white sweatshirts with the blue-and-red PC logo, clambered off and took their positions. The Mulroney itinerary was not released until the last practical moment, to preclude actual spontaneous demonstrations, which tended to be peopled by economic nationalists, trade unionists, left-wingers, and the idly curious. These types, in the eyes of the young Conservatives, were little more than flag-waving pus.

If word had leaked out and a crowd of protesters had gathered, the youths — "whiteshirts" to the press corps — would position themselves strategically, to force the protesters out of camera range. When Mulroney spoke, it was up to the whiteshirts to cheer his every pause; if hecklers rose to protest, it was up to the whiteshirts to drown them out. One of the whiteshirts confided to a Global television cameraman that he "felt like a stormtrooper."

"The effect was to have a bar, or a dance hall, or a skating rink, filled with people screaming Mulroney's name and creating an image of hysterical adulation," observed Tim Naumetz, a Toronto *Sun* reporter who campaigned with Mulroney. "The purpose was to turn Mulroney into a hero, into someone that people scream and yell for; and you have the TV cameras picking it all up."

Even the NDP, the party of the average Canadian, did not want to risk close encounters with average Canadians. At a campaign stop in Oshawa, for instance, Ed Broadbent was scheduled to meet the folks at a shopping mall. The stop coincided with the five-o'clock lull at the mall; the place was nearly deserted half an hour before the leader's arrival. Soon, though, a respectable crowd gathered: pensioners with party-manufactured orange banners ("This time, Ed") and mothers carrying tykes dressed in Li'l Critters overalls, with "Ed" buttons pinned to the straps. Dozens of these people, loyalist to the core, trooped in to provide the backdrop of proletarian devotion the party wished to project.

Not that the New Democrats were particularly devious, or lacked authentic support in Oshawa. Like all parties, however, the NDP worried that the television image would not project this support if the hand-held camera, in its search for conflict, focused on a handful of protesters. That the protesters might have come forth genuinely to make their voices heard, while the supporters were a fabrication, was irrelevant; it was necessary to invent a reality that would replace the real reality.

During the 1988 campaign there was great emphasis on the "controlled event," as campaign organizers called it. The controlled event was at least partially defensive. Just as the parties realized the importance of staged support, so they appreciated the damage that could be inflicted by staged opposition. Hence the practice of salting campaign rallies with hecklers. There was no evidence that these provocateurs were organized nationally. The few who fessed up to being partisan mischief-makers, such as the pro-free-traders who rallied against Turner in Ottawa, typically said they had organized locally, on the spur of the moment. It was a mark of their political sophistication that they knew their impact could so easily be exaggerated beyond their numbers; that the media, in other words, could so willingly be enlisted to distort the magnitude of their presence.

THIS EASE of manipulation arose partly from the refinement of the technology itself. In the early days of television, hecklers were easily controlled by the platform speaker, who had control of the microphone and the attention of a fixed-position camera. One celebrated master of the technique was Harold Wilson, who planned his 1964 campaign in Great Britain for television. When confronted with hecklers, Wilson talked down to them in a calm, jocular manner — he realized the microphone could pick up only murmuring from the floor, and the camera would remain fixed on him. His opponent, Sir Alec Douglas-Home, attempted to shout down the hecklers, thus losing control of the meeting, and of his image.

Wilson's technique simply would not work in 1988 — lightweight, portable video cameras had become standard equipment. When John Turner addressed a rally of a thousand people crammed into a high-school auditorium in Pierrefonds, Quebec, he had not yet opened his mouth when someone in the audience shouted: "You're a liar!" Pools of light swung away from the Liberal leader and searched the crowd, looking for the offender. From another corner, a second heckler upped the ante: "You're a *fucking* liar!" The light pools danced away from the first heckler and over to the second. Turner droned into his speech, unaware that he had lost the meeting.

The reaction of party loyalists to these shouts was instinctive and swift — they crowded around the hecklers and surrounded them with placards, a technique not unlike the one employed by security forces in South Korea. When putting down a demonstration, the South Koreans pull some young woman into a dark alley to kick the juice out of her. If followed by the cameras, they simply form a tortoise-shell of riot shields over the scene so that the beating can continue in privacy.

The Montreal-area Liberals lacked the discipline of the Korean security forces. Before long, the Pierrefonds scene dissolved into outright punching and shoving. In one case, a Tory youth threw the first punch; in another, the Liberals started the rough stuff. A thirty-year-old fellow named Graham Gleddie was the main casualty of the evening. Gleddie's sin was to ask, after a Turner campaign promise, "How are you going to pay for it, Mr. Turner?" For this he was struck by a sign-wielding partisan and knocked to the ground by a bop to the face. He rose from the floor with blood flowing from his nose and a gash in his forehead. Exactly how he received the gash is not known; several reporters believe he struck his head against a portable camera which had been rushed in to record the fracas.

Afterwards Turner said that, although he understood the incident, he regretted it. Emotions had run high, but he accepted dissent from the floor as part of the democratic process and enjoyed a "good heckler." Which perhaps is why the Liberals used hired muscle to rough up hecklers at Turner's next campaign appearance, in Ottawa — they were not good hecklers. The goons were recognizable by their blue uniforms, which identified them as members of the City of Ottawa police force. These were not officers on regular duty, enforcing the laws of the land; they were off-duty cops hired by the party to maintain security and order. That legitimate political opposition got crushed in the process was simply part of the nature of things.

The Ottawa event took place at the Château Laurier Hotel, across the canal from the houses of Parliament. The hotel had recently been renovated and, fortunately for the organizers, the ballroom wing was separated from the main lobby by a hallway. This hallway is bisected by a black wrought-iron gate. A few Liberal heavies manned the gate. Anyone who wanted through had to produce a ticket. Tickets had been distributed to Liberal youths — down to and including a children's school choir — and to Liberal senior citizens, both of whom were considered safe bets.

Outside the hotel, a group of people calling themselves the Alliance for Young Canadians had been milling about, bearing placards, trying to guess which entrance Turner would use. When the leader's black limo pulled up to a side entrance, they rushed to greet him. They wanted to call him a liar. Presumably this would not qualify them as good hecklers, so the Liberal organizers had them out-manoeuvred — a group of supporters lined Turner's short walk up the hotel steps, shouting hosannahs. For all the security, though, it was simple enough to infiltrate the hall. All a person had to do was jump into position directly behind Turner and follow him, limp for limp. A couple of reporters did this. One of them, a brash American, was so taken with the ease of access to Canadian political figures that he attempted to interview Turner on the spot.

"Later," said an aide.

For a party leader, the walk-about into a controlled event is, as Turner would say, four fingers of scotcherini. The leader is blinded by the halogen lights of the cameras, his vision reduced to a six-foot lagoon of adoring, worshipful faces, of hands reaching out for a blessing. There is the impression of thousands more just out of visual range, an overarching din of shouting voices, of canned theme music, of human closeness. The way is cleared by boom mikes and secret service; the sea parts, and the leader passes through. This is perhaps the headiest perquisite of power — to be the locus of bedlam, the unifying force in a field of human emotion.

BY THEIR WALKS shall ye know them. Sir Alec Guinness always perfected the walk of a character first; he said that the colonel's stride in *The Bridge on the River Kwai* was the triumph of his career.

Brian Mulroney had a universal joint connecting his legs with his spine. It allowed him to glissade on oiled hips, moving forward in an unctuous slither, nothing seeming to move below the waist. Above this joint, though, he was rigid; the prime minister of Canada cannot turn his head to the left or right without turning his shoulders with it.

Ed Broadbent had a subtler walk. He moved forward by shifting from side to side, his weight transferring solidly from one foot to the other. This suggestion of a skating motion was needed to maintain his balance, as his centre of gravity was always poised just slightly ahead of his waist. When Broadbent stopped, he braked like a train; his head stopped first, then, clack-clack-clack, the rest of his body collided with it.

John Turner, a nerve pinched in his back, walked in crazy clockwork fashion. His right leg lurched forward; the left leg, grinding over a chipped cog on the spinal crankshaft, swung out at ninety degrees from the intended direction before changing course and delivering a glancing, sidelong blow at the floor. Turner's legs were like a pair of quarrelsome drunks: the effort of pulling them apart set his face in a tight smile of concentration. From time to time, the drunks managed to land a blow on the barkeep, and Turner's eyes popped open in anguished surprise. The Toronto writer Ian Brown remarked that Turner's walk reminded him of the family dog whose hips had been crushed by a passing car. It was pathetic to watch him pulling himself across the carpet on his forepaws, demonstrating his pluck, eyes pleading for another chance. It broke your heart when you had to put him down.

Turner lurched to the stage of the Château Laurier, legs flailing, eyes bugging, face set in a constipated grin (it was about this time that his handlers believed he finally had the image thing licked, having "cooled off" for television) and proceeded to rattle off some concocted prices for his campaign promises.

"When you gonna tell the truth, John?" someone shouted — and said no more. The heckler was grabbed by Ottawa's finest, who hustled him out of the hall. He was followed by reporters and cameramen, but this irritant was handled by one of the police officers in the tradition of the warm-hearted Irish flatfoot of a Boy's Town movie. The police officer bodychecked a cameraman into the stone walls of the hotel corridor, grunting, "Stay the fuck out of my way." He then batted at the microphones and hand-held tape recorders until the heckler was chucked out the doors.

Next to go was a man with a cardboard rhinoceros horn strapped to his forehead, a fellow drunk or stoned or perhaps just high on life, shouting incoherently in French. Then a few hecklers — probably Tory plants — hit the sidewalk. Then a dwarfish Liberal organizer, smitten with power, began simply nodding at people who looked as if they might make trouble later on. They, too, were strong-armed from the hall.

The Liberals did not find it so easy to suspend civil freedoms because they are more evil than people of other political persuasion; nor are those involved in politics more or less innately fiendish than the population at large. Ordinary, unscripted people simply had no place in the theatrical events of the post-literate campaign.

WHEN MARSHALL McLUHAN predicted that television would create a global village, no one foresaw what an unusual village it would be. It was not a place where people gathered by the well to exchange stories, or sat in a longhouse to listen to village leaders. It was a place where everybody remained inside their huts, watching television. Through the medium of television, they experienced vicariously a reconstruction of experience — the chattering women by the stream, the talented story-tellers by the fire. No longer, though, were they able to experience those things other than vicariously. The streets of the global village were empty; dust-devils danced among the shadows of the village square.

Nowhere was this phenomenon more evident than at the 1988 summer Olympic Games in Seoul — the most crowded global village ever constructed, and the emptiest. At the Seoul Olympics, members of all national teams and the media were issued passes containing a magnetic bar code. Armed sentries demanded the pass and fed it through a verifying machine, at every entrance to every venue, along pathways in the Olympic Park, in the lobbies of all Seoul hotels, in bus queues, at diplomatic receptions — anywhere, in short, that the so-called Olympic family could be expected to gather. A high-ranking bar code meant the bearer could travel anywhere; travel became more restricted as the ranking fell; lack of any bar code meant the bearer had no status whatever. The security people refused to say whether the bar code also allowed the authorities to keep track of the holder's every movement.

The bearer of a bar code felt odd indeed as he strolled through the Olympic sites, not only because his steps were approved by a beeping machine, guided by eager volunteers, and protected by snipers perched on rooftops. The singular sensation was not of supervision but of loneliness. The broad avenues of the Olympic Park were built of meticulous cobblestone, lined with cherry trees, and bordered by the steel flanks of modern buildings. The way was decorated with the slogan of the Seoul Games — "Peace. Harmony. Progress" — and the skies were dappled with white banners the size of baseball diamonds, imprinted with the Olympic rings, held aloft by balloons. The grounds were inspirational, impressive, and orderly.

They were also, for the most part, empty. Outside the televised spectacles — such as the opening and closing ceremonies — the public spaces presented acre upon acre of hollow bijou. The authorities tried to explain: many Western visitors had stayed away, frightened by the terrorist threat, and Koreans themselves had little appreciation of Athenian track games, preferring the fighting sports.

Mostly, of course, people were at home, watching the Games on television.

The shortage of actual spectators soon concerned the authorities, who tried reducing ticket prices, then gave tickets away, then began to bus in spectators from elementary schools and homes for the elderly. This was not some altruistic outworking of the Olympic spirit; it was show business. The vacant rows of seats at track events had become an embarrassment, failing to provide an appropriately enthusiastic backdrop for the Games. No matter that the empty seats actually reflected a lack of enthusiasm for those events; the authorities invented enthusiasm. As those with magnetic passes went about their business, they regularly went by long, doleful rows of spectators who, having been press-ganged into a show of exhilaration for the Games, were being searched for articles which would betray a lack of the proper Olympian spirit.

One afternoon, a youth attempting to pass a security

179

checkpoint was found to be concealing several soda bottles, filled with gasoline and stuffed with rags. Exposed, the youth dumped his Molotov cocktails and tried to flee, but was tackled and dragged by his hair to a waiting van. It was a common sight; it hardly lifted an eyebrow. Overhead, a white blimp sashayed across the blue sky, its belly flashing the ubiquitous "Peace. Harmony. Progress."

IN BOTH the 1988 Summer Olympics and the 1988 election campaign, the "controlled event" did not mean the total eradication of public participation. It simply drove public participation out of sight, behind the walls of the village huts. The emotions felt in the privacy of Canadian homes were as sharp and immediate as anything experienced by the proxy participants at the Olympic stadium, or the Château Laurier. Sharper, perhaps, in the case of the Ben Johnson affair.

Ben Johnson's most astounding run of all was almost a private moment. It came not in the hundred-metre finals but a few days earlier, on a practice track normally reserved for college students. It was early morning, before the sun burned, and silent. Johnson appeared with some others from the Canadian team. Angella Issajenko, bulging in a skin-tight grey jumpsuit, zipped here and there at half-mast, resembled what the inside of a train engine must look like. Angela Bailey looked dolefully about while the masseur worked on her thigh. Ben Johnson loped around a while, then set up in the blocks. His coach, Charlie Francis, clapped his hands.

Johnson has superior dorsal muscle development, which made his rise from the blocks resemble a dolphin's back breaking water. After that it was difficult to follow anything clearly. Two eyes, like jaundiced lasers vaporizing the wind resistance; a set of pink palms cutting the air; a back like a knotted pile of rope. Only afterwards, as through water, did the sound of his feet register — the loud cracking of belt leather against glass, rapid as small-arms fire.

Francis made a few notations on a clipboard. He sauntered over to a reporter on the sideline, to mooch a smoke. He didn't say anything, but he seemed a little rattled — he had just witnessed Johnson run the fastest time ever posted by a human being over eighty metres. Francis's hands may have been shaking; for several moments, no one could think of anything to say. There are different

180

ways to describe what Johnson had just done. He had generated forty-five horsepower against the blocks and reached a top speed of forty-six kilometres per hour. For anyone close enough to feel the shifted air, however, numbers were a poor replacement for what they had sensed, which was a moment of human transcendence.

This was a very different emotion from the one generated two days later, when Johnson took the gold medal before the eyes of the world. Here was an emotion warped by the need of the global village to impose order and hierarchy on events, to create and resolve conflict, to concentrate the mind of the collective. Hence the promotion of the Lewis-Johnson rivalry, the overshadowing of other Olympic events, the focus on the ten seconds that would define Seoul, in the same way Mary Lou Retton defined Los Angeles, or Mark Spitz did Munich. It was a moment laced with nationalism, and injected with testosterone. Johnson's subsequent loss of the gold delivered a blow to Canadian complacency equal to that of the Watergate scandal to Americans. The scandal's proximity to the election campaign confirmed, while rendering scary, the Conservative assertion that the nation had to adjust to compete at the world level.

In another way, though, the whole affair contributed to deepening cynicism about the staged events of the global village. Canadians had dared to have faith in their own excellence, and the basis of their faith had been shown to be fraudulent. It was doubtful whether they could look on the next great stage-show — the federal election — with the same degree of innocence.

Consider the file kept by the Gallup organization on the Ben Johnson affair. Normally, Gallup surveys only the direction of opinion, not its intensity. The intensity can be deduced, though, by the degree of interest in a polling question. When, days after the fact, Gallup asked Canadians whether they were aware that Johnson had been stripped of his medal because of drug use, ninety-nine per cent said they were.

That ninety-nine per cent needs to be put into perspective. A couple of months earlier, in July, Gallup had polled Canadians on their awareness of the federal cabinet. The first finding was a clue to the others — one Canadian in three was completely ignorant of the cabinet. They could not name a single member. Quebec ranked highest among provinces whose residents confessed complete ignorance of the executive. There, more than four in ten of the people surveyed couldn't name a single minister.

The best-known members of the Conservative cabinet (besides Mulroney) were Joe Clark and John Crosbie. Clark had been, however briefly, a prime minister. One might assume that he would be well known, that people would realize he was still in the cabinet. For this survey, respondents didn't have to know Clark's portfolio was external affairs — they just had to name three members of the cabinet. Seven out of ten Canadians didn't name Clark. The same proportion held for Crosbie, a man who had nearly become party leader. Beyond these two high-profile ministers, awareness fell sharply. Five in six did not name Flora MacDonald, the most accomplished woman in Canadian politics. Seven in eight did not name the finance minister, Michael Wilson. Don Mazankowski, who had even more influence than the prime minister on the daily operations of government, was named by one in twenty.

It gets worse. Brian Mulroney had recently appointed an old friend and Quebec nationalist, Lucien Bouchard, as his secretary of state. The appointment was the sort of thing that led editorial writers, particularly in Western Canada, to fret about the composition of the cabinet; but on the prairies, apparently, only one person in a hundred had ever heard of Lucien Bouchard.

In Toronto, no doubt, they would smirk at that statistic — the colossal ignorance of the prairie redneck, too long in the sun, unschooled in history, lacking national perspective, yet presumptuous enough to criticize the structure of Confederation. Perhaps. In Ontario, only one person in a hundred named Marcel Masse, the minister of communications. Ninety-seven in a hundred did not — and probably could not — name Bouchard.

In another indication of political indifference, Gallup polled Canadians on their attachment to politics. Only one in six found politics an "absorbing interest" about which they enjoyed learning everything they could. Nearly forty per cent thought politics were too complicated; they didn't have the time or interest "to understand what was going on." Another forty-two percent agreed to the motherhood statement that it was their responsibility as citizens to learn about political affairs.

One wonders how this widespread ignorance affects horse-race poll results on issues such as free trade. How valid is the whole enterprise when only fifteen of every hundred people surveyed admit they have a voluntary interest in public debate, another forty per cent feign interest, and the rest confess to being dumb clucks?

Ask Canadians which factors influence how they cast their ballots on voting day and the majority will say they vote on "leadership" and "the issues." They must say this because it sounds right and because they like to imagine themselves as responsible voters. In reality, when Gallup asked people which leader came closest to reflecting their thinking on a variety of issues, most hadn't the foggiest notion. On abortion, the deficit, environmental protection, day care, federal-provincial relations, and national defence, the leader called "Don't Know" led all the rest.

In poll results, undecided respondents are usually weighted and redistributed in the same proportion as the decided. But at what point can the political potency of "Don't Know" be ignored? Brian Mulroney led all three party leaders in every one of the issue categories among decided respondents surveyed in July 1988, but only once did he score as well as "Don't Know." Mulroney was tied with the bewildered majority on the issue of free trade — about a third thought the prime minister best reflected their thinking on the issue; the same proportion thought "Don't Know" best summed up their opinion. No leader, however, could come even close to "Don't Know" on abortion. There, the Bewildered Party polled forty-one per cent; Mulroney, seventeen; Broadbent, fifteen; and Turner, eleven.

With Ben Johnson it was a different matter. For a start, ninety-nine per cent knew of him. (Perhaps the other one per cent had missed out on the Johnson affair because they were keeping such a close eye on Lucien Bouchard.) In that breathtakingly large group, virtually everyone had an opinion. On whether Johnson had taken drugs, admittedly, a third said they didn't know. But that could well have reflected an honest, and informed, bafflement over the questions Johnson had raised about the security of the drug-testing procedures. Canadians were far less equivocal on other related questions. More than three-quarters were certain Johnson was capable of beating that smug geek, Carl Lewis, even without drugs. All the same, three-quarters felt that, in the circumstances, it was fair to strip Johnson of his medal.

SUCH SUDDEN AWARENESS, such sure-mindedness, and such in-

formed opinion was strikingly reminiscent of what Donald Johnston had described as the hundred-monkeys effect. The same
process would be evident again a month later, on the nights of the
televised election debates. The resonance of both events through
the Canadian psyche was pronounced; and, to at least one man, it
would have been perfectly understandable. His name was Marie-
Joseph-Pierre Teilhard de Chardin, and he would have seen both
the Ben Johnson incident and the televised debates as heralding
the arrival — as he predicted — of something he called the
nöosphere.

Teilhard led an implausible life, and a fascinating one. Born
to an aristocratic family in the Auvergne in 1881 — the son of a
great-grandniece of Voltaire — he spent his childhood collecting
rocks. At eighteen, he decided to study geology and to become a
Jesuit, two pursuits he followed as a novice at Aix-en-Provence. In
1902 the religious orders were expelled from France. Teilhard,
disguised as a layman, fled to the Isle of Jersey. He taught chemistry
in Cairo, returned to England in 1911 and, after eleven years of
training, was ordained as a Jesuit. During the First World War he
spent four years in uniform at the front. He turned down a position
as chaplain and served as a stretcher-bearer instead, considering it
more useful. "Fundamentally, I'm glad to have been at Ypres," he
wrote. He considered it his "baptism in the real."

But "the real" was to haunt the rest of Teilhard's days. As
a boy, he had taken iron as a symbol of the element he sought in
life; as a Jesuit, he had adopted fire to symbolize love and illumination. The two, iron and fire, were not easily reconciled. This
conflict between the material and the spiritual was fated to lead to
censure from the Church, a life-long philosophical quest, and his
eventual postulation of the remarkable theory of the nöosphere.

Teilhard was drawn to paleontology, and eventually made
his way to China to study some important bones. His journey
entailed passage through bandit country: "It is the last country in
the world," he wrote, "where one would find peace and comfort."
He delighted in studying the past, and began to work his science
into his religion. For Teilhard, the mystery of God was "the
incarnate Being in the world of matter." It was the job of others,
he thought, to "proclaim [God's] splendours as pure Spirit."

He was bound for trouble. During a leave in Paris, Teilhard
worked on a paper questioning the doctrine of Original Sin. He left

some notes on his desk, which were stolen by a Jesuit busybody and sent to Teilhard's superiors in Rome. The priest was sent back to China in exile. He spent the next years a fugitive paleontologist-priest, wandering through China, Ethiopia, and remote Africa.

Teilhard was no tyro as a rock-digger. In 1929 he helped find and identify the skull of the 400,000-year-old Peking man. This discovery was of such scientific importance that the Church allowed him to return to Paris, but banned him from talking about anything other than rocks and bones. Teilhard kept busy writing both science and philosophy, and by 1946 he had developed, and circulated underground, his idea of the nöosphere. The Church, realizing his works were making the rounds in manuscript, issued a monitum against them — not a condemnation, but a very serious warning. The monitum was issued about the same time Teilhard was honoured with election to the French Academy of Science.

The Church never did allow publication of Teilhard's works in his lifetime. Only after his death in 1955, when the Church's jurisdiction lapsed, did Teilhard's notions reach a wider public. They caused a controversy and are still not accepted by the Curia. Teilhard had fused science with religion, using his knowledge of man's earliest roots and his belief in evolution to point the way to the future.

His postulation of the nöosphere "belongs to the class of idea," as Carl Jung wrote of his theory of the collective unconscious, "that people at first find strange, but soon come to possess and use as familiar conceptions." Essentially, Teilhard believed he had discovered the flip side of Jung, a collective *conscious*. It took the form of a layer around the planet — a "mind-layer," as the term nöosphere roughly translates. Just as scientists had earlier connected all the inorganic matter of the earth into a conceptual framework called the lithosphere, just as zoologists later identified all organisms as belonging to a living layer on the earth's skin known as the biosphere, just as this whole was surrounded by an atmosphere, so, Teilhard believed, we were witnessing the formation of a thinking layer, binding all.

The nöosphere came about, he believed, because of the unique nature of man. Teilhard viewed man as unique not only because of his self-consciousness, but because of his awareness of his self-consciousness. Man was, in comparison with the other creatures, consciousness squared. "Man is psychically distinguished from all other animals by the entirely new fact that he not only knows, but knows that he knows," Teilhard wrote. "In him, for the first time on earth, consciousness has coiled back upon itself to become thought."

The consequences were, by Teilhard's reckoning, enormous. While all previous evolution had patterned itself along the lines of greater complexity, the entrance of man on the field of life — for all life is "a single and gigantic organism" — turned evolution into a process of greater convergence. This convergence, Teilhard believed, would continue until the Omega point, his end-time vision.

Teilhard is not easy to follow and he fully satisfies neither theologian, scientist, nor philosopher. But, as his friend Sir Julian Huxley remarked, his ideas had the appeal of "the broad sweep and a comprehensive treatment." Given that Teilhard's ideas begin with genesis and end with the second coming, touching on all of creation along the way, it is hard to disagree with Huxley.

Teilhard never fully explored the actual workings of the nöosphere; like love and spring rain, he believed, it was just there, and vitally important. He would not find his theory out of place in the world of sound bites, program trading, Decima polls, minicams and satellites. Rather than bewail these developments as the death of one form of communication, he would hail them as the embryo of a completely new form. "No one can deny that a [world] network of economic and psychic affiliations is being woven at ever-increasing speed which envelops and constantly penetrates more deeply within each of us," Teilhard wrote. "With every day that passes it becomes a little more impossible for us to act or think otherwise than collectively."

That notion has been digested, and phrased more colloquially, by David Quammen, a columnist for *Outside* magazine. In his book *The Flight of the Iguana*, Quammen looked at the nöosphere this way: "More and more in recent years, we are all thinking about the same things at the same time. Electromagnetic radiation is chiefly responsible; microwaves, macrowaves, dashing and dancing electrons unite us instantly and constantly with the waves of each other's brain. We can't step out into the yard without being bonked by a signal that has come caroming off some satellite, and when we step back inside, there's Dan Rather, ready with the day's subject for thought. One day we think about a gutshot pope.

On a designated Sunday in January we gather in clusters to focus our thoughts upon the Super Bowl. Occasionally we ponder a matter of somewhat less consequence, like the early returns from the New Hampshire primary or the question of who shot J.R. Ewing. Late in the evening we think about what Ted Koppel thinks it's important we think about... My point is not that some of these subjects are trivial while others are undeniably and terrifyingly significant; my point is that we think about them together in great national (sometimes global) waves of wrinkling brows, and on cue. God himself has never summoned so much precisely synchronized, prayerful attention as Mary Lou Retton got for doing back flips."

Or as Ben Johnson got for doing steroids.

Quammen has reservations about this nöosphere business — a biologist, he doesn't think uniformity is good for any community of organisms. Evolution, after all, is a trend toward greater complexity, which leads to sturdier life forms. But he doesn't question the validity of the theory.

"The Age of Nations is past," Teilhard wrote, predicting a future informed by the nöosphere. "The task before us now, if we would not perish, is to shake off our ancient prejudices, and to build the earth."

# CHAPTER 11

# SHAKING THE
# BOOGA-WOOGA STICK

*O my brothers! Love your country.*
*Our country is our home, our home*
*which God has given us. . . Your*
*country is one and indivisible. . . Your*
*country is the token of the mission*
*God has given you. . . .*
GIUSEPPE MAZZINI

ABOUT THE TIME OF THE TELE-
vised campaign debates in Canada, the attention of the world was
focused on the fate of two whales trapped in ice off the coast of
Alaska. In this instance, very little impeded the functioning of the
nöosphere. The whales didn't say anything, for a start, so the
world's concentration was not interrupted by constant explanations of what they had just said. They didn't do anything, either,
other than bloody their noses on the ice, so there was no distraction
of shifting circumstances. They just stayed put, trapped, a global
problem demanding a solution. They remained number one on the
nöosphere parade until the two great superpowers, who couldn't
agree on seating arrangements at conferences to reduce the stock-
piles of intercontinental ballistic missiles, co-operated in a rescue
operation to set them free.

The Alaskan whales, Ben Johnson, and the televised debates during the 1988 campaign had one thing in common: all rose

rapidly to the nöosphere because all were relatively unfiltered events. People saw Ben Johnson run the hundred metres from beginning to end; they watched the whales bumping repeatedly against the ice; they saw the leaders exchange verbal blows. They remembered the images themselves, not the interruptions of the events-brokers.

The events-broker operates in the same manner as any other broker; he gets between the two ends of a transaction and grabs some as it goes by. This is what sports announcers do when, say, they get in between the golfer and the viewer to observe that a putt didn't make it in, something the viewer has already seen for himself. It happens every night on the news. The announcer introduces a story about an important announcement by Politician X. Then the reporter comes on, to say Politician X had something important to say today. Then, while footage of X rolls across the screen, the reporter tells you what X is saying. If X is lucky, he actually gets a nanosecond sound burst of his own — "truly shocking situation" — before the reporter comes back on to explain why what X said was important.

A good example of events-brokering could be seen after Margaret Thatcher was quoted by the *Washington Post* as favouring the Canada-U.S. Free-Trade Agreement. In the course of a 1,632-word interview about international issues, primarily the sweeping reforms introduced by Mikhail Gorbachev, Thatcher devoted 31 words — fewer than two per cent of the total — to the free-trade deal. "It would be a blow if that agreement were not ratified, a great blow," she was quoted as saying. She added that failure to ratify the deal would make it "very difficult for any prime minister of Canada to go and negotiate another agreement with another country."

Some of her other remarks cut rather more to the quick. While supporting Soviet reforms, she opined: "Marxism's had it." While encouraging the Palestinian Liberation Organization to recognize Israel's right to exist, she said, "The PLO is no favourite of mine." None of these other comments, however, would create quite the same stir in Canada as her untimely remarks about that life-and-death issue, the Free Trade Agreement.

From Thatcher's 31 words, the *National* on CBC television spun its top two news items of the evening — 838 words of news, or twenty-seven times the number Thatcher herself had used. (The

CBC was merely typical: Southam News devoted 2,066 words over three separate newspaper pieces to the Canadian leaders' reactions to the British leader's remarks.) The various CBC events-brokers mentioned Thatcher's remarks ten times, without ever quoting her directly. Of those 838 words of news, 220 words, about a quarter of the total, went to direct response from two of the Canadian party leaders. Only about two-thirds of the 220 words were about Margaret Thatcher. One reporter, who had been quoted in the newspapers as saying the leaders should be allowed more time to speak directly to the public but couldn't because of the demands of "precious air time," began an interview with Broadbent by showing a clip of the NDP leader mainstreeting in Winnipeg:

BROADBENT: Hi there, hi.

WOMAN ON STREET: Good morning.

BROADBENT: Your hairdo reminds me of my daughter.

And so forth. When such pleasantries are stripped away, Turner and Broadbent were allowed a combined total of 143 words to respond directly to Thatcher's "interference" in the Canadian election. Turner uttered 98 words — during which he remarked that Canada was no longer a colony and that no way, ever, would Britain get that submarine contract now. Broadbent had 45 words, during which he said twice that free trade was "none of Margaret Thatcher's business." Take away this repetition, too, and Broadbent's response finally equates with the 31 words Thatcher actually devoted to free trade.

This is no different from the approach of a newspaper. Television is not the sole purveyor of post-literate discourse any more than the Church was once the sole purveyor of Latin. Television, like the Church, may have introduced a new form of conversation; but it was so well suited to the age that it was soon adopted by all related forms of expression. Nobody wants newspapers to return to the days when they simply reprinted transcripts from Hansard — it is hidebound to deny the necessity of bringing order and structure to complex events — but the extent to which the process of public dialogue is drowned out by the events-brokers in every medium is remarkable. Television offers the promise of intimacy, but most of the time all it delivers is a quick peek under the kimono. Brokering, while useful in its way, prevents the nöosphere from working up a good head of steam.

"Campaigning by television was supposed to be like an

enormous town hall meeting," observed the Southam News political columnist Donald McGillivray. "But it is an odd kind of meeting, because political messages have to be inserted in a lot of other stuff — popular entertainment, and frothy songs, and messages about dog food and personal hygiene. People are drifting in and out to buy hot dogs and potato chips, and to go to the washroom. Every once in a while politicians get a few seconds to shout messages at the crowd. Usually, there's somebody else at the rostrum shouting louder, telling the town hall what the politician is saying. No wonder they over-dramatize."

THE GREAT APPEAL of the televised campaign debates was that they weren't brokered. Great care and attention had been taken, in the preparations, to prevent those two antiquated vehicles of expression — the people and the press — from interfering with the exercise. "[NDP strategist Robin] Sears wants to be sure his candidate will not have to go through pack at front door, people waving placards and shouting questions," note the minutes of a confidential pre-debate meeting between the networks and the party representatives, held October 18 at the Four Seasons Hotel in Ottawa. "[The prime minister's press secretary Bruce] Phillips asked where camera crews and reporters were going to be. He had no objection to pictures, but no scrums. [Liberal image-maker Henry] Comor thought the simplest thing would be to just drive around back and into trailers."

The party representatives debated other critical points at this meeting — they agreed that all three leaders would drink flat bottled water, as carbonated water brings up gas; and that the lecterns would be adjustable, so no leader appeared taller than another. They weighed the merits of bathroom locations and they negotiated arrangements for escorts for any leader making a fast sprint out of the studio, to ensure that he wouldn't run into a live camera.

One of the party representatives' major preoccupations was how to keep the debate free of spontaneous questioning. "Someone thought that since it's a photo-op [we] shouldn't have the press — just cameras," the minutes record, referring to the leaders' walk through the set just before the debate. "Phillips wanted to be assured that candidates not going to be interfered with by having questions shouted at them."

The absence of events-brokers explains why, when John Turner repeated, on the night of October 25, 1988, exactly what he had been saying for the past eighteen months, it finally got through. Nobody got between the two ends of the transaction. What got through was a genuine, almost mystical commitment to duty, loyalty, and nation. Engraved in rosewood above the door to Turner's office are the words: "Fear God; Honour the King."

"On the one hand, he's devout to the point of being a fanatic Roman Catholic," said his aide, Peter Connolly. "At least, on the things Catholicism may have something to say to him about — he just ignores all the other stuff. He says that comes with the baby, the bathwater. But he's a deeply religious guy, he loves this country. He sees it as a manifestation of what you can do for mankind, what mankind can do for itself, given an appeal to its higher motives — however imperfect and unfinished that appeal."

Covering the debate, the two hundred or so journalists assembled at the CJOH broadcast centre in Ottawa were safely locked in a cage. They found themselves in exactly the same position as everyone else in Canada — they watched it on television. Actually, there was one dissimilarity: the gathering of journalists was infiltrated by high-profile political figures from each party. Their function was to spin-doctor the reporters' assessments of the leaders' performances. This task at first was left to the usual press flacks. They sat around on the makeshift bleachers, watching the debate with everyone else. Occasionally a reporter would talk to them, but the room's attention was focused on the television screen at the foot of the stands.

Then Senator Alasdair Graham, the Liberal campaign co-chairman, slipped through the studio door, a look of roguish innocence on his face. His pockets were stuffed with dangerously addictive, mood-enhancing quotes, which he intended to peddle to the would-be junkies of the press corps. A small group sidled over to Graham and began taking notes.

"I think John's doing very well," Graham purred. "Don't you?"

A buzz went through the hall when Graham was joined by André Ouellet, the other Liberal campaign co-chairman. Ouellet, remember, was one of those named in the CBC's report of the "coup" against Turner. If Ouellet's here, went the buzz, the coup must be over.

Members of the other parties, meanwhile, fearing they were about to be outspun, stepped up their efforts. The former Saskatchewan premier, Allan Blakeney, managed to worm his way in front of a CBC camera. Hey! went the buzz. A New Democrat who's actually been elected! Let's get him!

Blakeney, with sober directness, allowed as how he thought Broadbent was doing very well.

Then the professional gadfly and former Trudeau aide Patrick Gossage hit the room, waving a censer of praise for the new leader.

"Dr. Phillips is here!" announced Brian Mulroney's press secretary, Bruce Phillips, shouldering his way into the room, his manner a declaration that the Tories were not about to be outspun by anyone. "Dr. Phillips will soon be joined by a few of his colleagues."

The Conservative Party had an ace up its sleeve: the magic spinning cabinet. Phillips was joined by Finance Minister Michael Wilson and Communications Minister Flora MacDonald. They both allowed as how they thought the prime minister was doing very well indeed.

By the time the three leaders began debating women's issues, barely a media soul was paying attention to the screen. The journalists' studio had been transformed into a carnival, the spinners and the spun. It was, as the Ontario New Democrat leader Bob Rae termed it, a "political bazaar." And yet a curious phenomenon was evident, something as indicative of the pivotal nature of the 1988 campaign as anything that happened during the debate itself. Everyone wanted to talk to the spin doctors, yes, readily ignoring what was happening on the screen. But no one pretended to care a whit for their opinions. Everyone wanted to do a story on spinning.

"I just think it's exciting to be a part of all this," said an ingenuous Flora MacDonald, asked what she was doing in the room. Michael Wilson, who beguiles with all the enthusiasm of a faithless priest giving last rites, avoided pretence: "We just thought we'd better get down here to give you the straight goods." Someone asked Wilson if the timing of his appearance didn't show that his party cared little about women's issues, the Tories having stacked the room just as the women's debate began. "Uh, not at all," said Wilson, his eyes dodging in search of an aide.

Reporters kept asking Gossage what it is, exactly, that a

spinner does, and Gossage kept avoiding an answer. "It's so White House," he camped. "We ought to be able to come up with something else — something Canadian."

"A good spin has to be believable," offered Doug Kirkpatrick, deputy principal secretary to John Turner. "If someone throws you a curve, you know it's a curve, and not a fastball."

Nothing neuters subterfuge like recognition. Safe to say that the public response to the televised debate was unaffected by the spin doctors. Whatever conclusions people drew from the debate, they drew on their own. The spinners simply cancelled each other out.

WHAT PEOPLE really wanted to see on their screens, of course, was a contest. As Marshall McLuhan observed, television thrives on the process and virtually overlooks the resolution. The televised debates offered a dramatic process of confrontation; it was up to the viewer to determine how it was resolved.

In the view of Derek De Kerckhove, who teaches at the McLuhan Program in Culture and Technology at the University of Toronto, televised debates are appealing because they offer a return to single-warrior combat. Single warriors were once known as champions, a word that still retains that meaning when we speak of "championing" a cause. The tradition was established under Anglo-Norman law, which rendered it uncommonly suitable to Canadian politics. Trial by battle was a recognized method of settling legal disputes; women, minors, and people disabled by age or infirmity were permitted to appoint champions to fight on their behalf.

So entrenched was this historic notion, and so apt in post-literate circumstances, that commentators found it difficult to describe the televised debates otherwise: "They fired away at close range tonight, hoping to get their shots in while dodging the ones aimed their way," Peter Mansbridge told his CBC audience. "The weapons were words." Good thing, too.

In France, the clergy were represented by champions; in England, the kings were. There was even a patronage position, known as the "campio regis." The king's champion rode into the coronation banquet, clad in full armour on a warhorse, and challenged to single combat anyone who thought his master unfit to reign. He threw down the gauntlet three times, calling out the medieval equivalent of, "Anybody got any obs?" The king then toasted him from a gilt cup; the cup was given to the champion as a fee. If anyone had actually taken up the challenge, the fee would have been the champion's armour and his horse, the second-finest in the king's stable.

There is no record that the challenge was ever taken up, and the role of campio regis fell into disuse — only to be revived, in this century, by Bill Fox, the prime minister's press secretary. When Mulroney was a newly minted prime minister, Fox didn't like the looks of a story written by a *Maclean's* correspondent. He showed up at the reporter's door early next morning, while the reporter was still in bed, and informed his wife: "Tell him I'm looking for him." Later, when the *Toronto Star* reported on expensive renovations to the Mulroney residence, Fox left word for the reporter with the *Star*'s receptionist: "Tell him from me I'm going to rip his fucking lungs out." Unfortunately, no one ever picked up the gauntlet. Fox has since taken good-humour pills and returned to private practice, a gilt cup over his mantel; in October 1988, it was left to the leaders themselves to play the role of champion.

IF IT WERE NOT FOR this concentration on fighting imagery, it might very well have been Ed Broadbent, not John Turner, who seized the high ground of meaning during the televised debates. Everything Turner was to say later, Broadbent said in his introductory remarks. Because he delivered these remarks as part of his opening statement, however, Broadbent was merely parading in front of the reviewing stand. He was not in actual combat, and so the focus was lost. But it's right there in the transcript: not ten seconds into his introduction, Broadbent said that free trade "threatens our families, our environment, our medicare, and pensions; that it jeopardizes regional development and sets back programs for our farmers." It was exactly these fears that made Turner's later joust with Mulroney so plausible; by articulating these fears early on, Broadbent was performing an invaluable service to his opponent.

Mulroney, in his walk-past, clung to the "managing change" theme which had been so effective in the early part of the campaign. "We have set this country, our beloved Canada, on a new course," he said, and while he undoubtedly loves Canada, he loaded so much syrup into the word "beloved" that he might have been auditioning for *Rose Marie*. "We have a stronger Canada today, better able to make our own future in a world of change and uncertainty." The choice offered in the election, he argued, came down to this: "What group of men and women should you choose to maintain Canada's strength and the growth and the prosperity and our standard of living in a complex and changing world?" Mulroney was doing an admirable job of following his pollster's advice to soothe the electorate's broader millennial anxieties; but he was doing a lousy job of providing a glimpse of his soul.

Not that Turner started out any better. "Mr. Mulroney and Mr. Broadbent will talk to you about leadership," he said. "They mean leadership of the party. What they should be talking about is leadership of a country. Canada is more important than any single one person."

Six million viewers watched, transfixed, as Turner committed ritual hara-kiri on prime time. He had just reminded them that he couldn't control his own party. They had just realized he now wanted to lead the country. And they had just been told that the country was more important than any single person — John Turner, for instance. "This election is not a popularity contest," Turner added. "The issue is the future of Canada." Like the plain girl who had hoped to win the title of homecoming queen on the strength of her baton-twirling, Turner was whimpering that no one had told him it was a beauty contest.

The transcript of the English televised debate runs to 168 pages, but the critical two minutes occupy only four of those pages. This exchange came to be known as the Two Minutes that Changed the Election, or TMTCTE. (As the *Ottawa Citizen* columnist Charles Gordon pointed out, however, the actual exchange — starting with Turner's first "You sold us out" to Mulroney's final "Please be serious" — lasted two minutes and thirty-eight seconds. Thus, instead of TMTCTE, the exchange ought to have been referred to as TMA38STCTE. Gordon's intention was humorous, but he has the disadvantage of a readership of public servants, who thought his point valid.)

Several things made the exchange riveting. For a start, it was clearly a two-hander: Broadbent had already been eliminated from the debate. The NDP leader's attempts to define himself as the logical opposition to the government had amounted to little more than bickering. During his exchange with Turner, Broadbent had reached back four years to use Mulroney's line from the 1984 debate: "You had the same option open to you, sir," he berated Turner, "and you said no." Mulroney had used a similar line in reference to a Liberal orgy of patronage. Broadbent was using it in reference to Turner's refusal to spend federal money on municipal sewers. It didn't have quite the same zing.

No one realized it at the time, but Broadbent blundered further when he attributed one scary quotation about free trade to the Canadian Chamber of Commerce, which hadn't issued it; and when he quoted the president of the Canadian Manufacturers Association, Laurent Thibault, as predicting that free trade would erode Canadian social programs. He used the present tense: "He is saying this," said Broadbent, "and I quote" — but the quotation was eight years old. Thibault issued a protest the next day, saying that his thinking had "evolved" on the matter. (Once the election was over, Thibault's thinking evolved again — eight years into the past. He pressured Finance Minister Michael Wilson to cut social spending now that free trade was a fait accompli. Do not, as the magicians say, try this stunt at home.)

Mulroney's response to the Thibault quote was blink-eyed astonishment. "I know nothing about that," he said. "I would have to examine the context in which he said it." Evidently, Turner and Mulroney had decided they had endured enough of the NDP pest. In their next exchange, they portrayed him as the gawky kid who is sometimes allowed to play backfield. Challenging Mulroney to a special debate on free trade, Turner said: "Why don't you and I have a head to head? Invite Mr. Broadbent, fine."

"Isn't that nice," Mulroney replied. "You are going to invite Mr. Broadbent?"

"Yes, I would indeed," Turner said. "Have a head to head and let's deal with the issue the way Canadians expect — "

"It seems to me you were very gracious to decide you were going to include Mr. Broadbent," Mulroney said. (Say what you like about the prime minister: while blindfolded in a well at midnight he could spot a chance to belittle an opponent.) "He will be relieved to hear that."

"Now, let's not get sarcastic," Turner replied. "He has a perfect right to be there."

"Of course he does," Mulroney smiled.

If Broadbent hadn't been undermined by now, any hope he had of recovery was dashed a few minutes later, when the two-minute exchange began. The exchange actually had three parts. In the first, Turner defined the issue of the campaign. No wonder he did so well at it — he had six runs at it:

"I happen to believe that you have sold us out," Turner said. "I happen to believe that, once you — "

"Mr. Turner, just one second."

"Once any region — "

"You do not have a monopoly on patriotism," Mulroney said.

"Once — "

"And I resent the fact that your implication is that only you are a Canadian."

"I am sorry," Turner responded. "I — "

"I want to tell you that I come from a Canadian family —"

"Once — "

" — and I love Canada," said Mulroney.

"Once any — "

"And that is why I did it," Mulroney concluded. "To promote prosperity — "

"Once any country — "

" — and don't you — "

"Once any country yields its economic levers," Turner gasped.

"Don't you impugn my motives or anyone else's," Mulroney warned; but nothing was going to stop Turner now, not after seven "onces."

"Once a country yields its energy — "

"We have not done it."

"Once a country yields its agriculture, once a country — "

"Wrong again."

" — opens itself up to a subsidy war with the United States — "

"Wrong again."

" — in terms of definition, then the political ability — "

"You — "

" — of this country to sustain the influence of the United States, to remain as it is, a competitive nation, that — "

"Mr. Turner."

" — will go on forever, and — "

"Mr. Turner."

" — that is the issue of this election, sir," Turner said, at long last.

In that halting exchange John Turner had, if only through sheer perseverance, defined the terms of the 1988 election.

THE SECOND PART of this exchange, which has come to be known as Brian Mulroney's Log Cabin speech, illustrated how painfully awkward it was for Mulroney to bare his soul. In 1984, he had managed to say that Canada was a land of "small towns and big dreams," a phrase that had the benefit of simplicity and the resonance of a shared truth. When he attempted the same trick in 1988, he not only built the town, he showered its bricks with kisses:

"Mr. Turner, let me tell you something, sir. This country is only about one hundred and twenty years old, but my own father, fifty-five years ago, went himself, as a labourer, with hundreds of other Canadians and with their own hands, in northeastern Quebec, they built a little town and schools and churches and they, in their own way, were nation-building; in the same way as the waves of immigrants from the Ukraine and Eastern Europe rolled back the prairies and, in their own way, in their own time, they were nation-building because they loved Canada.

"I, today, sir, as a Canadian, believe genuinely in what I am doing. I believe it is right for Canada. I believe that, in my own modest way, I am nation-building because I believe this benefits Canada and I love Canada."

Turner did not attempt to match his opponent, did not utter the phrase "I believe" four times. If he loved Canada he apparently felt that the assertion of his sentiment, like an avowal of genius, was best left to others. It may have been, as his aides were saying, that Turner's antagonism to free trade had grown into a full-blown obsession. If so, then what he saw in Mulroney's protestations of patriotism must have been loathsome. Whatever he saw, it galvanized him into a rare moment of calm:

"I admire your father for what he did," Turner replied. "My grandfather moved to British Columbia. My mother was a miner's daughter there. We are just as Canadian as you are, Mr. Mulroney, but I will tell you this. You mentioned one hundred and twenty years of history. We built a country east and west and north. We built it on an infrastructure that deliberately resisted the continental pressure of the United States.

"For one hundred and twenty years, we have done it. With one signature of a pen, you have reversed that, thrown us into the north-south influence of the United States — "

"With a — " Mulroney interrupted.

" — and will reduce us, I am sure," Turner continued, "to a colony of the United States, because when the economic levers go, the political independence is sure to follow."

There was a slim chance Mulroney could still have salvaged it. Perhaps he could have handled it with the proved technique of Lloyd Bentsen, who, during the American debate, deflated his opponent's stridency with a knowing grin, a shake of the head, and: "You're no Jack Kennedy." It's hard, though, to think of a Canadian patriot on the spur of the moment; and understated irony is not Mulroney's strong suit. Instead, the prime minister made an astonishing statement which, however true, reduced his Log Cabin speech to nothing more than a maudlin platitude. Moments before, he had said free trade was the stuff the pioneers were made of — grit, resolve, love of the new land. Now, cornered, Mulroney said the deal was "a document that is cancellable on six months' notice. Be serious."

"Look," said Turner.

"Be serious."

"Cancellable?" Turner gasped. "You are talking about our relationship with the United States. Once that — "

"A commercial document that is cancellable on six months' notice," Mulroney repeated.

Turner had trouble believing his ears. "Commercial document? That document relates — "

"That is what it is, a commercial treaty," Mulroney added, nonchalant.

"It relates to every facet of our life."

"It is a commercial treaty."

"It is far more important to us than it is to the United States."

"Mr. Turner — "

"Far more important."

"Please be serious."

"Well," Turner said, "I am serious, and I have never been more serious in my life."

That was the fall right there, the moment after which every

step the Conservatives took would be a step of recovery, every act an act of redemption. Brian Mulroney had not in any way misrepresented the truth or misled the public. But he had stripped the free-trade issue of any talismanic quality it might have held for the Conservatives. He had exposed it for what it was — a commercial document, cancellable, nothing more. That was the truth, but the post-literate election is not won on truth; it is won on imposed meaning. Mulroney had just rendered free trade a neutral object — the first of Pavlov's three steps — and given his opponent the opportunity to imbue this neutral object with meaning. He did this at a moment when every microwave launcher in the country was beaming the exchange into the nöosphere and the collective consciousness of the six-million-odd Canadians who were watching — the hundred monkeys, who in turn had the power to transmit their knowledge to all the other monkeys.

It may be of no consequence, or it may explain a great deal, that the live camera during the "signature of a pen" exchange was behind Mulroney's head. With each new assertion by Turner, Mulroney's head moved slightly. He was actually bobbing forward, anticipating a counterpoint, but the camera angle made it look as if he was jerking back from physical blows to the face. Turner was beating him up. It's what people had turned on their television sets to see.

IN HIS MEMOIRS of his work as a campaign adviser to John F. Kennedy, *Getting Elected*, J. Leonard Reinsch provides an extremely detailed account of the Nixon-Kennedy televised debates — right down to who controlled the thermostat. Before those debates, and contrary to popular memory, Kennedy was not the favoured candidate. "Here was a highly articulate, personable candidate," Reinsch recalled, "who, in the eyes of extremists, had Catholic horns; who, in the eyes of Republicans and some Democrats, lacked experience; and, in the eyes of many, was much too young to be President." Nixon's offer of a televised debate was snapped up by Reinsch: "In a joint appearance with Richard Nixon, Kennedy had nothing to lose and everything to win." The assessment was shared by Kennedy himself. Asked if he had any instructions for Reinsch, who negotiated the terms of the debates, Kennedy replied: "Just one. Don't let him get off the hook."

Like John Turner, Kennedy rehearsed heavily for the debate; like Brian Mulroney, Nixon rested beforehand. For the reasons mentioned earlier — Nixon's bad knee, his light suit, his sweaty brow — Kennedy won the first round. As Reinsch cheerfully admits: "Few could recite exactly what was said during the debate. But Kennedy. . . had enhanced his image — and image won out over content." An overnight poll gave Kennedy the win, 39 per cent to 23.

Reinsch was stunned by the brave new world of television celebrity. Cash flowed in to the Kennedy campaign, women threw themselves at the candidate, crowds fought to touch his car. "You had to see all this Kennedymania to appreciate it," he said. "But many still wondered: how much of it would translate into votes?" Reinsch took his cue from the bookies — after the fourth debate, six Las Vegas bookmakers had made Kennedy the better-than-even-money choice to defeat Nixon.

Since 1960, no political leader in North America has allowed himself to lose as badly as Nixon. Handlers learned their lesson, and extraordinary care was taken with such matters as lighting, camera angles, make-up, and presentation. Subsequent debates thus provided a more level playing ground. Through the years, a conventional wisdom evolved. It holds that televised debates have little immediate impact on the public. Those viewers who already support one candidate will believe their candidate performed well, and continue to support him. Those floating on the uncommitted margins will remain unsettled. Over a period of days, a consensus will emerge in the media, reinforced by polls, and mediated in public conversation. Once this process declares a winner, goes the conventional wisdom, support tends to shift in the direction of previous opinions. Debates, in other words, reinforce an existing trend; they do not create a new one.

The televised debates in Canada in 1979, for example, when Broadbent, Pierre Trudeau, and Joe Clark duked it out, had little impact either on voter preference or on campaign agenda. The contest itself was indecisive, and voter positions were firmly fixed before the debate. The televised debates during Brian Mulroney's first campaign, in 1984, on the other hand, triggered the largest movement of voter support ever recorded to that date. But popular support moved away from an already crumbling Liberal campaign and toward the clearly resurgent Conservatives. Public-opinion polls indicated that party support before the debates was "soft" and susceptible to a mood shift, and the media were quick to declare Mulroney the winner. This judgement blended well with the popular impression that the Liberal campaign was becoming unravelled and the Conservatives were gaining momentum. At the time of the 1984 debates, Mulroney may have been in second place, but he was not the underdog.

Over the years, political strategists had concluded that, while a good televised debate could reinforce a winning campaign, it could not salvage a losing one. But if a candidate could not score a reversal on image, perhaps he could succeed in applying his definition of the campaign issue, to imbue it with meaning. This would be of consequence only if campaigns had evolved to the point at which they possessed little intrinsic value and were thus susceptible to imposed values. Which, by 1988, they were. As Allan Gregg had found in his deeper soundings of voter sentiment, the only way for a politician to lead the electorate down that path was through a clear demonstration of spontaneity, emotion, and motive. People can still be led, Gregg had said, but they want to be led by someone demonstrating those qualities.

Mulroney, who thumbed repeatedly through his four fat briefing books in the days before the 1988 debate, had these qualities effectively drilled out of him. Turner, though, clearly demonstrated them during the televised exchange — if only because they were all he had left in the world.

In the months before the election was called, Turner felt he had clearly beaten the Conservatives in his Commons speeches against free trade. He had also been well received outside Ottawa, at gatherings such as his Quadra nomination meeting. But he was concerned that his message wasn't getting through, that he was unable to link free trade with his broader concerns of nationalism, social policy, and sovereignty. His instructions to his debate negotiators were therefore the same as Kennedy's — get one, at any cost.

"We were terrified we would do or say something so that we wouldn't get a debate at all," recalled his chief adviser, Peter Connolly. "We told our negotiators, 'When push comes to shove, swallow your pride, swallow your brains, swallow your balls, just get us a debate.' Because we knew we had to show Turner to the people. Well, he knew it. And he was right."

Unfortunately for Turner, reports of the "coup" the previous week had left him forsaken. His first rehearsal was scheduled for the Friday before the French debate, which was held on Monday, October 24. He had taken no time to prepare, relying on his headquarters in Ottawa to draft a briefing manual. The manual was shipped to him the day before the rehearsal so that he could read it on the flight back to Ottawa. "He was relying on the description of a briefing book that wasn't produced," Connolly recalled. "He had a briefing book, but it was of zero value. It was for both the French and English debates, and it was less than an inch thick. Utterly worthless."

When Turner arrived at the studio for rehearsal, things were no better. "There were a whole bunch of people who were supposed to be there, and there was nobody there," Connolly recalled. "People had abandoned him. The actual rehearsal was a disaster. His French was bad because he was tired, and his answers were worse. The questions — I don't know, it was just a disaster. Same for the English rehearsal. He was tired. The expectations of most insiders were pretty low." Turner was sustained by just one thing: his conviction that Mulroney was destroying the country. As Connolly put it: "He just wanted to get 'im."

When Connolly and an aide, Doug Kirkpatrick, drove to Stornoway to collect Turner on the night of the French debate, Turner was already out on the driveway, pacing up and down. He jumped in the car and barked, "Let's go! Go, go!" The two aides attempted to cool him off but Turner wouldn't be cooled. "He couldn't wait," said Connolly. "Grrr, let me at him. He didn't say that, but that was the mood."

After the first two hours of the English debate the next night, Turner returned to his briefing trailer annoyed by what he considered the unwarranted interruptions of the moderator and the checkerboard pattern of questioning. As he walked back into the studio for the last segment, Connolly recalls, Turner said, "I don't care what happens in there, I'm going after Mulroney. I don't care what she [the moderator, Rosalie Abella] says. I'm going to get him."

ODD, THE WAY it worked. The CBC was careful that night not to pick a winner, although the network did select as one of its highlights the two-minute exchange. Newspapers the next morning also focused on the exchange, although the reviews were mixed. Turner got muted support, at best, as the winner. The *Toronto Star* led with a neutral headline: "Sparks fly as leaders clash in TV debate." The subtitle read: "Turner: 'You sold us out.' PM: 'I love Canada, too.'" The lead paragraph of the main story was impartial: "In a gripping exchange with Liberal leader John Turner, Prime Minister Brian Mulroney last night declared that he signed the free trade deal because he 'loves Canada.'"

When the *Star* isolated a winning issue for Turner, it chose patronage, not free trade. Another front-page headline said: "Turner jabs on patronage put Mulroney on defensive: 'I didn't do as well as I should have,' PM says." One of the paper's political columnists, Carol Goar, in a front-page analysis, gave Turner the victory by decision: "Debate win gives Grit campaign momentum." Goar wrote: "The winner: John Turner. The Liberal leader looked poised, confident and clear headed. . . ."

The Toronto *Sun*'s political columnist, Joe O'Donnell, by contrast, judged that Turner had "checked his brains with his coat," and was the clear loser. *The Globe and Mail*'s Jeffrey Simpson wrote a column called "His best hour," but his assessment was mixed: "Liberal leader John Turner exorcised the ghosts of the 1984 debates last night," Simpson wrote, "but he didn't conjure up any new ones to scare Conservative leader Brian Mulroney." The *Globe*'s main news headline, meanwhile, was neutral: "Turner, PM turn trade deal into scrap over patriotism."

Outside Toronto, the message was the same. "Trade dominates debate," read the headline in the *Vancouver Sun*: "Tenacious Turner riles PM to cite patriotism." The Montreal *Gazette*'s headline was flat: "Debate turns into shouting match; PM, Turner clash over patriotism in nasty exchange over trade deal." The *Gazette*'s snappiest writer, Hubert Bauch, gave the win to Turner in an analysis headlined: "Turner steals show with crisp performance." Bauch knew a blood sport when he saw one: "Leading the series of round-robin confrontations, Turner liberally boxed Prime Minister Brian Mulroney's ears about patronage — the very topic that had turned out to be the Liberal leader's Armageddon in similar debates four years ago." The *Ottawa Citizen* submerged the question of who had won beneath what was, quite certainly, the least inspired headline of the entire campaign: "After debates, leaders on road again." (This is what prompts writers at the *Citizen* — of whom, I must add in the interests of full disclosure, I am one — to imagine the headlines their editors would assign to other great stories, had they lived in other times: "Hotter than normal for this time of year" [Hiroshima]; or, "No building permits issued for wall construction" [Berlin].)

The following night, the CBC cautiously identified Turner as the winner of the debate: "There are no sure answers," Peter Mansbridge said on the *National*, "but it's fair to say that John Turner has come out looking pretty good on most scorecards." This was followed by David Halton's report on reaction across the country, which concluded: "It'll take another round of opinion polls to prove that and to prove that Turner has actually had any real impact on the voters."

What Halton didn't know was that polls had already been taken, and they showed that Turner had disproved the conventional wisdom about televised debates — he had, miraculously, performed the Kennedy turnaround. There are many indications that Turner's exposed heart swayed voters at once, before they had a chance to be influenced by the events-brokers. Some of these signs were unscientific — the CBC "panel of average Canadians" picked Turner, as did members of a focus group assembled at Concordia University in Montreal.

None were as convincing, however, as a Gallup poll released two days later. Gallup had interviewed nearly seven hundred English-speaking Canadians, including anglophones in Quebec, on the night following the debate. The interviews were conducted by telephone no later than 9:30 p.m. The morning headlines would have been available to respondents, but the CBC's Wednesday night identification of Turner as the likely winner would not have. Gallup found that 72 per cent of respondents believed Turner won the debate. Only 17 per cent believed Mulroney was the winner, and 11 per cent picked Broadbent.

This response was not an empty victory for Turner; it promised to translate directly into votes. Fifteen per cent of those surveyed said they were more likely to vote Liberal as a result of Turner's performance. That was more than twice the number of respondents who shifted to the Conservatives, and four times the number who moved to the New Democrats.

Lorne Bozinoff, the head of Gallup in Canada, said that the poll indicated that Liberal support had been picked up from undecided voters. His hunch, though, told him Turner had bled off Conservatives as well. Respondents who said they were previously undecided may have been displaying "an artefact of memory," as Bozinoff put it. "People don't like to admit they've switched loyalties."

Gallup was concurrently conducting at-home interviews for its weekly assessment of party strengths. "The general population survey had some uptick for Turner on the night of the debate," Bozinoff said. "For the next several days, as the impact of the debate was still being processed, it continued upward." Bozinoff is convinced the change took place in the voters first, and was picked up by the media and the pollsters only after the fact. He watched, astounded, as the daily reports from field workers came in. Not only had Turner reversed his party's slide overnight, he was gaining on the Tories at a rate of one point a day — the same rate that Tory support was eroding. At that pace the Conservatives would be trailing in a week.

The aphorism that a party cannot reverse its fortunes during a campaign debate was consigned by the election of 1988 to the dusty heaps of political myth. Somehow, somewhere, John Turner had set the minds of the hundred monkeys in motion, and all the other monkeys were getting the same idea.

It was up to the Conservatives to find out how he had done it, and to counter the trend. Not that it would seem to affect the ultimate outcome. There was another piece of conventional wisdom out there, which even the most optimistic Tory strategist must have found daunting in the wake of the debate. No federal party in Canada had managed to reverse a mid-campaign slump and come back to win. Ever.

# CHAPTER 12

# DAMBUSTERS

*All advertising, whether it lies in the
field of business or of politics, will
carry success by continuity and
regular uniformity of application.*
ADOLF HITLER

I'VE NEVER SEEN VOTER MOVE-
ment like this," said Allan Gregg, shaking his head, his hair
brushing his shoulders like the automated rags at the car wash.
"Never, ever, ever."

In his playpen-office at Decima Research in Toronto, Gregg
took the thick wad of printouts — the previous night's tracking —
and dumped it on his desk. "People are getting fatigued," he said.
He meant the voters but could easily have meant himself. Two
weeks before the election, Gregg looked spent. Still, there was a
spark of manic energy behind his darkened lids; something beyond
agitation to his shifting heels, his clicking lighter, his clucking
tongue; something almost fanatical. It was the fanaticism that
comes from certainty. In the past few days he had been sucked into
the dark whorl of a collapsing campaign, seen the bottomless gyre
of the electorate's heart — fickle, frightened, impulsive. He had
emerged, clutching an answer; but he never wanted to go down
there again.

Yes, Gregg confirmed, the Conservative vote had fallen
apart after the televised debates. Yes, the Tories were bleeding,
from all support groups. "And you could isolate one hundred per

cent of the vote shift on the basis of free trade."

Gregg's task was to find the source of John Turner's extraordinary and unexpected resonance among the public. It was clear enough that Turner, during the debate, had demonstrated the qualities of spontaneity and emotion Gregg believed so central to the post-literate campaign; the mystery was exactly what damage had been done to the Tories, and where. By all the old measures of political wisdom, the damage should have been limited. Mulroney was still leading his opponents personally by 11 points; his party still ranked 18 points higher than either opposition party. "But all traditional cues have taken a back seat," Gregg said. The Tory party was like a body invaded by cancer. The body was fundamentally healthy. If they could only remove the cancer, it would heal itself.

If they couldn't, Gregg knew, the disease would spread. His tracking had shown an immediate swing toward Turner, and some of this new support was coming at the expense of Conservative loyalties. Moreover, there was a ripple effect — one of Gregg's most surprising findings was that the number of respondents who said they had seen the two-minute exchange during the debate increased sharply in the days following the debate. They had probably seen the rebroadcast on news reports; their internalized belief that they had witnessed the live exchange indicated to Gregg that they were rationalizing their decision to change loyalties.

MANY OF GREGG'S findings were supported by the findings of the federally funded 1988 Canadian National Election Study. When results of nightly surveys taken for that study are divided into three periods — pre-debate, the ten days following the debate, and the final weeks of the campaign — it becomes evident that public support for free trade slumped in the middle, post-debate period. The numbers also show that Turner's gains were made not only from undecided voters but from Tory and NDP loyalists. Not just the levels of free-trade support had changed; so had the party structure of that support. Moreover, Turner had transformed free trade into a galvanizing issue among those who opposed the agreement, while Mulroney had failed to make it a decisive issue among those who supported the deal.

Working on his mainframe computer at the University of British Columbia, Richard Johnston was able to cross-reference such indicators as party identification, attitudes toward free trade, and voter intention. When these three indicators are laid on top of each other, a clear pattern emerges. Before the debate, opponents of free trade from all parties — including the roughly one-quarter of voters who had no party loyalty — were not terribly inclined to vote Liberal. Among people who opposed free trade, about 40 per cent were prepared to vote Liberal, another 40 per cent NDP. A further 15 per cent were intending to vote Conservative, despite their dislike of free trade.

After the debate, however, Turner's support among all-party opponents to free trade soared to 54 per cent — up an astonishing 14 points. Broadbent's support declined about five points, and the Conservative vote was nearly wiped out. Just 5 per cent of all opponents to free trade said they were still prepared to vote Conservative. Turner's opposition to free trade was attracting considerable all-party support.

A glimpse into the ranks of Conservative Party loyalists simply confirmed the larger trend. This was the figure that got Gregg thinking of cancer: before the debate, more than two-thirds of Conservatives opposed to free trade remained loyal to the party. (Yes, Virginia, there was such a thing as a Tory opposed to free trade — at the outset, one in six free-trade opponents was Conservative.) But after the debate, the number of Conservatives willing to hold their noses on free trade and vote the party line was sliced in half. Their vote switched overwhelmingly to the Liberals. Before the debate, Turner had been polling only 16 per cent of the vote among Tories who disliked free trade; just after the debate, that figure rose to 43 per cent. Any politician able to triple hard-line votes stolen from the other guy's ranks should finish the day off by parting the Red Sea.

Curiously, though, the election study's numbers do not lead to the conclusion that this switch grew out of nationalist or left-wing sentiments. Richard Johnston was also able to correlate attitudes toward free trade with nationalist issues. The number of opponents to free trade who also opposed the Meech Lake Accord fell three and one-half points after the debate — not significant, in this size of polling sample.

Nor was there significant change in the correlation between free-trade opponents and those who also opposed the privatization of Air Canada; or who also favoured greater extension of bilingualism; or who also opposed the purchase of nuclear-powered submarines; or who also favoured more government subsidies for child-care centres; or who also wanted more done to promote French; even, surprisingly, between those who opposed free trade and those who also opposed closer ties to the United States. The only significant correlation between opposition to free trade and "left-wing" sentiments was found in the number of free-trade opponents who felt the government was doing a "poor" or "very poor" job of protecting the environment — that number jumped seven points after the debate. That was the one exception. Otherwise, the change in support for Turner — despite his flag-waving during the debate — was not scanning as a simply nationalist one.

JOHN TURNER had succeeded, during the debate, in linking free trade with nationalism; and nationalism, in all its guises, has always been a potent force in Canadian politics. Allan Gregg reckoned that nationalism had dug a conduit for Turner. By gaining credibility on the nationalist linkage, Gregg believed, Turner had created a channel for everything else he had been saying about free trade. And through this channel flowed the apocalyptic sludge, the millennial anxiety, that was so much a part of the popular culture in Canada in the fall of 1988.

"The effect of the television debate," said Gregg, "was that it moved all that millennial anxiety from an unfocused anxiety about the future to the realization that they'd found the Beast — the Beast is free trade.

"Are you worried about medicare?" he said, running through the list. "Hey, remember John Turner saying that, under free trade, they'll check your wallet before they check your pulse? Afraid of running out of clean water? John Turner says we're going to have to sell all our water to the Americans. What about your cities? Under free trade, we'll have American cities. It goes on and on."

The Conservatives had held to the naive belief that the free-trade agreement would be judged as a commercial document. Turner had transformed free trade into a talisman; once he began shaking the booga-wooga stick, there was no end to the fears that could be associated with free trade. And no end to the voters motivated by those fears.

Before the debates, Gregg's regression analyses had pretty well divided free-trade sentiment between those who hoped to benefit from the deal (high-income earners, men, urban-dwellers) and those who expected to lose from it (women, youth, the poorly educated). These latter groups had no real evidence on which to base their fears; they had simply learned to expect the worst from whatever came along. But millennial anxiety cut across all social classes and income groups, across sex and colour. Millennial anxiety was shared by everyone; after the debates, when Gregg tried to decipher the tumbling Tory numbers around free trade, he found that "the split between those who benefit and those who lose just disappeared. It fell apart overnight. Suddenly, everybody felt at risk."

Just as suddenly, the Conservatives saw their "managing change" theme turned against them. "That whole issue got shifted back on us," Gregg said. "Rather than managing a packet of vague anxieties, we came to represent the packet. Once free trade adopted the quality-of-life variables, it fit that exactly." As an illustration, Gregg pointed out that, before the campaign, two-thirds of all poll respondents believed social programs were not threatened by free trade. Immediately after the debate, that number fell to 40 per cent. What had happened? "I've never felt that confused before," Gregg admitted. "Do you realize we were doing focus groups on Thursday" — the English debate had been Tuesday night — "and the people were feeding back to us, verbatim, John Turner's arguments against free trade."

How, he was asked, could that have happened?

"It's something to do with resonance," said Gregg. "This population is wildly whipshod. In 1979 and 1980, people said, 'Something is fundamentally wrong here,' and we asked them, 'Do you want four more years like the last four?' In 1984, we said, 'We've got to change the way we do things.' In 1988, the feeling out there was, 'Boy, are things ever good, and it's not going to stay this way.'

Convinced that free trade had become a roll of flypaper hanging in the scary attic of the Canadian psyche, Gregg set about determining what exactly served as the glue. His instinct was to test a concept that had become a corporate buzz-word around the Decima offices, "proxy." To Gregg's mind, the fundamental questions a voter answers at the ballot box are: "Who is most like me, and who is most for me?" The voter does not so much match his opinions on a particular issue with the opinions of a leader, as

212

choose the leader most likely to represent his interests on all sorts of issues. Voters, that is, select political leaders much as they choose lawyers or doctors. They are willing to put decisions on complex issues in the hands of professionals, but first must have a relationship of trust.

If so, Gregg reasoned, then the voter support Turner drew from the fears that stuck to free trade was linked to his own trustworthiness. Gregg checked the polling data — sure enough, his bingo card was filled. So, too, in Richard Johnston's national election study — the number of respondents who thought Turner could be trusted "a great deal" or "somewhat" climbed 9 points after the debate among the electorate as a whole, the same as among opponents of free trade. Over the same period, Mulroney's trustworthiness rating fell 10 points among the electorate at large, 11 points among free-trade opponents.

An even stronger indication of the linkage Gregg was looking for — the connection between the voters' opposition to free trade and their trust of John Turner — is provided by a nifty little device known as the Kendall statistic. This measures the overall coupling of two survey responses — how tightly the nut of one is screwed to the bolt of another. It is helpful, in understanding the Kendall figure, to imagine a public-opinion survey as a "snapshot" of the electorate. The Kendall takes such transparencies and places one on top of the other. If the images produced were exactly the same, the Kendall figure would be 1. If the snapshots were of two entirely different images, with not a single tree or shrub in the same place, the Kendall would be 0.

It is hard to imagine two survey questions that would yield a Kendall of 1. Rarely does a Kendall climb higher than 0.5. But a respectable Kendall would be produced by, say, laying the transparency of a question about opera over the transparency of a question about mud wrestling (assuming that people who love opera hate mud wrestling, and vice versa). Kendall measures a linkage, but not a direction. If people who love opera also love theatre, for instance, laying the transparency of a question about opera over the transparency of a question about theatre would also yield a high Kendall.

The Kendall figure linking Turner's trustworthiness with attitudes toward free trade increased by 35 per cent after the televised debate. The linkage between Turner's credibility and public attitudes had tightened considerably. The Kendall does not judge whether it was a movement away from free trade or toward it; whether Turner's credibility helped or hindered. It merely says the nut was tightened. Taken together with the other findings, though, the conclusion was inescapable: a bond had formed between the two issues, to Turner's benefit. The same Kendall figure for Mulroney and free trade also jumped 24 per cent over the same period. In his case, though, the closer connection worked to his disadvantage.

On the Friday after the debate, at the weekly meeting of the top Tory strategists — Senators Lowell Murray and Norman Atkins, consultant Harry Near, and strategy adviser Hugh Segal — Allan Gregg told the others: "Guys, we got some real serious problems here." But he also proposed a solution: "The bridge between the fears of free trade and John Turner is John Turner's credibility. We've got to bomb the bridge."

ATTACK JOHN TURNER'S credibility — now here was a prescription that offered some hope. Credibility, after all, is a matter of perception, and perception is the stuff of which campaign discourse is made. The problem lay in determining exactly how to alter the perception of Turner's trustworthiness. There was no time for detailed market research, for running test messages past focus groups. There was little to be gained by a subtle nudge. So the Conservative strategy committee hit upon the simplest expedient available. The Tories would call John Turner a liar, over and over and over again.

They had no proof, of course, that Turner was lying. In the beginning they didn't even believe he was lying. But people come to uphold what emerges from their mouths, and it is now hard to find a Conservative strategist willing — on the record or off — to allow that the Tories' late campaign tactics may have tiptoed over the line of slander. Granted, Turner had been drawing speculative conclusions from the text of the free-trade agreement, assembling a mental image of the elephant from the pieces at hand. Granted, too, that parts of his vision were clearly implausible and offered purely as rhetoric — the bit about checking your wallet before checking your pulse, for instance. Still, to make the "liar" charge stick, the Conservatives had to do exactly what Mulroney, in the debate, had objected to so strongly — impugn motive.

If Turner's motive could be shattered, his credibility would follow. So the Tories said that Turner was lying to save his job. In other words, the campaign theme that was to lead the Tories to their first back-to-back majority governments in more than a century was based on an outrageous plan to undermine a man's reputation in public, to portray him alternately as a conniving grasper, a deceitful fraud, and a dangerous lunatic. As a political strategy, it was brilliant. It worked.

The one person in the Conservative Party who did not need to be instructed on how to proceed in the wake of Turner's miracle comeback was Brian Mulroney himself. Mulroney had arrived at exactly the same conclusion by Thursday — the day before the strategy committee met. Whatever that says about him as a person, it speaks glowingly about his political instincts. Even before he received his pollster's findings, his reflexes had told him to go on the attack.

"At its worst, the tactics of Mr. Turner and Mr. Broadbent are shameful and dishonest," Mulroney told a gathering of small-business leaders in Toronto on Thursday. "At the least, they are an attempt to hide the fact they offer Canadians no realistic alternatives, no plan of their own. . . . It is classic negative politics — if you shout long and loud enough about what you are against, perhaps people won't notice there is nothing you are for."

Mulroney did not single out Turner at once, but he was on the right track. Certainly, the Toronto speech was a marked departure from the subdued, elevated tone of his campaign to date. "Our opponents. . . . have impugned our motives. They have insulted the intelligence of the Canadian voters. And they have resorted to the most shameful kind of scare tactics, telling Canadians, as the NDP have in their television advertising, that the trade agreement jeopardizes medicare; telling senior Canadians, as Mr. Broadbent has, that their pensions are in danger.

"Mr. Turner has told you what he would tear up, but he has not told you what he would put in its place," Mulroney railed. He said that Turner's campaign promises costed out at $33-billion, and "that means that the deficit would go through the roof again, driving interest rates sky-high, driving away investment and driving down the Canadian dollar." Turner had promised a daycare package, Mulroney told the crowd, which the Liberals said would cost $4-billion one day and $10-billion the next. "What does that tell you about the competence of Mr. Turner and his party to govern this country?"

Ah, Mulroney. He rises to a brawl the way old hunting dogs feel a stir when the leaves change colour. Over the next few days, he would heave "managing change" out the window and narrow his attack on Turner. In speeches the next week, he did the following:

He deflected anxiety about the economy away from free trade and attached it to Turner's credibility. "Mr. Turner's platform would put our economic growth in jeopardy. . . . The damage (of a Liberal win) to economic activity in southern Ontario would be swift, dramatic, and powerful," he told one gathering. "Earlier in this decade," he reminded another, "Canadians suffered through the worst recession in post-war history. Do Canadians want to risk a return to that?"

He took the public's second major anxiety — environmental collapse — and laid it next to the first, severing its connection with free trade and associating it with Turner's credibility. "Does Mr. Turner really believe he could tear up the trade agreement with the Americans one day," Mulroney asked, "and sign an acid-rain agreement with the Americans the next? No one in this room could believe anything that preposterous."

He stirred the latent fears about personal economic security and attached them to Turner's credibility. "Let Mr. Turner tell you," he said, "which of those two million Canadian jobs he intends to let hang in the wind of American protectionism."

He attached suspicions of a profligate and ineffective central government to Turner's credibility. "Mr. Turner has made extravagant spending promises — billions and billions of dollars — and the meter is still running. And he refuses to tell Canadians how he would pay the bill."

Finally, having loaded all these fears into Turner's arms, he put Turner's credibility to the sword. "Those are the basic facts of this agreement, and no amount of misrepresentation or mistruth will change them."

Later, Mulroney said: "He wraps himself in the flag, in the hope you won't notice he is naked underneath."

"It is easier to peddle fears and lies than to build a nation."

"Don't be fooled by Mr. Turner."

Tories such as Near, Atkins, Derek Burney, the prime

minister's chief of staff, and Marc Lortie, the prime minister's spokesman, watched Mulroney's performance in the days following the debate and marvelled. Here, truly, was the soul of a great politician.

So excited was Mulroney, so pleased to be back in the kind of campaign he understood, that he waved at a tree. Entering the studios of the multicultural television station MTV at the foot of Bathurst Street in Toronto, Mulroney and Mila turned to perform one of their patented cheek-by-jowl wavey-wavey numbers. The reporters on hand turned to see at whom the prime minister was waving. There was nothing in that direction but a park, nothing in the park but a tree.

The campaign of 1988 to this point could be summed up by these verifiable facts — the prime minister of Canada was deliberately vilifying his main opponent, he was persuading the electorate they had nothing to fear about the approach of the millennium, and he was waving at trees.

THE TORY TROOPS hustled into action. Speeches were written to inflict maximum damage to Turner's reputation. The speech prepared for Joe Clark was particularly precious, cloaking an act of violence in the velvet cape of piety. "I want to speak for a moment," it began, "about standards in public life." Clark went on to set the standard, by eviscerating the Leader of Her Majesty's Loyal Opposition. "The system assumes that parties will. . . . tell the truth," Clark said, adding that John Turner's campaign was based "upon a deliberate lie. Mr. Turner is a desperate man, leading a shattered party. That does not excuse his tactics."

The irony of that reasoning is that the Conservatives, when they wrote the speech, were themselves desperate; and their tactics were quite new to Canadian politics. "John Turner," said Clark, "has let his party drift and disintegrate around him, so that now, in an election, all they offer is fear." There was more than a grain of truth to that. As Clark pointed out, the best and most capable in the party — Donald Johnston, Doug Frith, Jean Chrétien, Donald Macdonald — had been alienated by Turner; some of the Liberal premiers stood against the national leader; Liberal policy seemed to be emanating from the left fringe and from the boisterous, inexperienced group of federal MPs known as the Rat Pack. "What kind of cabinet would he form? What kind of national consensus would he fashion?"

"John Turner runs on fear, because that is all he has."

Clark's speech was pivotal: it offered Turner a blackboard and chalk, an offer the Tories made repeatedly over the next week. On this blackboard Turner was able to sketch only the same old argument he had relied on in the televised debates. As the Conservative strategists predicted, once Turner's motive had been called into question and his credibility undermined, his nationalist rhetoric played about as well as Frank Stronach's little satellites and pyramids.

The Clark speech was delivered to the Confederation Club, a gathering of business leaders in Ottawa. At least, the people in attendance appeared to be business leaders — each table sported a corporate name tag, and the bunting and banners were those of the Confederation Club rather than the Progressive Conservative Party. Like everything else in the campaign, however, this gathering was not what it seemed. The Confederation Club is a Tory front, assembled every time a cabinet minister or Conservative leader wants a friendly crowd. It was pure theatre. And though the television reporter might mention that this was a partisan crowd, the pictures showed a non-partisan one; and the pictures always win. Television viewers see people who look just like their boss under patriotic-sounding banners, seated at tables with name-tags like "VaxData Systems Inc." They see Joe Clark appearing to tell a respectable, non-committed gathering that John Turner is a liar, and they see the audience cheering its rabid assent.

A speech was also drafted for Michael Wilson. "Now, Mr. Turner says, join his crusade," the speech went. "If you are the leader of a crusade, you have to be a leader. You have to have courage. Does it take courage to lie to senior citizens about their medicare, just to get a vote?. . . Is this the type of man you would like to lead a crusade? No wonder half his caucus told him to quit."

Wilson, like Mulroney, was ahead of his speech-writers. On the Monday after the Friday strategists' meeting, before his speech was even written, he was on the road complaining about the "lies and distortions" of the opposition. Asked a few days later why he had adopted this tack, Wilson reflected the assessment of his strategists: "Fear is something that has clearly affected this campaign. The purpose of our election campaign from here forward must be to expose the reasons why people have been scared."

OCTOBER 30 TO November 5 was the week of the Tories' counter-attack. It was also the week that special-interest groups began to wade in with their assessments of who was telling the truth about free trade — as if anyone could. Some claimed to have stepped forward on their own: the retired Supreme Court judge Willard Estey, who assured Canadians the deal was a "good, sound, solid agreement"; the founder of medicare Emmett Hall, who assured them it did not threaten the federal medical-insurance plan; even Simon Reisman, the free-trade negotiator once considered among Turner's closest friends and most trusted confidants.

In an interview on the CBC program the *Journal*, Reisman called Turner "a traitor" for opposing free trade. Treason is a crime punishable in many countries by death and in Canada by life imprisonment. Reisman had put Turner on the same moral level as a rapist or a murderer. He gave no indication that he was speaking figuratively. "I think the man who is selling out Canada is John Turner because he's reckless, he's betraying the country and he's playing with the future of our children and grandchildren," Reisman said. "I challenge him, I accuse him of being a traitor to Canada for saying the things he is saying."

This vile little outburst was typical of Reisman's corrosiveness. By their friends shall ye know them: the first to spring to Reisman's defence was Mulroney himself. "I didn't use those particular words and I don't think they're in my vocabulary," Mulroney said. "That would not have been my choice of word." Nonetheless, said the prime minister, Reisman was justified in using the word traitor. "To be accused by Mr. Turner of having sold out Canada is the ultimate indignity of accusations," he said. "And so Simon blew his cork." He added, as only Mulroney would, that Reisman had "fought for his country" in the Second World War.

Mulroney had thus defended Reisman's slander with the same logic as someone who says, "I would never boil a kitten. Boiling kittens is wrong. Do not count me among the kitten-boilers. But when my friends boil kittens, it is quite understandable." To a moral philosopher, this is known as relative ethics; to others it is known as weak-mindedness. If, at the same time, you yourself were not boiling kittens but skinning them alive — if, that is, you disapproved of calling Turner a traitor but happily called him a liar instead — there would be another word to characterize your behaviour. The word is hypocrisy.

Mulroney had said Reisman was justified because he was merely responding to the charge that he had "sold out" the country, "the ultimate indignity of accusations." But Turner had levelled that charge at Mulroney, not Reisman. If you approve of others boiling kittens on your behalf, then you are a coward and possibly a voyeur. Now, Brian Mulroney is not really all these nasty things — he was perhaps best described, by his former press secretary, Michel Gratton, as a "decent, flawed man." But on this particular day, attempting to reverse Turner's remarkable recovery, the prime minister managed to embody much of what's reprehensible in an election campaign.

Turner waited a day to respond to the charge. There were no saints or martyrs anywhere this far into the campaign. Turner had to skate delicately around the fact that he had started it all with his assertion that Mulroney had sold out Canada — an accusation which was itself rather close to treason. "I haven't got into that kind of vocabulary," was Turner's careful rebuttal. "I have never challenged the prime minister's patriotism. I just challenged his bad judgement."

WHILE THE MAJOR parties were occupied in the exquisite exercise of slitting throats while not being seen to wield the knife, a parallel campaign had been launched by citizens wishing to save the electoral process from the politicians. These citizens were operating on the mistaken assumption that the election still revolved around free trade, rather than credibility. For this reason, their efforts must be judged noble but tangential to the actual campaign.

The right of citizens' groups and business coalitions to involve themselves in the campaign had been established four years earlier. During the 1984 campaign, a right-wing pressure group called the National Citizens' Coalition went to court to defend its right to spend $100,000 attacking the NDP. Canadian election law is a byzantine regulatory tangle that attempts to steer a moderate course between vote-buying and legitimate campaign expense. The law restricting such advertising had stood since 1974, but it was possible to mount a defence based on public interest. The 1974 law still allowed outside advertising "for the purpose of gaining support for views held. . . on an issue of public policy, or for the purpose of advancing the aims of any [non-partisan] organization." This defence allowed political advocacy, and would have permitted the pro-free-traders to spend to their heart's content during the 1988 campaign.

In 1983, however, the law had been changed to prohibit the incurrence of "election expenses" during a campaign by people who were not candidates or the agents of candidates. The public-interest defence was removed because of the danger that it would be used by "front" organizations whose real purpose was partisan. The thinking behind the 1983 law was fairly clear — a party was limited in the amount it could spend, both locally and nationally. Unfortunately, the restrictions could be easily circumvented if someone else spent money on the party's behalf.

The National Citizens' Coalition argued that taking away this public-interest defence meant that the law went beyond the "reasonable limits" to free expression allowed under the Charter of Rights. The coalition argued that the amended law violated its right to free expression, and spent $300,000 arguing the case. In June 1984, Mr. Justice Donald Medhurst of the Alberta Court of Queen's Bench ruled in the coalition's favour. The chief electoral officer decided not to appeal.

In essence, the election law seeks to limit the amount of information controlled by any one party during a campaign. The money is not important — but the information that money can buy is. It is a curious law, since information is supposed to be what campaigns are all about. It reflects the spirit of tolerance and fair play we like to think of as part of the Canadian political landscape. But information flows two ways — from the people to the party, and back again — and only the second part of this flow of information was affected by the law.

Spending limits restricted the amount of advertising any one party could buy, and the amount of media attention it could command. The parties, in their ability to speak to the public, were thus on relatively equal footing. But in the other direction of the information flow, money still talked. A wrinkle was added to the law which made it possible for parties to exclude polling costs from their election expenses. It is up to a party to decide whether a poll is conducted for the purpose of ongoing party support (in which case it's not an election expense) or for partisan campaign ends (in which case it is).

Because of this wrinkle, it will never be known exactly how much the Conservatives spent on polling during the 1988 campaign; certainly, they had far and away the most extensive polling data available. Under Canadian election law, all parties have an equal chance of speaking to the public, but an unequal chance of hearing what the public has to say.

Did a party's public message make any sense or not? Did it strike a resonant chord? Did it draw votes? The party with the most money to spend on polling was best able to answer these questions. It is rather like having a law which says each party gets equal time at the podium, but only the richest would know which language the audience understands.

Things like this happen when governments attempt to legislate information, an effort doomed from the start. People like to talk. During an election campaign, some people feel compelled to talk. A law that seeks to gag the utterance of public sentiment, while allowing the political élites to plumb that sentiment in secret, is stupid and anti-democratic.

The Canadian public spent about $4-million talking to each other about the 1988 campaign. They conducted this conversation through advertisements placed by muffin makers, multinational corporations, writers, postal workers, peaceniks, and arms manufacturers. Democracy did not crumble.

A group opposing free trade, the Pro-Canada Network, spent about $750,000 during the campaign. Most of that went to the production of 2.2 million copies of a twenty-four-page booklet. The booklet was a breezy explanation of how the free-trade deal would destroy the nation, complete with caricatures by Terry Mosher, a.k.a. Aislin, the Montreal *Gazette* cartoonist. In response, the group called the Canadian Alliance for Free Trade and Job Opportunities spent about $1.5-million. On Thursday, November 3, the week of the Tories' counterattack, they circulated a grey, reasoned defence of the free-trade agreement as an advertising supplement in six million Canadian newspapers.

"We had been waiting, working on the right time," said Peter Lougheed, the former Alberta premier and a founder of the group. "The problem was, people said they wanted information on free trade, but they don't read it until they're deeply concerned. It was straight copy. Some people criticized it as too dense. But my judgement was that we'd come at a time in the campaign when people were ready to digest it."

DURING THE 1988 campaign Canada even created its own Betsy
Ross, a retired family-court judge named Marjorie Bowker. Granny
Bowker's 58-page critique of the agreement was neither intellectu-
ally challenging nor dishonest — it was a straightforward account
of what the deal meant, from her perspective. She thought the deal
failed to guarantee the market access Canada had sought, while
offering too many trade incentives in return. She could not entirely
resist, though, the temptation to guess the size of the elephant.
Although she claimed to be in favour of free trade as a principle,
she wrote: "Such a union can have but one result — the smaller
[country] is swallowed by the larger." Bowker was noteworthy not
for what she added to the debate, but for the enormous spontaneous
demand her little tract elicited.

This demand was triggered by an innocent meeting between the *Ottawa Citizen* columnist Roy MacGregor and the
former Liberal cabinet minister Eugene Whelan. As usual, Whelan
was committing savagery on whichever language came his way —
that day, he was particularly interested in Mikhail Gorbachev's
program of "pesterikee." He was toying with the idea of entering
the campaign late; so he continually interrupted himself to ask:
"Whattya think, Roy? Think Gene should run?" At one point, he
tossed a dog-eared photocopy over the desk to MacGregor. "Here
y'are, Roy. Take a gander at that." The manuscript was titled: *What
Will the Free Trade Act Mean to You and Canada?* Under the title,
Bowker had written: "Kindly circulate."

MacGregor was taken with the little booklet, and wrote a
column about it. The next day, the office receptionist estimated
she fielded nearly a thousand requests for a copy — the phone
literally never stopped ringing. By the week of the Tories' counter-
attack, a printer had run off twenty thousand copies, which were
snapped up. Free-trade books, for and against, suddenly became the
rage — hastily written, cheaply produced, densely worded, and
wildly popular.

Perhaps people bought those books because they wanted
to know about free trade. A better guess, though, is that they were
trying to find out enough about free trade to decide whom to
believe. They sought this information from credible sources, and
Bowker represented two of the most trustworthy icons of our
popular culture — judges and grandmothers.

The Tories, for their part, dashed off a four-page tabloid to feed the insatiable demand for information about free trade. Within five days of the strategists' meeting, five million copies of the pamphlet had been printed and distributed. Soon they were to be found everywhere: in party offices, mailboxes, supermarkets, doctors' waiting rooms. The Tories infested the country with this little brochure, which was ostensibly about the free-trade agreement but was in fact aimed directly at John Turner's credibility. The front-page headline, in blue-and-red party colours, read: "What you should know about THE FREE TRADE AGREEMENT." Under the headline was a photograph of what appeared to be a normal, happy family. Beside the photograph was another large headline, in blue: "WHAT IS IT?"

The first thing the Tories told you was: "It is an agreement about trade — and only trade." This was followed by hundreds of words indicating it was about a hell of a lot more. Another blue headline: "THE AGREEMENT WILL PROTECT PRESENT JOBS AND HELP CREATE NEW JOBS IN THE FUTURE." Under the fold was another photograph, of a couple in advanced middle age, and the information that free trade would benefit each average family by $800 a year. Another headline: "THE AGREEMENT IS AN INSURANCE POLICY AND A SHIELD AGAINST U.S. PROTECTIONISM." Then, in their continuing battle against the scare tactics of the Liberals, the Tory writers advised: "If your job (or any jobs in your community) depends on trade to the U.S., take a hard look at the alternatives before you let anybody 'tear up' the agreement." The kicker came when the unwary reader turned the page. The centre-spread headline was a blitzkrieg in gaudy red letters the width of your hand: "THE TEN BIG LIES."

Lie Number One, according to the tract, was, "The Trade Agreement Will Destroy Canada's Social Programs." "Next time a Liberal or a New Democrat candidate comes to your door," the tract advised, "ask them to show you the clause in the agreement that takes away your pension or your medicare." This was the print equivalent of the leaders' demagogic call to "read the agreement." One could as easily have asked the candidate to point to the clause where it says the agreement "will help create new jobs in the future."

The pamphlet listed nine other lies. Lie Number Eight was, "The Americans Get to Take All Our Water." "The critics usually point to Chapter 22 of the Customs Tariff (Item 22.01) when they try to make this argument," the tract said. "One thing they don't always tell you is the title of Chapter 22: 'Beverages, Spirits, and Vinegar.' Lakes and rivers are not 'beverages,' even when you're desperately trying to get elected."

In a box with a red outline, the paper asked: "SO WHY ARE THE LIBERALS AND THE NDP TRYING TO SPREAD ALL THESE LIES?" Answer: "The federal election campaign may have something to do with it. The Liberals realize that they need something big to direct the public's mind from the Liberal Party troubles. . . . John Turner has no credibility as a national leader; he cannot even lead his own caucus."

This tabloid, which became known as the "big lies" paper, was a classic of the propagandist's art. It had the qualities of the best posters (such as Kitchener's famous "YOUR country needs YOU") and was, in fact, designed to be displayed on the office bulletin board. It also had the literary devices (the unnecessary choice, the false premise) which distinguished such influential propaganda journals as Mao's *Literary Gazette* in China and *Der Stürmer* in Weimar Germany.

The very name — "The Ten Big Lies" — was a brilliant stroke on the part of the Conservative propagandists. In his seminal study of propaganda devices, *Mass Persuasion in History*, the Glasgow University scholar and advertising director Oliver Thomson identified Hitler's tenets of propaganda from a study of *Mein Kampf*: "One should avoid abstract ideas and appeal instead to the emotions; one should constantly repeat a few stereotyped phrases, never be objective; in other words only put one side of the argument, criticise the enemy violently and always try to identify one special enemy." Hitler used the "big lie" to vituperate first the Versailles traitors, then Communists, then Jews. In their not-so-subtle way, the Conservatives were equating Turner's stance against free trade with Hitler's attack on the Jews. "The most dangerous propaganda," writes Thomson, "is the kind which is not recognised as such at all, either by its audience or even by its perpetrators."

The Conservatives also planned to launch an advertising blitz that would maintain the "proxy" format of their earlier television commercials. In these commercials, others spoke on the Conservatives' behalf. The proxy ads had, at the outset, quoted newspaper editorials as saying "Free trade is good for Canada," and other such uplifting stuff. Now, in the new wave, the newspapers would be quoted as saying: "John Turner is lying to save his job." These ads ended with an unflattering freeze-frame of the media-hot leader, the Mutant Ninja Liberal from Outer Space.

THE LIBERALS, OF COURSE, objected to the Tories' use of negative advertising. Oh, irony — the Liberals themselves had aired nothing else. Their most celebrated commercial was called "Map." According to the market research and tracking data compiled by Martin Goldfarb, Map was the most successful advertisement produced by the Liberal Party in twenty years. Filmed at Casa Loma in Toronto, it opened on two men huddled over an outline map of North America. "Since we're talking about this free-trade agreement," says one of the men, "there's one line I'd like to change."

"Which line is that?" asks the other.

The first man picks up an eraser and begins to rub out the border between Canada and the United States. "This one here. It's just getting in the way." The two men shake hands while the voice-over asks: "Just how much are we giving away in the Mulroney Free-Trade Deal? The line has been drawn. Which side do you stand on?" Then, as the Liberal logo flashes across the screen, the voice instructs: "Vote for Canada. Vote Liberal. It's a vote of confidence."

David Morton, a vice-president of Quaker Oats, who led the Liberals' Red Leaf advertising wing during the 1988 campaign, explained: "We wanted it to be hard-hitting but not brutal. The rule we went by was if people saw the commercial and smiled, as opposed to winced, that's the line we didn't want to cross." The Map spot received rave reviews from the Goldfarb focus groups, from subjects who thought the item "thought-provoking." Which it was. Had the commercial shown a giant comet called "free trade" crashing through downtown Toronto and killing thousands, that would have been "thought-provoking," too, and about as likely as the free-trade agreement erasing the Canada-U.S. border.

By the fall of 1988 it had become almost irrelevant to talk about truth in advertising. Advertisers go to great lengths looking for "authenticity," but that's not quite the same thing. Morton knew, for example, that Mulroney had spoken out against free trade in 1983, and Red Leaf's advertising agencies had devised a spot called "Both Sides Now." In one concept, they would alter the image so Mulroney would appear to be speaking out of both sides of his mouth — but this was judged too rough. Morton wanted simply to run footage of Mulroney's 1983 statement, and play it next to his 1987 comments in favour of the deal. This would have attacked both Mulroney's credibility and free trade — two of the key Liberal advertising strategies adopted in August. Try as they might, however, the people at Red Leaf could not find Mulroney denouncing free trade on camera.

One day, driving from his Peterborough home to an agency meeting in Toronto, Morton heard the statement, which Mulroney had uttered during an interview on the CBC radio program *Sunday Morning*. He got a copy of the audio tape, and Red Leaf went to work dubbing it over film footage of Mulroney in the Commons. Then they flipped the same footage, so that Mulroney was pointing the other way, and dubbed his more recent, pro-free-trade, remarks. "What better way to question his credibility than to do that?" asked Morton, proud of the spot. They are very clever down at Red Leaf. They should all get jobs on the *National*.

The Conservatives also knew that the Map spot was working to the Liberals' advantage, so they fell upon the inspired response of copying it — except for the ending. In the Conservative version, the Canadian hand reaches out to stop the American as he attempts to erase the border. "John Turner says there's something in the free-trade agreement that threatens Canadian sovereignty," intones the announcer. The Canadian takes the pencil and redraws the border as the announcer says: "That's a lie — and this is where we draw the line."

And this is where the battle of perception, the struggle to control meaning, the conduct of the post-literate campaign had taken us by the first week of November, 1988: the Conservative Party of Canada planned to produce this ad — a symbolic rebuttal of a complex package of anxieties and fears tied to a cultural totem — and broadcast it during a children's television program called *Romper Room*.

MANY PEOPLE BELIEVED the Conservative advertising strategy — the Tories also bought heavily into *The Young and the Restless* and *Days of Our Lives* — betrayed a party that was rolling in money and simply out to buy a federal election. Not so. The Conservatives bought television time on soap operas and children's programs because their research told them there was little point buying it anywhere else.

"Starting tomorrow," said Allan Gregg, "we have these ads using a word which has never been used before during a political campaign. We're calling him a liar." Gregg still had the look of the prophet about him. He reached toward the television screen in his office, in a gesture of entreaty. "'Liar! Liar!' And we have even nastier ones coming out in the days after that. And where are we putting them?

"Traditionally, the best spot available for political advertising is news adjacency. What you ideally want to do is book-end the *National* and the *Journal*. Now, if you did that today, you'd merely be talking to the decided. So we're trying to get the elderly, the young, the stay-at-homes. Big TV consumers. We're trying to get — and I say this without a hint of condescension or of attempting to be patronizing, but there's no other way to say it — we're trying to get the real dumb ones."

Sheep are dumb, and what had happened to the Canadian electorate over the past couple of weeks was analogous to what happens to sheep in a pen. As any stockman knows, sheep respond to their master's voice. They are anxious about the world. They don't have a lot of natural defences or much ability to shift for themselves, so, while they are skittish, they are also trusting. This explains the comfort they derive from being with their shepherd; it may also help enable them, like birds, to change direction all at once.

Science has never really explained how a herd of sheep or a flock of birds can signal each other to reverse course, simultaneously, in formation, just as science cannot yet explain the hundred-monkeys phenomenon. Yet the phenomenon itself is indisputable. Two weeks before the election, the Canadian electorate resembled this group of sheep, having to choose which voice to follow. At the outset, Mulroney had been cooing softly to the sheep, and they were drawn in his direction.

"Don't go over there!" Turner had shouted. "Wolves are out there! Come over here!"

So the sheep had changed direction and taken off toward Turner's gate.

"He's lying to you!" Mulroney had shouted. "He's the wolf!"

At this point, sheep freeze. The Conservative counterattack had indeed frozen the electorate — halted the flow of votes to the Liberals. Yet the sheep could not remain frozen forever. They had to pick a gate, and this knowledge heightened the awareness of their predicament. The question in the mind of the electorate was, according to Gregg: "Who's going to protect me in my confusion?" The dumb ones could still be influenced by blandishments and fears, but the others would look for some other clue. The competing shepherds had cancelled each other out. The sheep were now seeking a third voice, an arbitrator. But they would not trust a third voice that was closely identified with the competing shepherds.

The attitude of Canadian voters at the start of the campaign's most crucial week could, in Gregg's view, be summed up as follows: "Okay, so he's lying. So now what?"

The pile of tracking data on Allan Gregg's desk on Friday, November 4, confirmed this cancelling out. John Turner had accomplished the Kennedy trick during the debates, the miracle turnaround. While Kennedy's mystique had endured for twenty-five years, though, Turner's had stalled in a week. And then the damnedest thing had happened. Turner's stall was followed by a sudden and precipitous dive.

"Last night's traffic shows another strong tumble back in our favour," said Gregg. Turner's peak had come about on Wednesday, the eighth day after the debate. There was some disagreement about exactly how high he had flown; there would be no doubt about how far he would fall.

This return of support to the Conservatives clearly baffled Gregg. He hadn't expected the party to do so well, so soon. He had expected the strategy of undoing Turner's credibility to freeze the sheep, that's all, not start a headlong dash back toward the Tory gate. There should have been a gradual return to pre-debate Conservative sentiments. But there was nothing gradual about what Allan Gregg had seen. "We are constantly behind the eight-ball," he said. "The technology that's available — it allows us to unearth what's going on, but we can't respond fast enough." What had gone on was that the third voice had spoken. In the week to come it would speak even more powerfully, though it never had to shout.

It spoke calmly, dispassionately, barely noticed by those paying attention to the din. It was an unmistakable clarion, though, for those ears attuned to this kind of signal. It was a voice so impartial as to be nearly insentient. It was the voice of the market.

CHAPTER 13

# EXITING CONFUSAO

*Confusão is a good word, a synthesis
word, an everything word. . . .
Confusão means confusion, a mess, a
state of anarchy and disorder. . . .
Confusão can reign over an enormous
territory and sweep through millions
of people. The best thing is to act
slowly and wait. After a while
confusão loses energy, weakens,
vanishes. . . . We start gathering
strength again for the next confusão.*
RYSZARD KAPUŚCIŃSKI

ALMOST EVERYONE HAS EXPERI-
enced a personal confusão, at home or at work. A national confusão
is something else altogether. Much of the news you get from other
places is news of a national confusão. A national confusão will get
inside your home; it also envelops your home, and everything else.
You can't get away from it. I have recently been part of a national
confusão in Korea and another in Haiti, and I can report that
Ryszard Kapuściński's advice is solid. If you find yourself in a
national confusão, stay low and move slowly.

The way people behave in a national confusão is not unlike
the way they behave during sex. Canadians, being a passionate but
northern people, spent most of the week of their national confusão
indoors, holding their breath and moaning slightly. The free-trade

confusão, when it hit, was inescapable, worse than the damn heat wave. There was a party in Ottawa, attended by a diverse group of people who had never met — university teachers, Polish intellectuals, solid-thinking nurses — and they were all wrapped up in confusão. They tried to have a good time but couldn't. One man shook another's hand and said it was the first time he'd met a right-wing demagogue. They looked at each other — the second man said he'd never before met a son of a bitch. Their wives fluttered in nervous confusão; the meat on the barbecue got burned. Neighbour was divided against neighbour, working relationships suffered, everyone suspected everyone else, though nobody knew quite why, or of what. In Toronto, at least for a while, talk of the national confusão even drowned out talk of real-estate prices. People tried to turn the conversation elsewhere; it always came back to the confusão.

The CBC — the country's limbic system — was overloaded with nervous messages. The corporation did its best to impose order on the confusão but only got caught up in the confusão itself. "It's an issue most Canadians say they do not understand and perhaps because of that it has become the issue of the election campaign," Peter Mansbridge said. "It seems that everyone is now trying to make voters understand it to see it as either very good or very bad."

"I'm very scared, I'm very nervous," said a respected economist, Sherry Atkinson Cooper. "It might very well be the first made-in-Canada recession." This was followed by more such pessimism. But the CBC was trapped by balance. At the end of one item, the corporation's economics reporter, Der Hoi Yin, contradicted every message the limbic system had just sent out: "But opponents of free trade say scrapping the deal won't spell disaster. Not scrapping it will." What could Canadians do, but hold their breath and moan?

IN MOST PLACES confusão comes and goes, but there's one place it never leaves. Here people have learned to live with confusão, to float like a cork on its whirlpools and undertows. This is the Chicago Mercantile Exchange. The place is a thirty-storey grey granite building on top of a mall with neon-lit bars bearing names like "Limit Up." The place is also a lesson that, as you move toward the centre of things, you're bound to encounter confusão.

Inside, from the catwalks encircling the trading floor, you see hundreds of traders in jackets of different colours, jostling and rushing between "pits," which are rather like small amphitheatres. The tiny amphitheatre where the value of the Canadian dollar is established is about the size of a bathtub, with stairs all round. About twenty traders cram around, along with equal numbers of runners, order-takers, and pit-monitors.

When the place is in action, it's living confusão. The dealers shout, push, jump to attract the attention of other dealers; they pound themselves on the forehead, they stroke their moustaches, they wave fingers in frantic, intricate patterns. The confusão of the Chicago Mercantile Exchange is not what can be seen, however, but what this activity represents. What can be seen is in fact quite orderly. Each gesture is a buy or a sell order. Each stair around the bathtub represents a different trading month. Each brightly coloured jacket represents a different trading house. Perhaps the single most impressive aspect of the Chicago Mercantile Exchange is the order cards. A trader can throw these cards about thirty feet, with pinpoint accuracy, into the hands of a runner. But the air is filled with them, which adds to the illusion of confusão.

There is no sign of political ideology on the floor of the exchange, even though most of the traders are small, self-employed businessmen, passionately devoted to free enterprise, the American Dream, and Pepto-Bismol. The strongest form of political expression one finds is a lapel pin that reads: "Free markets, free men." In the hurly-burly of daily trade, nobody has time to dwell deeply on politics. Most people here are motivated by reflexes and experiences which they articulate as a set of aphorisms. Scared money goes nowhere, fast. Buy a rumour and sell a fact. Bulls get fat, bears get fat, pigs never do. These people do not care a fag-end whether the currency they are trading respects human rights or observes the Geneva protocols, whether it is backed by a right-wing or a left-wing government. Often they don't even know.

There are two types of trader, the chartist and the fundamentalist. The chartist believes that a currency has no fundamental value and changes price in strict accordance with how it is traded; he expects that a spike in the price of a currency will be followed by a decline; he does not care, or believe in, what may have caused either. The fundamentalist, on the other hand, feels the price of a currency responds to events in the world; he believes

233

that the market is trying to sense the "real" value of a currency. Even this concept, however, must be tempered by the reality of what the traders are doing. They are selling and buying not currencies but currency futures.

Whether the futures speculator trades in Chicago, New York, or Toronto, the last thing he wants to do is take delivery of Canadian dollars. He trades promises to buy the currency at a fixed price some time in future. Whether motivated by charts or by events, whether hedging or speculating, the trader operates in the fictitious realm of expectation. Nothing traded on a futures market has intrinsic worth, since nothing changes hands but a prediction. The "real" value of currency futures depends entirely on the market's perception of where the currency will go. The currency pit is a place where perception and reality are fused — permanent, institutionalized confusão.

Chicago is the centre of commodity-futures trading for North America, but the enterprise has spread. The greatest growth in currency trading has taken place in the quiet hum of centralized brokerage houses, where currencies are shifted by computer bit. Starting in 1982, the Philadelphia Stock Exchange began trading Canadian-dollar currency options, a slightly different wrinkle. Vast amounts of currencies are also shifted around in hopes of a profit at the margins — a process known as arbitraging — by automated computer program. On one thing all traders, and even dumb computers, agree. As a Canadian-dollar trader on the Chicago Exchange, Gary Segal, put it: "When political news hits, you may as well throw the charts out the window."

The Chicago floor receives news the same way most of us do — in fast bits. The floor has screens that monitor and condense the events of the world. These are not unlike the screens found in the rapid-transit systems of Toronto and Vancouver, which feed fact bits to commuters, who in turn feed these bits to the heart of the city. The screens are reminiscent of the news-bulletin channel on television. No scandal is so complex, no tragedy so heart-wrenching, no government so convoluted that news of it cannot be reduced to ten words. Often, the traders on the floor in Chicago and the commuter on the SkyTrain in Vancouver are getting the same ten words. The SkyTrain is a green-and-white cylinder which rolls on tracks without any driver. "Former BCEC president Murphy resigns from gov't fold," the message board said one day. This was followed by: "Abortion debate will highlight day in the Commons." At the Chicago exchange, traders pick up loose sheets of information bits, which are changed every couple of hours. These also carry few words, but then it doesn't take more than a few words — "Reagan shot," for example — to send the market into panic.

THE FIRST PUBLICLY available opinion polls showing that John Turner's performance in the televised debate had caused a decline in support for Brian Mulroney and the Conservatives were released on Sunday, October 30. On that day, Insight Canada issued a poll commissioned by the CTV television network which gave the Liberals an astounding four-point lead over the Tories.

Same thing next day. "Liberals Gain Support After Debate," read the Gallup news release. "Tory Majority Threatened." The poll registered a four-point increase for the Liberals and a two-point decline for the Conservatives, placing the three national parties at 38, 32, and 27 per cent support. Moreover, Turner's ranking as the best prime minister for Canada had risen from 10 to 19 per cent among respondents, while both Mulroney's and Broadbent's rankings had dropped. Gallup added its seat projections, calling a close result, and advised: "Even a slight change in voter preference would translate into a minority-government situation. Such a scenario would probably ensure the demise of the free-trade initiative."

That was more than enough information for the markets.

In the wake of the polls showing a decline in Tory fortunes, currency dealers the world over, starting with the Japanese, began dumping their Canadian-dollar holdings. The sell-off began overnight in the Far East, giving the central bank time to orchestrate a response. In times of a plummeting currency, the Bank of Canada rushes in to buy the dollar, increasing demand for it and helping to stabilize its price. The beating was so severe on the day of the Gallup, however, that the Bank of Canada spent hundreds of millions of dollars without staunching the flow. Running low on available resources, the Canadian bank called upon the Bank of England for help. Despite this joint intervention, the dollar had fallen a mighty one and a half cents against the U.S. dollar by the end of daily trading. This news was reported under a front-page banner headline in *The Globe and Mail*: "Dollar takes nosedive as

Conservatives fall in opinion poll results."

"Ten days ago markets were absolutely confident about what would occur," the Royal Bank vice-president of trading, Bryan Griffiths, told the *Report on Business*. "Now we have uncertainty, and markets don't like uncertainty." Rod Fowler, head of foreign exchange for the brokerage firm Wood Gundy, added: "The market is shocked by the amount of support for the Liberals." One trader in Chicago put it succinctly for the Dow Jones Wire Service: "The world is bailing out of Canada."

Politics has always engendered the exercise of two related forces. The closer you get to political power, anywhere on the planet, the more clearly you see the indispensability of these two forces. They may be used subtly or blatantly, in public or in private, separately or in combination. These two forces are money and violence.

Money had just talked.

John Turner, in perhaps the dumbest political move of his career, attempted to redress the situation by reminding the world of his record as finance minister: "You can reassure the money markets. . . that I will act. . . in a responsible manner as I acted when I was minister of finance for four years."

Ah, confusão. Turner's stint as finance minister in the Trudeau government, from 1972 to 1975, came at a time when the Liberals were coping with oil-price shocks and burgeoning inflation. While in office, Turner increased spending an average 21 per cent a year, taxes an average 18 per cent. During his time as finance minister the annual deficit of the federal government more than trebled — from $1.6-billion to $5.8-billion. Chicken feed by today's standards, and out of Turner's control, but enough to earn him an accurate though unfair reputation as the father of the Canadian deficit. The perception of the markets was that a Liberal win on November 21 would fuel Canada's deficit and wipe out the free-trade panacea. That, at least, was the perception of traders concerned with such fundamentals — the others just rode the current, swimming in confusão.

Michael Wilson tried to be reserved: "I'm not going to comment on that. I don't think it's appropriate for me to comment." A sober sentiment, considering that anything the finance minister said had great power to fuel the confusão. He could not, however, resist adding: "The marketplace works in a very dispassionate way. People speak with their money. They don't speak with great emotion. They just decide what is better for them economically."

Any doubt that the dollar's value was being influenced by poll results was erased in the next few days. On Tuesday, *The Globe and Mail* published a poll by the Environics Research Group which showed the Liberals in the lead. More significantly, the most recent wave of polling, conducted over the previous weekend, showed that "the Liberals would now have enough votes to form a minority government."

The previous polls had merely weakened the markets at the knees. With the Environics poll, the market swooned. That poll was enough to drive down not only the dollar but the entire Toronto Stock Exchange. The market's basket of 300 stocks, the TSE 300, retreated sharply in brisk trading. The TSE 300 was off 18 points, enough to be newsworthy, though insignificant compared with what was to come. Over the next week, as poll after poll confirmed the Liberal upsurge, the TSE plunged. By the time the market responded to the Gallup of November 7, the Toronto Stock Exchange had dropped 136 points.

The Dow Jones Industrial Average, on the other hand, was retreating on news that Dan Quayle had cribbed on his bar exams.

NEXT CAME YO-YO TIME for the Canadian dollar. Public opinion, speaking through the pollsters, had the boys and girls in the Chicago Mercantile Bathtub doing the sleeper, round the world, walking the dog. The dollar fell another two-thirds of a cent with the November 7 Gallup, then promptly recouped three-quarters of a cent on news that the Conservatives were regaining ground.

"The volatility of the dollar is directly affected every time a poll is released. It's a whiplash market, and the polls are the driving force," said a vice-president (foreign exchange) at Citibank. "In terms of the Canadian dollar, almost eighty per cent of the market movement is based solely on polls these days," said a vice-president (trading) at Deak International. "Dealers around the world are watching the polls and reacting to them immediately."

Here's how to make your fortune. Hire a bunch of high-school dropouts and rent a telephone bank. Hang out a shingle as a pollster. Offer your services free to a major newspaper or television network. Then invest heavily in the futures market, leveraging extensively, because you now have more power to influence the currency than all the bullion in all the vaults controlled by John Crow, the governor of the Bank of Canada. "I would certainly trade all my positions if I had advance information," said the Deak vice-president. "We're talking millions of dollars changing hands based on that sort of information."

But the influence of polls on markets worked both ways. The market responded to the polls; public sentiment responded in turn to the markets. This connection may have been the single most decisive factor in turning the course of the election. Consider: Turner started to drop in the polls in mid-week, right after the market declines. Emmett Hall's Liberal-bashing came later. Simon Reisman's Turner-bashing came later. The Ten Big Lies came later. The negative advertising came later. The Alliance For Free Trade and Job Opportunities newspaper insert came later. The muffin-makers for free trade and the artists for free trade came later. The Clark speech came later. The Wilson speech came later. All these things undoubtedly hurt Turner and the Liberals, but they were already hurting. Something had triggered an abrupt, negative reaction among the public. And only the market scare fits the timing.

Brian Mulroney had been saying, as early as November 1: "[Turner's] choices are massive tax increases, or massive deficits, or both. And just as surely as summer follows spring, higher deficits lead to inflation, which lead to higher interest rates, which lead to unemployment." If the market had responded positively to Turner's rise in the polls, Mulroney's credibility would have suffered. Credibility was crucially important at this stage of the campaign, and the markets laid a barrage into the side of the good ship John Turner. The markets also helped Mulroney strip millennial anxiety away from free trade and load it onto Turner's foundering ship.

What better indication, for a population beset by anxiety and fearful that the good times could not last, than an advance ruling by the markets? Dealing in future expectations and wedding those expectations with reality, the markets provided an alarmed and confused populace with an answer to the question, "So they're all lying. So now what?"

Some people felt the futures market was displaying "bad will" toward the Liberals and John Turner. They felt the market behaved as it did because it represents big corporate Tory interests, and big corporate Tory interests are always out to screw the little guy. People like Ed Broadbent talk that way. But that kind of thinking attributes a degree of anthropomorphism to the market that the market does not deserve. The computers whose programs dumped dollar options in Philadelphia did not even know, as Al Capone put it, which street Canada was on. The traders on the floor of the exchange knew that Canada was cold, and maybe they'd like to go there one day and shoot a moose.

If the market drew a collective judgement about free trade, it was neither more nor less informed than the judgement of the commuter on the SkyTrain. The commuter is simply reacting to the information at hand. Why assume that the market had a "motive," that it was "punishing" the Canadian people for liking John Turner? Why not assume that people were "using" the market to look six months into the future? They wanted to see what John Turner's Canada would look like, and the market gave them an answer. In any case, to get wrapped up in motive is to overlook the simple symmetry of the thing. When the opinion of one affected the opinion of the other, what followed just happened, just was. The public said "I am," and the market said "I am." Both "were," and both knew they "were" — creating, as Teilhard suggested, a state of consciousness squared.

Those who decry the passing of what was, historically, a brief and shining interlude between pre-literate and post-literate discourse, should consider this. The intricate and laminated network of information that now connects the trading houses of Tokyo and Hong Kong with those of London and Toronto moves more merchant traffic in a single day than the entire Phoenician navy could ship around the world in the span of an empire, and does so by means of tiny little bursts of information. By 1988 this network had become plugged into every other laminated network zooming around in the nöosphere, so that the slightest rumbling of leaders triggered a seismic response on these markets; and the sentiments of an entire nation, reduced to another set of information bits, were more than enough to start an avalanche.

These were the days, as the pop star Paul Simon put it in a song popular in 1988, of staccato signals of constant information, of lasers in the jungle somewhere. When the Canadian electorate pondered, briefly, the idea of John Turner as leader, the collective response of the markets was doom; so the Canadian electorate pondered again.

THE GALLUP POLL released on November 7, 1988, two weeks before the election, has been condemned as the greatest polling mistake since the infamous *Literary Digest* poll of 1936 in the United States. The November 7 poll was tagged the "rogue" Gallup, that mysterious one time in twenty that, mathematics predict, will yield a bad result. Every twentieth poll is a rogue poll; it's just that nobody ever knows when that "twentieth" time will come around and nobody can say for sure whether the November 7 Gallup was one such poll. Pick up a die and roll it: your odds of rolling a six are 16.66 per cent. Throw a six ten times in succession and your odds of throwing a six on the next roll are 16.66 per cent. Go fifty times without rolling a six and your odds of rolling a six on the next attempt are 16.66 per cent. Like the six on a die, rogues come and rogues go. One is always coming, but you never know when.

Pollsters like to illuminate their science by referring to a Greek urn. Imagine there is a Greek urn filled with billiard balls of different colours. You can empty the urn, and count every single ball, to see how many there are of each colour. Or you can pull out a small number of balls as a representative sample, an indication of what else is in there. Mathematics dictates that the first few balls you pull out will yield the greatest information for the smallest effort. After that, your information yield decreases exponentially. After so many balls, the additional information that each new one provides becomes almost insignificant. Pull out half the balls and you'll have a pretty good idea of what's in there.

The statistics behind this are not mysterious, just complicated, like logarithmic tables. In fact, each pollster relies on a little slide rule that allows him to compute the size of the population surveyed against the number of random samples pulled out of the urn, then tells him what his "margin of error" will be and how often his result will fall within that margin.

In the language of nuclear-arms talks, this margin of error is exactly the same as the CEP — circular error probable — of an intercontinental ballistic missile. When arms negotiators sit down at the table, they compare not only warheads and nuclear payload, but also CEP. Say, for example, the CEP of a delivery system is 1,000 yards at 50 per cent. That means the warhead will fall within 1,000 yards of the target half the time; the other half, the warhead could land anywhere — in your backyard, for instance. And of the half that do fall within 1,000 yards, none of them — or all of them — might actually land on the target.

Polling is just like that. When a pollster admits to a margin of error of four per cent, 19 times out of 20, and his poll indicates 40 per cent support for the Conservatives, you cannot conclude that the Conservatives have the support of 40 per cent of the population. You can conclude only that the pollster is 95 per cent sure that support for the Conservatives is somewhere between 36 and 44 per cent. It is probably closer to 40 per cent than any other number in that range, but there is no way of knowing for sure.

If the pollster were allowed a lower confidence rating, he could offer a narrower margin of error. If the same poll was said to be accurate nine times out of 10, rather than 19 times out of 20, then the margin of error would shrink by half. A pollster's confidence is inversely related to his precision. Throw a snowball at a barn door with your eyes closed. With some confidence, you can say you hit the door. With more confidence, you can say you hit the barn. On a given survey, a pollster can say he's 95 per cent sure of a result within a four-point margin of error, or 90 per cent sure within a two-point margin.

Back to the Greek urn a moment. Say the urn has 50 red balls, 30 white balls, and 20 black. If the pollster removes half the balls, he will — most of the time — get about 25 red, 15 white, and 10 black. It is conceivable, though, that he could draw all 50 red balls before drawing a single ball of another colour. That possibility is remote, but it exists. That would be the rogue poll. It happens.

A margin of error of three to four per cent, 19 times in 20, is almost the industry standard for a national poll. It doesn't make much sense to speak of a result "between x and y" — such fuzziness would only make it difficult for the consumer to grasp the import of the poll. Still, consumers should be constantly reminded of the potential margin of error, particularly in the case of a poll result that indicates change only within that margin of error. Such results are often reported as indicating shifts in party support, but they are simply not statistically significant.

Remember the New Democrat upsurge in the polls in mid-1986? John Terry, a political and social-affairs researcher with the Library of Parliament research branch, reviewed the Gallups from several years against the margin of error. "The data... offer no statistical evidence whatsoever of increased — or decreased — support for the NDP over the past two years (1985 and 1986)," he concluded. "The one-poll surge for that party in the summer of 1986 gives the appearance of being precisely what one would statistically expect: the one poll out of twenty that is wrong."

Similarly, a rash of poll results between June, 1986, and January, 1987, gave the New Democrats support levels in Quebec of between 16 and 32 per cent. It was enough to start speculation about an NDP swell in that province. "One talks of changes or trends in party support in a single province at one's peril," Terry wrote. "Given the margins of error for Quebec in the different samples, the answer to... which poll is wrong and which right about Quebec must be: all of them or none of them." The fact is, not one of these polls, to which NDP supporters pointed with pride, showed a shift outside the margin of error.

AS WELL AS THIS inherent uncertainty, polls also carry the risk of bad method. That is what happened with the infamous *Literary Digest* poll in 1936. *Literary Digest* was a magazine that had correctly predicted the winners of the last few U.S. presidential elections; it sent out more than 10-million ballots to a sample drawn from telephone directories and automobile-registration lists. A sample of that size is astonishing. *Literary Digest* claimed to have polled every third registered voter in Chicago, for example. The polls were returned by mail; over the summer more than 2.3-million responses were tabulated. It was an enormous survey — in Canada, where about 1,000 people are sampled for a typical survey, the equivalent poll would encompass 230,000 respondents. The magazine gave the election to the Republican Alf Landon.

The electorate gave the election to a rather better-known figure named Franklin Delano Roosevelt.

Although everyone speculated over the years on what had caused the *Literary Digest* fiasco — it probably set back the efforts of a determined young man named George Gallup a decade — no one had ever conducted a serious investigation of what went wrong until 1988, when the University of Iowa professor Peverill Squire published the results of his research into the matter. Squire concluded there was some truth to the idea that the poll sample was biased — that people who owned telephones or cars during the Depression may have been slightly more in favour of voting Republican. That had been the conventional wisdom for years.

But he also uncovered another distorting factor, which remains a problem to this day — a phenomenon known as non-responsive bias. Put simply, this meant that people who supported Landon were more likely to fill in the ballot, buy a stamp, and post it back to *Literary Digest* than people who supported Roosevelt. Why, Squires does not say. Maybe people who supported Landon felt more strongly about their candidate. Maybe Democrats felt Roosevelt had the advantage of incumbency, and did not need a boost in the polls. Whatever the cause, the effect was a warped result — even in a poll sample hundreds of times larger than anything used in the Canadian federal election.

Non-random polls are still conducted during campaigns and reported as news, which does a great disservice to pollsters. The *Toronto Star*, the biggest blatherer of Mickey Mouse poll results during the 1988 campaign — particularly, it seemed, if the poll helped Turner — was most obviously guilty of this. On the crucial day after the televised debate, the *Star* printed not one but two wildly unscientific "poll" results saying Turner had won the contest. Neither was worth the smudgy stock it was printed on. Deep in the copy, each story carried the caveat that the poll was "informal" or "unscientific," but this information was greatly out-cued by the serious treatment given the stories. One was printed under the headline: "Turner won TV debate, callers say."

The callers had been people who felt sufficiently motivated to call a local television station and register their vote by pressing a touch-dial on the telephone. A station spokesman said gee whiz, no, he didn't think the Liberals could have got together to tie up the phone lines, stuffing votes. The *Star*, which would run a post-election apologia explaining that their coverage had been balanced and responsible, put this piece of nonsense on its front page. Which only proves Val Sears' old saw that some newspapers — he was referring to the defunct *Telegram* — come with the garbage already wrapped in them.

Some news organizations and pollsters were careful to report the sample size, questions asked, and polling period — the CBC and *The Globe and Mail* were admirable not only in this respect but also in reporting their own polls in the context of competitors' polls. But even the most respectable poll-users were guilty of failing to report response rates. "Those who conduct the most reliable surveys are concerned with this problem, and much effort is expended devising ways to cope with it," Squire concluded, in his study. "Failure to properly handle participation problems can damage the results produced by any poll, but many surveys do not report or discuss their response rates. Consumers of public opinion surveys. . . must be reminded of this potential problem in order to avoid a future disaster like the *Literary Digest* poll."

Hello? *Toronto Star*? Anyone listening?

THERE ARE PROBLEMS with polls, certainly, but there are also knocks against them that do not stand up under scrutiny. The most common of these is the idea that polls "influence voters" in some pernicious manner. So much has been written about this supposed phenomenon, so many politicians have threatened to ban polls because of it, that the matter ought to be laid to rest.

First: there is simply no conclusive evidence that polls influence people in this way. When you poll people on this very question, of course, about 85 per cent say that polls do change the way other people vote but do not change the way they themselves vote. Those who argue that polls should be banned point to the "bandwagon effect" — the idea that certain regions, such as Quebec, always jump on board the winning party, once the winning party has been determined through polling. This is tautological. Quebec may end up on the winning side because it jumped on the bandwagon; or Quebec may itself be the bandwagon, given the importance of the Quebec vote to the national outcome. When Gallup polled Canadian voters in early November, 1988, a couple of weeks before the election, it found that 43 per cent of respondents intended to vote Liberal. But only 28 per cent thought the Liberals would win. At that point — this was at the height of Liberal popularity — 52 per cent still believed the Conservatives would win the election. Some bandwagon. (The support for the New Democrats, incidentally, was 22 per cent; but only 3 per cent thought the New Democrats would win. So much for a party of idealists.)

Second: what is wrong with a bandwagon effect, anyway? Politicians oppose it because it loses them elections they feel they might otherwise have won. But the people who jump on board obviously feel they have good reasons for doing so. In other words, politicians would ban polls because they presume they know better than the voter what's good for the voter — a notion that's self-serving, patronizing, and insulting.

Third: those who would ban polls during elections do not propose banning all polls, merely public ones. The political parties would continue to poll in private and base their campaign strategies on these secret polls. Isn't that a democratic notion? It ranks up there with election laws that would gag the people, but not the politicians, during campaigns. If there is one overpowering lesson to be drawn from the 1988 campaign, it is precisely that the electorate has become attuned to electoral manipulations, from television images to the partisan use of poll results. When the people have the same information as the politicians, they know why the politicians do and say things — why, for example, they say ad nauseam that an election is about "managing change." Politicians don't like that.

Politicians didn't like television at first, either, but they adapted to it. And they found, to their amazement, that people who are given more information know more. There is a persistent notion among politicians that the electorate must be protected from itself, that its representatives know what is best for the voters. This strain of thinking would ban polls, gag the public, and say: "Leave the thinking to us." Holders of this view gum their lips, stamp their canes against the floor, and say TV reduces politics to image and polls render politics a horse race. They're the same sort of people who reckon that if God had wanted women to ride bicycles, He wouldn't have given them skirts. Both television and polls are popular because they work. Image is a convenient arbiter, after all, and if elections aren't horse races, why does the first one past the post win?

Another notion in partisan politics is that people express a collective wisdom greater than its individual parts. So what, they ask, if people can't name anybody in the cabinet? Army ants are among the world's dumbest creatures; but put a few hundred thousand of them together and they are cunning and resourceful tacticians, builders, and workers. There are those in politics who view voters the same way, but the view has faced two obstacles. The first is cultural — western liberals are not raised to think in collective terms. The second is rational — even if the popular wisdom is valid, how can it be expressed? With army ants, scientist are at least researching the role of pheromones, which play a part in many animals' sense of smell. People can also smell, but not over great distances. What people can do better than army ants is think. Nowadays, they can think over virtually any distance, with unprecedented speed. Polls help each person to know what the other people are thinking.

Senator Michael Kirby worked for Pierre Trudeau, off and on, between 1974 and 1982. In those days he knew the prime minister about as well as anybody. As vice-president of the Liberal Party's polling firm, Goldfarb Consultants, he once conducted a national survey on the personality traits of Trudeau and a provincial premier. Kirby was astonished by the results — the national electorate had composed a picture of Trudeau "uncannily similar" to the man he knew personally. So he asked a dozen others who knew Trudeau well to answer the same survey questions. The two sets of answers to the question — what kind of person is Pierre Trudeau? — were identical.

These results made a believer of Kirby. People had formed their impressions of Trudeau from television, but their perceptions were no less valid than those of people who had worked next to the prime minister for years. When Trudeau's colleagues tried to imagine his likely reaction to a given situation, in other words, they were working on the same understanding of Trudeau's personality as people had formed in their living rooms in Halifax and Victoria.

Kirby has come to believe that the only problem with television is that there's not enough of it — or, at least, enough of the right sort. "Print cannot convey emotion, personality, like television can," said Kirby. "But there's too much of the sixty-second, or six-second, clip. It's rare people get a chance to spend much time with a leader, like they did during the debate." And what they concluded from the 1988 debate is something that John Turner's aides had known for months, but that Turner himself had been unable to communicate, to move past the events-brokers, the static on the line: that free trade was, for him, a sovereignty issue, and one about which he felt passionately.

You could also argue — so long as you believe that people are able to process information and draw rational conclusions — that the only problem with polls is that there aren't enough of them. There were twenty-four polls publicly available in the 1988 campaign, more than twice as many as in 1984 and three times as many as were available during the campaigns of 1979 and 1980. Perhaps next time out the polls will finally take their rightful role and place in a campaign — a daily tracking of the horse race, the issues, and the reactions to yesterday's events, right there on page two next to the weather map.

CONSERVATIVES, PARTICULARLY, like to complain about the harmful influence on their campaign of the monster Gallup of November 7. But if it had not been for the fact that thirteen different public-opinion polls were conducted in the two-week period before and after the Gallup, the expectation left by that one poll — certain Liberal victory — would have been left unchallenged.

The Gallup released on November 7, two weeks before the election, bore the press-release headline: "Grits surge to lead — Liberal majority likely." The poll gave the Liberals 43 per cent of the vote, 12 points ahead of the Conservatives. The debate is continuing about whether or not it was a rogue poll. Lorne Bozinoff, Gallup's vice-president, pointed out that the poll was on the same "trend-line" as those around it. But Norm Atkins, the Conservative's chief organizer, said that the Gallup was not in keeping with Decima's own tracking. "We knew that our data was in the field exactly the same day as Gallup," he said. "Ours was thirty-four, thirty-four, twenty-nine. We knew we were even."

The Conservatives learned about Gallup's numbers on Sunday night. They realized the harmful impact would be felt not by the electorate but by their troops on the ground. "It had an incredible impact on the organization, on the morale of the party cadre," Atkins said. "Fortunately, we were able to get out enough information to reassure people."

Atkins is painfully modest — in fact, he had worked two years preparing for just such an eventuality, and the November 7 Gallup put his organization to the test. Organization, he believed, was the line of defence in an election campaign: "While you can't win with an organization, you can lose without it."

In 1986, two years into Brian Mulroney's first term as prime minister, Atkins had devised a model of national campaign co-ordination to prepare the party for changing electoral bound-aries, a high number of independent-minded incumbents, some fresh-faced new candidates, and riding associations that would have to be rebuilt. "You start with a concept," he said, "and my view is, before you even look at people, you want to make sure you have a solid, realistic plan." His approach grew out of the line-supply, pyramid organization he had learned in his youth in the U.S. army supply corps. He had to devise a system to control the supply of information, rather than of ammunition; but the principles were the same.

Atkins talked about his organizational plan at meetings with his regional chairmen in Ottawa, and as he outlined his ideas one of his listeners — the northern Alberta chairman, John Chomiak, who happens to be an engineer — decided to transfer them to blueprint paper. The resulting series of overlapping circles and chains of command took on a pattern. Atkins was describing something similar to a three-dimensional chessboard, with one exception: players could move over the surface of any one board, but could drop through to the layer below only on the corrresponding square.

The Tories' national office would be organized into about two dozen divisions: platform policy, party youth, volunteers, and so on. This structure would be mirrored at the regional level — same boxes, different names. This same division of labour was repeated at the local level. This, Atkins felt, would allow flexibility and discipline while avoiding the problems that had attended the Conservatives' 1984 campaign.

In 1984, the technologically minded Conservatives had created a vast data network for their workers: briefing books by the dozen, a personal computer in every campaign office, electronic mail, a national bulletin board. The system had got plugged up when everyone started talking to everyone else, sticking their noses in where they didn't belong. The controls imposed in 1988 would mean that any riding worker would be only two steps away from his counterpart in national headquarters; it would also mean that the national worker would not be bothered by stray requests from other departments.

This discipline was imposed on both the workers and the machines. The Conservatives stuck with their electronic mail system but changed the access. Gates were installed on the computers so that, for instance, only two people — the national operations director, Harry Near, and his co-worker, Marjorie Le-

Breton — had the ability to send out an "all hail and distress" message to the troops.

It was a happy coincidence for the Conservatives that the monster Gallup of November 7 fell on a Monday. On Mondays, the prime minister was regularly in Ottawa, resting for another week on the trail. Taking advantage of this rest day each week, the party's central strategy committee held a breakfast meeting. On this particular Monday, there also happened to be a meeting at the Westin Hotel of the national campaign executive — about forty-five middle managers.

Marc Lortie, the prime minister's press secretary, arrived at 24 Sussex Drive about 7 a.m. Mulroney was just stepping out of the shower. The prime minister did not stand on formality; he met with Lortie right away.

"Marc, what do you think of the poll?"

"Not very useful at this time," Lortie responded, in his unflappable, silk-stocking manner, "because it does not correspond to the reality. But it has an influencing effect on the workers. I think we should address it."

"So do I," said Mulroney.

To Lortie, the prime minister seemed uncommonly cool. Mulroney repeated what he had said many times since the campaign began: "Marc, it's your first campaign. There's going to be a pattern to the campaign, there's going to be a dip. It's in the nature of things. Never underestimate the Liberal Party — it's a grand institution. There's going to be a dip and then, if we're good, we will go up again."

In retrospect, Lortie wonders how the prime minister knew that. Lortie wasn't alone. Mulroney had said the same thing to Derek Burney, his chief of staff, and Norm Atkins, to name two; he'd been saying it even when all indications were that the Tories would take the election in a waltz.

Lortie and Mulroney decided to spend the afternoon in an impromptu visit to Hull, just across the Ottawa River. The objective: to inform the media that the Gallup did not reflect the party's own numbers, but regardless, the Conservatives were working hard to win.

At the breakfast meeting, the central strategy committee decided to encourage the troops. Near strolled over to his computer terminal and sent out a memo, which read in part:

"RIDING BULLETIN NO: 50

"TO: Riding campaign managers

"FROM: National campaign HQ

"DATE: Nov. 7, 1988

"RE: The Gallup Poll Nov. 7

"URGENT!!

"This Gallup poll is wrong. WRONG. It is at total variance to our own polling which was done over the same period of time as Gallup. Our own polls show that the election is very much a horse race; that we and the Liberals are neck and neck on a national basis.

"In addition, in Quebec our polling shows that we are not behind, we are very much ahead.

"Tell your workers not to panic. The Gallup is wrong. It is a bad poll and other public opinion polls confirm our own numbers.

"Now is the time to keep a cool head and continue to work hard.

"Harry Near. Ops/Dir."

To reinforce the message, Atkins took Allan Gregg along to the meeting of the national campaign executive. "The atmosphere over there was a lot of concern, people didn't know what was going on," Atkins said. "But I didn't say very much of anything. On the way over, I asked Allan whether he still believed in his numbers, and he said he did. I said, 'My job this morning is for me to open the meeting and for you to tell them the Gallup is you-know-what.'"

The Conservative organization did not buckle with news of the Gallup. It didn't even creak. That's a testament to its strength and flexibility, and to the two years of planning and refining that had gone into it. On voting day, two weeks after the monster Gallup, the Conservative workers were on the ground, undaunted, getting out the vote.

"I think we started the campaign by saying we had a plan [for the country], and we had the people that could implement the plan," Atkins said. "In the last two weeks, that's what we got back to. We said, 'You have four seconds when you go into the voting booth to make a decision — but that decision is going to last four years.'"

Atkins, as usual, was at the heart of the Conservative

campaign, privy to its inside intelligence and responsible for maintaining its strength and momentum. His analysis of what happened on November 21 is a fetching blend of simplicity and truth, instructive both for what it reveals and for what it doesn't: "Generally speaking, those people who were with us in the beginning, and who had some doubts about us during the centre, were the ones who came back to us at the end."

CHAPTER 14

# ONE HUNDRED MONKEYS

*Mukubili is not the only genius*
*among Japanese macaques, and,*
*indeed, she is rather overshadowed*
*by the inventiveness of Imo, a female*
*who came up with two clever ideas*
*on the little island of Koshima in the*
*extreme south of Japan. . . .*

A COMPLETE GUIDE TO MONKEYS, APES, AND OTHER
PRIMATES, GENUS: MACACA — MICHAEL KAVANAGH

T HE FATEFUL MORNING HAS AR-
rived," wrote Senator Arthur Roebuck in 1945, in the little pamphlet entitled *Campaign Management and How to Win Elections.*
"Drivers, footmen, telephone operators and scrutineers have each
been handed their instructions. Now the telephones are ringing
and the pleasant voices of the women operators are politely urging
the favourable voters to come to the polls at once. The foot workers
are hurrying down the various streets calling at the houses of the
friendly voters, with their cheerful persuasion to remember without delay the first duty of citizenship, and the drivers of the cars
are darting away for supporters who require to be conveyed to the
polls. In every Polling Division, [workers] are shepherding, coax-
ing, dragging the favourable voters to the polls. The object is to get
the favourable vote in the Ballot Box."

The fateful morning of November 21, 1988, broke cold and
overcast for Mac Harb. The Liberal candidate in Ottawa Centre

closed his eyes a moment, to see if he could feel what was coming. He couldn't feel anything except nerves.

Harb dressed carefully — this could be *the* day. He wore a basic navy two-piece suit and, to dress it up a bit, a red foulard necktie with matching pocket kerchief. Red was a good colour. A good Liberal colour. A David Peterson look. The shoes he picked were good, solid shoes, good for walking. He told himself: "You feel good. You look terrific." But his stomach — the knot there, a bundle of nerves. He drove to his campaign headquarters, a rented office in downtown Ottawa. In compliance with the instructions in *Ready, Set, Go!* Harb had chosen a highly visible street-front headquarters with plenty of glass, much of it plastered with his name and smiling mug.

Dalton McGuinty was there. What a combination: Harb, the Lebanese immigrant with the knock-em-dead looks; McGuinty the Irishman with the silvery tongue. They were like a Mafia hit team of charm. McGuinty was a big man with a careworn face and an ironic smile. He knew all the angles. He could slip in the side door of a convent and overwhelm Mother Superior with his flattery and roguish piety; he could catch the elbow of the Holy Father after Mass and slip a few words in his ear. Harb was of slighter build, dark and sharp as a razor. He was still learning, but he knew the ways of the ethnic ward heeler. Ottawa Centre was like an atlas to him: here the Greeks, on this block the Italians, a pocket of stray Turks over there. Together, Harb and McGuinty had at their fingertips every vote not directly descended from the two conquering nations of Canada.

Harb looked up to McGuinty. McGuinty had got himself elected to Queen's Park. He and Peterson were like *that*. He'd been through this sort of day before, he'd know what to do. Harb poured himself maybe his tenth cup of coffee.

At campaign headquarters, the voices of the women operators on the phones revealed a polyglot of languages. The drivers and footmen were busy as well. It's a miracle people weren't hurt. Harb was trying to have a little chat with his publicity chairman when two drivers burst through the door, half-dragging an elderly woman, shouting. There was a lot of back and forth, Harb soliciting the old woman's name and address, all of it in another language. She was a new Canadian, she'd been left off the voters' list, they wouldn't let her vote.

Harb sent the drivers packing, with instructions to try again. "Problems," he said.

McGuinty took a careful stroll past the telephone banks, noting the orders for rides. "Oldest trick in the book," he said. "They tie up your phones, and tie up your cars. Get half your fleet driving out to some gravel pit to pick up a vote."

The most recent poll had shown Harb in a neck-and-neck race with the New Democrat incumbent, Michael Cassidy. Harb had studied every word in *Ready, Set, Go!*, especially the chapter titled "Getting Out the Vote." On the wall-sized calendar in his headquarters, November 21 had been marked "E-Day." That morning, someone had printed in bold, red letters across the entire calendar: "GOTV." Getting out the vote. The difference between winning and losing.

"Oh, it would be a shame if it's close," Harb said. "To lose by just a few votes would be unbearable. I hope it's decisive either way."

Harb thought about what he had just said, rocking on his heels, reconsidering: "Having said that, I would be pleased and delighted to take this riding by one single vote."

"Mac," said McGuinty. "Put on your coat."

The two men strolled out to McGuinty's brown Cadillac. As Harb climbed in the passenger side, McGuinty held back. "It's best just to keep the candidate busy today," he said, over his shoulder. "No sense leaving him around, stewing."

McGuinty had barely placed the key in the ignition before Harb was urging him on, bouncing on his seat, checking his watch. "Come on!" he said. "Step on it!"

McGuinty nodded sagely, and hit the gas pedal. The Caddy swerved across Somerset Street as if through West Beirut. Two sedans came to a nose-diving halt. McGuinty waved. "Isn't that incredible?" he asked. "Just a wave and a smile, and they're happy to see you." He made his way, waving a lot, to one of Harb's outlying offices.

Harb didn't like it inside the office. Too quiet. "Any Italian-sounding names, francophones, Chinese, drag 'em out," he told a poll captain. "Don't wait, no time to lose." En route to a seniors' residence, he suddenly turned to McGuinty: "Stop the car!"

McGuinty hit the brakes — had he run over a cat? Worse?

"I want to knock on that door," Harb said. "There's a family of eight in there."

"Lord," said McGuinty, sardonically. "They must be Irish Catholic."

"Asian. Listen, I'm a believer in big families. They tend to vote Liberal."

"In you go, then."

McGuinty lit up a smoke. In Harb's absence, he said: "I'd be surprised if he pulls five votes today. But look at him, excited as a puppy. You've got to let him out to run."

"IT IS NOW AFTERNOON," wrote Senator Roebuck. "The names of the supporters still appearing on the list are steadily growing fewer, but time is flying. It is becoming a race between men and minutes. Not a moment to be wasted! Now only a few stragglers remain, but the clock is ticking. Method lengthens the passing minutes and gives wings to flying feet. 'Hurry, hurry, or you'll lose your vote. We've got to have you; you must come. Hurry! Hurry!'"

Harb climbed back in the Cadillac and told McGuinty to drive over to a low-income housing development. He had a feeling about the place. When they got there, every single patch of lawn was sporting a Cassidy sign.

"Mac, you're wasting your time."

"Oh, yeah?" he replied. "Just watch me."

Harb hit the doors on the run, and he was, as they say of the Gurkhas, the equal of five ordinary men. He didn't waste time; his first words were: "Canadian citizen? Are you a Canadian citizen?" The families, most of them immigrants, eyed Harb suspiciously — he could be from Immigration. If they simply shook their heads in silence, he would never know. Harb sprinted on to the next door.

"Step on it!" he shouted in a stifling unit upstairs, where a young woman had said she'd like a ride to the polls. She just had to use the powder room, first.

Harb grabbed her little brother, a boy of about eight. "Go upstairs," he said. "See what's keeping her. That's a good boy."

"She's doing her stupid make-up," the boy reported.

"You don't need your stupid make-up!" Harb shouted up the stairs.

The doorbell rang. It was a campaign worker for Michael Cassidy. Harb shooed her away. Outside, it was dark. The polls would be closing soon.

The woman descended, a vivacious brunette in a floral print dress, excited and chattering. Harb hustled her into the car. In the approximately ninety seconds it took to drive to the polling station, Harb had determined that she was a belly dancer in her spare time, told her she must be a wonderful belly dancer, and invited her to belly dance that night at his victory party.

His crowning glory, however, was the Cambodian woman. The Cambodian woman was a registered voter but couldn't get out of the house. Four kids, all under eight. Grandmother here, she's seventy-eight and only been here two months. She can't see too good, can't look after the children.

"Hey!" said Harb. "I know what. I'll baby-sit your kids. I love kids. In fact, I love your kids."

The kids started jumping with excitement. Harb started jumping, too. He jumped up and down with the kids.

"Woo-woo! See? Your kids love me."

The grandmother smiled, although she could hardly make out the strange man in this strange country, and understood even less about what he wanted. The mother relented, drawing on her coat.

"Hey, you know who I am, don't you?" Harb asked. The woman looked a little unsure. Before she left, Harb took a felt tip, and wrote his name on her hand, in block letters: "H-A-R-B."

The woman stepped into the car. She was clearly thrilled to be taking part in her first Canadian election, and to be riding in such a sumptuous car. She looked around at all the room, sank back into the velvet seat, marvelled at the opera lamp.

"Tell me, madam," McGuinty asked, delicately. "Do you know the name Mac Harb? H-A-R-B?"

"Dalton," someone interjected. "He already wrote his name on her hand."

"Really," McGuinty replied. He looked straight ahead, deadpan. "On the palm, I hope."

"GONG! THE POLLS have closed," wrote Senator Roebuck. "The field force gathers in the polling booths to watch the count, and, in the lull which precedes the torch-light procession, the Block

Chairmen call up the Campaign Manager. Every supporter who could be reached has voted.

"It was a good fight."

And, for Mac Harb, a rewarding one. It was close, but he beat Michael Cassidy by 671 votes. His election-day workers prodded some three thousand recalcitrant supporters to the booth on election day. Harb's victory was greatly aided by a general swing to the Liberals in eastern Ontario, a trend that was devastating for Ottawa Conservatives. Bureaucrats have long memories; for four years they had remembered Mulroney's words about their swank offices and soft lives, the "pink slips and running shoes" they should all receive. The federal public service was not the most carefully tended constituency under Mulroney, and the election-day choice of the voters in Ottawa Centre was entirely rational.

The Liberals won 83 seats in all — more than double the 1984 number, but still a disappointment. The vote for the Liberal Party — which Mulroney had called the "grand institution of Canadian politics" — had simply not reassembled along traditional lines. In Ontario, the party had improved from 14 to 40 seats. Much of this growth was centred on Toronto, where Liberal support was concentrated among urban ethnics, working women, and the working poor. Partly, they were allowing their long-standing party loyalty to determine whom to believe about free trade. To a much greater extent, they were basing their choice on the expectation that free trade would create continentalist pressures to dismantle Canadian social programs (of which they were the beneficiaries) while creating new jobs (from which they did not expect to benefit). Subtract the political rhetoric and their support of the Liberals was based on an entirely rational, self-interested way of looking at things.

In Quebec, the Liberals' share of the popular vote fell from 35 to 30 per cent, their seat total from 17 to 12. The party found new strength in the Atlantic provinces, where they gained 46 per cent of the popular vote (versus 35 per cent in 1984) and 20 seats (versus 7). Except for 5 seats in Manitoba and Turner's lone stand on the far rampart of Vancouver Quadra, the party was shut out of the West.

John Turner had pledged not to relinquish his leadership until he had repaired the party's finances, established party unity, and prepared a strong list of contenders to replace him. He had waged a campaign to save Canada from free trade. Five months after the election, having failed to achieve a single one of these goals, he resigned.

In York-Simcoe, just north of Toronto, Frank Stronach also failed in his quest. Despite his fabulous wealth, despite owning half the real estate and being one of the largest employers in the riding, he polled 6,700 fewer votes than the ghost of Sinc Stevens, a fellow named John Cole. Stronach had a dream, but Canada in 1988 was no place for dreamers. In this sense his riding reflected the country at large. Driven by fierce will and unbridled ambition, Stronach offered the people prophecies. Driven by anxiety, the people wanted plans.

IN THE EASTERN Townships of Quebec, Paul Vachon didn't even come close to taking Brome-Missisquoi for the New Democrats. The Butcher got about 5,500 votes, or 13 per cent of the total. The riding was carried by the Conservative widow, Gabrielle Bertrand, with the Liberals placing second. Vachon finished third, 16,794 votes short of victory.

If he'd been able to pull 10 more votes at each polling station, he would have hit 15 per cent of the popular vote. That would have meant a federal rebate of $14,000 — half his election expenses. If — the saddest word in politics. Vachon had to come up with the money from his own pocket.

He tried to figure it out. For long hours he'd sit in his upstairs room in the house his father built — it has new windows now, so the snow doesn't blow in during the winter — and try to figure where things went so wrong. "I know it's easy for a candidate to dream in technicolour," he said, "but I even thought I was ahead."

It all changed after some NDP nationalists made militant remarks against English rights in their province. A New Democrat nationalist in Quebec is a particular breed. Brian Mulroney had already snapped up all those who were merely moderate separatists and appointed them to his cabinet and crown agencies. This left slim pickings for the NDP. Ed Broadbent's response was that he couldn't really comment on a provincial matter. Broadbent must have been sleeping when, in 1984, the newly minted Liberal leader John Turner began his long slide in Quebec with exactly the same comment about the rights of Manitoba francophones. Mulroney's defence of the same linguistic minority raised hopes he might even care about the English minority in Quebec.

All of this was somehow tied in with the founding of the country, the supposed role of the Senate, and the unique nature of Vachon's area — "the Townships," or "the cantons." It was all tied together, The Butcher knew, but, as he'd be the first to admit, the whole thing was a little beyond him. "What the heck," he said. "It was a good experience. I'm just sorry about what happened to the party."

What happened to the party was that it got relegated, once again, to the status of regional protest rump. Oh, the New Democrats won 43 seats, their best showing. They increased their share of the popular vote two-thirds of one per cent in Atlantic Canada while failing to win a seat. In Quebec, their share of the vote was unchanged, as was their historical distinction of having never won a single seat in the province. In Ontario, they dropped two-thirds of one per cent in the popular vote, and from 13 seats to 10. In Manitoba they lost 2 seats, in Alberta they gained 1. Only in Saskatchewan did they gain significantly — from 5 seats to 10. Nearly half the NDP seats were won in the highly polarized political climate of British Columbia.

Ed Broadbent, a popular leader between elections but a miserable, crabby campaigner, had once again led his party to mediocrity, a draw with itself. Four months later, broken by defeat, the NDP leader announced his resignation.

THE ONLY TRULY national party in the 1988 election, the Progressive Conservatives, filled 169 of the 295 seats in the House of Commons. Brian Mulroney's weird coalition of francophobes and francophone nationalists provided the backbone of his electoral support. In Quebec and Alberta alone, where the Tories' percentage of the popular vote exceeded even that of the 1984 landslide, they carried 88 seats, more than half the party's total.

This was understandable enough. Those two provinces share a centrifugal view of Canada, in keeping with Mulroney's own. In both provinces free trade was perhaps viewed most clearly as an economic issue, one that provided a means of prying the provincial economies free of Ottawa's control. The prospect of free trade appealed as much to the prairie protest movement of reform as it did to the Parti Québécois, whose leader, Jacques Parizeau, hailed the free-trade agreement as creating the preconditions of a sovereign Quebec. Voters in those provinces, like John Turner, knew that once the economic levers were gone the political levers would follow.

Unlike John Turner, the voters in Quebec and Alberta thought this was a good thing.

Part of the Tories' success grew out of their mastery of technology, from deft application of polling results to their understanding of television to their blinding internal communications network. And just as they achieved fluency in these technologies — which had become, by 1988, fairly traditional — they took the first steps along a causeway of newer technological innovation made possible by the computer. These steps led to a project so secret that the few senior Conservative organizers aware of its full scope had taken, in the words of one, "a blood oath not to discuss it with anyone."

The program was called Target '88, but it was actually launched during the 1984 campaign, after the Conservatives recruited an Oklahoma-based Republican organizer, Mary Ellen Miller. The Tories' decision to call on Miller was as significant in its time as the Liberals' decision, twenty years earlier, to recruit the U.S. pollster Lou Harris. Miller, whose computer programs assisted both Pat Robertson and George Bush in the U.S., introduced the Conservatives to a world in which telemarketing, direct mail, and polling were meshed into a unified force by the awesome, grinding gristwork of the computer. The end result is a sort of electoral techno-massage.

In 1984 the effectiveness of the program, which operated out of a sealed room in the L'Esplanade Laurier office building in Ottawa, was not accurately assessed by the Conservatives. Their massive 1984 victory was viewed as a national sweep, and the L'Esplanade Laurier project — which focused on individual ridings — was seen as only mildly significant. This lack of interest irritated some of those who worked on the project. To anyone who would listen — which was nobody of importance — they pointed to figures that showed the Conservative vote was 10 to 15 points ahead of the national sweep in the ridings where the project was used. In these target ridings, they estimated, 65 per cent of the undecided vote had gone Conservative. If this were true — even if only partially true — then the L'Esplanade Laurier people were on to something big.

The decision to review the project was not made until mid-summer of 1988, a few months before the election call. The Conservatives asked Pierre Fortier, a consultant with the octopus-like lobbying firm Public Affairs International, to test the program on four select ridings. Fortier took a scaled-down version of the program and tested it on three ridings — the fourth served as a blind control.

Fortier had experience as a fundraiser and a thorough acquaintance with techniques that combine direct-mail and target-audience lists; he expected about a two per cent response rate to the Target '88 program. When the results poured in, they were, in his words, "absolutely unbelievable." Sixty-five per cent of those reached by the program had responded — about 30 times higher than expectations. The results were taken to the prime minister. Brian Mulroney not only agreed to an extension of the program, he helped draft the target letter.

One reason for this extraordinary response rate was that Target '88 invited involvement from an electorate that had previously felt disenfranchised, voiceless, and powerless. Another reason was that the person seeking their involvement was none other than the prime minister himself.

Here is how it worked. A target list was drawn up of about five thousand voters in each riding, designed to reach as many undecided voters as possible — the program has no interest in core supporters of either party. To reach the undecided voters, Fortier consulted Decima's riding-profile polls and national tracking. The idea was to draw up four "lifestyles" — for example, single mothers with jobs — that contained a high ratio of undecided voters. A database company called InfoDirect provided a list of all voters in the riding who fitted those lifestyle categories; another company attached addresses, telephone numbers, and postal codes to the names. The whole process took a couple of days.

A laser printer then generated a customized letter to each undecided voter, signed (mechanically, of course) by Brian Mulroney. The letter was standard pap: "As you know, this is an extremely important election. I wanted to take the opportunity to share my views with you. . . ." The key to the letter is what organizers called the "magic paragraph" near the bottom. Imagine, as you read what follows, that your mental state is one of anxiety about your future and the course of government; that you have been denied all other means of involvement in the campaign; and that you want, more than anything, simply to be listened to:

"We need your help in shaping and implementing a bold new plan for Canada's future. The old ways simply won't be good enough for the 1990's. I want to start by hearing from you. Please write me at the address shown on the envelope. I know that you and your family probably have concerns and thoughts on how government can serve you better. I want to hear them." Signed (well, sort of) by the big guy himself.

No questionnaire was attached: people were expected to reply in longhand, or on a typewriter. And reply they did. By the time the election rolled around, about 200,000 of those letters had been sent to a selected 40 ridings across the country. Amazingly, some 130,000 of the recipients wrote back. You'd be lucky to get that level of response to an offer of free twenty-dollar bills.

A few days later, the respondent received a telephone call: "Hello," the voice said, following a prepared script. "I'm calling for the prime minister. Did you receive his letter? Great! Did you write Mr. Mulroney? Thank you for writing. The list I'm calling from was compiled before we received your letter, but since I have you on the phone, could I get you to tell me what you think is the most serious issue facing the country today?"

Some time later, the voter received yet another letter from Brian Mulroney. Hard to believe this was fake. After all, the letter referred specifically to the voter's circumstances, and, using information gathered from the telephone survey, alluded directly to his concerns. There was also an extensive response to what the voter had identified as the key issue.

This lengthy response had been pulled from a list of thirty-three such stock responses at national headquarters, replies to comments that ranged from "I just can't trust Mulroney" to "I think we're giving too much away to Quebec." The letter was partly intended to disabuse the voter of his critical opinion; the real intent, though, was to persuade him that what he thought actually mattered.

After this letter came was a second phone call, again from someone "calling for the prime minister." Finally, on election day, the "prime minister's office" called again. Have you voted yet? Do you need any help getting out to vote?

"Chinese water torture," as Pierre Fortier put it. "Except

that you're not bugging people when you get hold of them during a campaign. They expect it. The more you see them, bug them, phone them, show you want their support, the more likely they are to vote for you."

What the voter saw was only the outer layer of this highly sophisticated program. The information generated by this repeated contact with undecided voters was put to use by the local campaign, and by national headquarters as well. The program was structured so that the local riding gathered information of tactical interest; national headquarters retained control of its strategic value.

The telephone calls were all made locally; the person calling "for the prime minister" was actually calling from the local candidate's campaign headquarters. The information thus gathered was tabulated on computer-readable index cards and couriered nightly to Ottawa, where the analysis was done.

In the local riding, the candidate held on to information that allowed him to canvass for support and recruit volunteers. For instance, the caller's prepared script provided for a rising level of involvement and intimacy, so that voters identified as influential in their neighbourhood — doctors, say — could eventually be asked to write a little note to their neighbours explaining why they intended to vote Conservative.

In the national campaign, the information served a number of uses. A voter might have written to say he appreciated the government's economic policies, as he now had a job at the local mine. This information was shipped over to the tour desk, which made sure Mulroney could refer to the mine-worker in his next speech to that community. Target '88 supplemented Decima's national tracking by providing the equivalent of a 5,000-member "focus group" in a single riding.

Because the computer software was provided by a U.S. Republican, it was geared to a two-party system. The Target '88 group found, as a result, that in two-party races their vote projections and strategic advice were deadly accurate; in tight three-way races, however, they often strayed from the mark.

The implications of Target '88 on the broader issue of campaign management are sweeping. The program shifts, for instance, the focus of message development away from the broad band of television to the narrow band of the computer. It also demonstrates why the new technologies have a centralizing effect and tend to relegate local party organization to a supporting role.

The effectiveness of the program in a race as volatile as the 1988 campaign is a matter of some dispute. The program appears to be most effective in tight races in swing ridings. A number of Conservative strategists credit Target '88 with helping Barbara McDougall defeat the Liberal Aideen Nicholson in a tight race in Toronto St. Paul's; David MacDonald defeat the Liberal Bill Graham in an even closer race in Toronto's Rosedale; and Rob Nicholson defeat the Liberal Gary Pillitteri in a squeaker in Niagara Falls, Ontario. Swing ridings can shift a campaign — Norm Atkins estimates that the Conservatives won 35 ridings in the 1988 campaign by less than two per cent of the vote. A program that targets such ridings could well mean the difference between winning and losing an election — particularly one that lacked the overarching diversion of an issue such as free trade.

But in a campaign so distorted by a single issue, such a program is of naturally limited value. As Gregg noted: "In this sort of campaign, with numbers swinging like this, it's like pissing in the wind." But it has awesome long-term implications. It has since been turned into a continuing program by the Conservatives. Now called the Incumbency Protection Program, it is intended to secure the Conservative majority in the Commons. The 1988 campaign director, Atkins, calls it the "way of the future," and the program chief, Fortier, calls it "the new dawn."

TO SIGN ON WITH Target '88, a local candidate had to dedicate about $5,000 of limited campaign funds and ten volunteers to a program controlled by headquarters. It's ironic that one of the candidates who embraced the idea was Bill Domm, a veteran Conservative MP from Peterborough, Ontario. In fact, despite Domm's reputation as a dinosaur, he had been doing his own version of the techno-massage since 1979. "He contacts everybody in his riding through the twelve-month period [before the writ is dropped] using direct mail and telemarketing," explained a senior Conservative organizer. "That's how he stays in there."

It's even more ironic that, when organizers approached Maureen McTeer about the Target '88 program, they were turned down. "She said, 'It'll never work in Carleton-Gloucester. I want eight-sided colour brochures going to 60,000 homes, I want billboards at all the major intersections, on the backs of the buses, I want the plastic lawn signs' — which were not party standard, by the way, because she wanted her own logo.

"So what you had in McTeer was a recalcitrant candidate who should be part of the modern era and want to move forward; and how many times have you heard people call Bill Domm a dinosaur? He's using modern techniques, and this woman's going back to the thirties."

The Conservative Party did all it could for Mo-Jo. It offered her a campaign vehicle complete with armour plating, flashing roof lights, and ride-a-matic suspension; she preferred to stand on the curb, show a bit of leg, and hitch-hike. She had fallen prey to the most common of electoral misconceptions — that the candidate actually matters.

One day during her faltering campaign, McTeer arrived for a meeting with her strategy committee. The group consisted of the Conservative power brokers Jodi White, Pierre Fortier, Bill Neville, David Small, and Tim Ralfe — a committee, as one of them noted, "remarkably similar to the one that ran Joe Clark's leadership bid in 1983." This was not a coincidence. Even though McTeer is, irrefutably, her own person, she couldn't pull enough organization as her own person to carry a casket. Out of loyalty to Clark, the committee did its best for McTeer.

The strategy committee had in hand a thorough riding survey which probed strengths and weaknesses of four hundred voters, their voting intentions and underlying attitudes. It was good work, and expensive, and the committee had spent considerable energies analysing the results. One of the findings was that McTeer had the kind of name-recognition most politicians only dream of — eighty-five per cent of her voters could identify her as their Conservative candidate. But the effect was wasted, because in those parts of the riding that were traditionally Conservative, McTeer's name actually hurt. Her fame was giving her a boost in polls she could not hope to win, while damaging her chances in polls she should have carried.

The strategists encouraged McTeer to abandon her free-lance campaign and jump on board the national bus. From her lawn signs to her speeches, they suggested, she should drop the emphasis on herself and join the Mulroney team. McTeer looked at the poll results, which told her she wasn't popular. She announced, "These aren't right," tossed the printouts aside, and walked out.

And lost the election, falling some seven thousand votes short of one Eugène Bellemare, a municipal alderman of uncertain talent who carried of Carleton-Gloucester for the Liberals.

IN HIS HOME TOWN OF Baie-Comeau on the north shore of the St. Lawrence in Quebec, the prime minister of Canada delivered his acceptance speech. Finally, he would tell the nation what the election had been all about.

"This campaign has shown that Canadians agree on what it is that we most cherish in our national life," he said. "Our sovereignty, the protection of minority rights, our unique social programs, our concern for the environment, our commitment to regional development — these have their source in a Canadian tradition of tolerance and sharing."

For a brief, chilling moment, it appeared as if Mulroney were admitting that John Turner was right. But no, he was just seizing meaning:

"The election, then, has been not about those values, but about the means to give them greater effect. So now, it is a time for healing in the land. For in the end, irrespective of party preference, we are all Canadians, we all love our country, and we all put the national interest first.

"And so, I say to all the people of Canada: the mandate you have given us tonight is to affirm these Canadian values at home and to promote them in the world."

That was nice. People do not like to be divided, and no one fears polarization more than a politician. There had been a time of confusão, and now Mulroney was softly and tenderly singing a few bars of "Don't Worry, Be Happy." "Healing in the land" is a sentiment close to the heart of Mulroney.

"Canadians. . . have spoken with a loud and clear voice of their desire for unity," he added. "And that's what the election was all about." So it was about unity. Mulroney had kept it a secret until the very end, like the toy at the bottom of the Crackerjack box.

Free trade, together with Meech Lake, he said, were the means to bring about unity. "The Free Trade Agreement and the Meech Lake Accord are the chief instruments of our prosperity and unity," he said. "They constitute a brilliant affirmation of the new spirit of national reconciliation and economic renewal that benefits us all."

And why not? Perhaps, finally, all that needed to be known about Meech Lake was that Quebec had signed it. Perhaps all that needed to be known about free trade was that the market liked it. Perhaps Canada no longer needed to be bound together from the centre. Perhaps, when the centre does not hold, things do not fall apart; each of the pieces just finds its own centre.

Mulroney tossed the rest of his prepared speech away, winging it. This was rare for Mulroney. The crowd was swelling with the elemental force of the wave, victory was his, he had secured his place in history. The glasses were off. It was time for a glimpse of his soul.

In French, he said: "We are picking up the shield again with pride, knowing that together we are going to build a more prosperous Canada, more tolerant and more unified.

"And inside this Canada, you'll find a strong Quebec. Strong provinces, and a lasting unity and a solid unity for all of Canada."

Switching to English, he said: "And so tonight is a night about unity. It is a night about Canada, the splendour of our nation, the coming together of East and West, the Atlantic provinces, the West, the great industrial heartland of Ontario and the province of Quebec."

Somewhat different emphasis on Quebec in the two versions; but let that pass.

"Coming together in a great affirmation of solidarity and unity and saying to Canada, and saying to the world: 'We are a proud nation that stands before you — one Canada with equality of opportunity for all — Canadians from Newfoundland and Labrador to British Columbia.' That is the message of tonight. Voila, the result of the election — Canadian unity!"

The good people of Baie-Comeau cheered. And Martin Brian Mulroney, the happy Bürgermeister of the cantons of Canada, danced a little jig.

SOME DAYS LATER, a memorandum was circulated among the five most senior strategists in the Conservative campaign. Had it gone any higher it would have been gospel by definition. There was no secret agenda in the memo, unless there is a devious undertone to such ringing items as, "The Continuation of a Positive, Outward Orientation for the Government and the Prime Minister." This orientation will include "The Prime Minister championing Canada's role as a moral leader in the International Theatre," and "The Heightening of Programs and Efforts which relate to Transition and Adjustments flowing from Free Trade's implementation." Not to imply that the transition would be more difficult than expected — the section merely suggested that, in addition to cushioning the negative effects, the Tories should put in place programs "to let the average Canadian participate in the benefits of free trade."

What is notable about the document is the extent to which the policy initiatives flow from the election results. To groups among which the Conservatives did poorly — among the poor, seniors, and women, for example — the document called for creative, non-expenditure means of improving the government's delivery of services.

"In order to diffuse their concerns and ensure that these groups are not mobilized against us at every turn, it would seem... essential that the party be seen to be reaching out and addressing their concerns, i.e. tangibly building on the post-election statements of the Prime Minister."

This document is significant not for what it says, but for what it means. It means the political process does respond to the expressed will of the people. It means, moreover, that the method of assessing this will has improved dramatically from the days when a leader could only deduce his support from regional voting patterns. A leader can only shift around those pieces he can see; the old situation therefore reinforced the traditional regional-brokerage role of Canadian prime ministers. With the help of pollsters, the leadership can now broker the interests of smaller and smaller target groups. This may prove to be the gravitational field that holds the country's newly liberated regions together.

In their analysis of the election, four political scientists — Richard Johnston, André Blais of the University of Montreal, Henry Brady of the University of Chicago, and Jean Crête of Laval University — concluded that the free-trade issue had possessed the ability to cleave through all groups in Canadian society. Although there is support for the notion — as the Conservative memo suggests — that the issue followed some social and economic patterns, the "core anxiety" about free trade "must have seeped into virtually every social category in the electorate and into every locale. This time, Canadians could not simply agree with their neighbours, co-workers and families, and compartmentalize disagreements into the usual tribal categories."

The Conservatives had won control of the Commons with slightly less than half the popular vote; this led, inevitably, to the observation that "more people had voted against free trade than for it." It even led some people to argue that the government had no "moral right" to proceed with free trade, although this reasoning fell to tatters when placed against a century's worth of election results that had failed — with very few exceptions — to produce a "moral right" to govern at all. Still, the question lingered: had everyone voted on the basis of free trade? And, if they had, did their votes reflect their feelings about the agreement itself, or about the myriad of secondary meanings attached to it?

At a seminar at the University of Chicago in April, the authors confirmed that free trade had indeed served to mediate a host of other concerns. For that reason, it is difficult to say whether the election of 1988 drew a new political map of the country. Did the Mulroney victory grow out of a lasting coalition, or one created by the dominance of a single issue?

The four scholars looked at the election results from every conceivable perspective; they considered social class and income levels, party loyalties and regional ones, ethnic backgrounds and education. Their conclusions are, at first blush, a curious composite. There was a high correlation nation-wide, for instance, between take-home pay and support for free trade. Households with incomes of more than $50,000 were more than twice as likely to support free trade as households with incomes below $50,000. That seems logical enough. But how to explain some of the other findings? Support for free trade was highest in Alberta. Given the opportunities for a secure energy market, and the province's reliance on energy exports, it would seem that Alberta voters had based their voting choices on the free-trade issue. But even there, the choice had talismanic overtones: "All of Albertans' relative aversion to the NDP," the authors concluded, "also got routed through free trade agreement opinion."

There were tantalizing findings across the country. The authors deduced, for instance, that federal civil servants in Quebec, being tied to a concept of nationhood that extended beyond the provincial border, were more than twice as likely to oppose free trade as other Quebeckers. But the lesson of the campaign wasn't that one social group, such as high-income earners, felt a particular way about free trade. It was that the issue sliced through so many social groups. Conventional methods of predicting and analysing voting trends simply fell apart in the face of the talismanic power of free trade. "This was especially true for Conservative preference [voters]," the authors wrote. "Union membership, self-employment, Alberta or Atlantic provinces residence, low and high income, sex, unemployment, French language use, and Catholicism had no direct effect" on Conservative voters' attitudes to free trade.

How, then, did voters make up their minds? In the opinion of the four academics, they did so the old-fashioned way: on their own. "We get an image of a powerful, yet remarkably free-standing division of opinion," they wrote. "Opinion formation on the free-trade agreement, although anchored to some degree in simple economic and social-policy interest and even in traditional party coalitions, arguably derived *mainly from Canadians' deliberations as citizens.* [Emphasis added.] The weakness of its social foundations should not be taken to indicate that the opinionation was bogus. When called upon to choose a party, the overwhelming majority of respondents chose the right one."

The case simply cannot be made that the Canadian voter acted in a manner that was irrational, or contrary to his own interest; that he was helplessly manipulated by image and advertising. The churlish losers of the election campaign whined that big business "bought" the election for the Conservatives. This would be possible if all Canada were a single ward, all its voters under the influence of Tammany Hall. As the only bribes and threats were those of corporate propaganda, however, such an assessment presumes a voter both weak-minded and timorous.

The victors pointed to their own success in having seized the high ground of meaning during the latter stages of the campaign. That, too, would have been possible if only one meaning could be ascribed to free trade. But many meanings were offered, and voters were free to choose among them, or to choose a leader to "proxy" their choice.

Neither the Liberals nor the Tories like to admit that the voters simply made up their minds on their own. But that's exactly what the voters did; and they did so on the basis of rational and enlightened self-interest. This self-enfranchisement is seen as remarkable only by those people — pollsters and spin-doctors, strategists and consultants — who make it their life's work to prevent this very thing from happening. That it happened in 1988, at a time when political campaigners were perfecting the tools intended to remove this capability from the electorate — or at least to warp it to their own ends — suggests more than mere coincidence. It suggests that the seeds of the triumph of popular wisdom were sown by the technology itself.

SUCH TECHNOLOGIES did not exist, of course, the last time a federal government hitched its fortunes to the notion of free trade. Yet in some ways the campaigns were oddly parallel. When, in 1911, the Liberal government of Wilfrid Laurier proposed a reciprocity agreement with the United States, Western farmers who favoured the idea — because it meant cheaper implements and wider markets — were assailed, on nationalist grounds, as traitors. Big business attempted to buy the election — at that time, the interests of big business were protectionist. Then, as in 1988, there was third-party interference, and the overlaying of a secondary meaning. Beyond those similarities, however, there was one striking difference — Laurier, the leader of the party that favoured free trade, lost the election.

In 1911 the free-trade issue consumed English Canada more fully than it did Quebec, which was diverted by a naval question. "In many ways, the idea that preoccupied debate about free trade in 1988 simply didn't exist in 1911," said Richard Johnston. "That is the idea of Canadian identity. In 1911, our identity was simple to define — we were British." It was easy enough, then, to portray those who favoured closer ties with the United States as anti-British.

It was not as simple, three-quarters of a century later, to regard those who favoured free trade with the U.S. as anti-Canadian. This led to the other striking difference between the two free-trade elections: in 1911, voter preference was readily predicted by region, class, and ancestry — in many ways, those tribal attributes *determined* attitudes toward free trade. In 1988, free trade had the ability to sunder such tribal groups.

If something made tribalism a spent force in Canadian politics in 1988, then something must have taken its place. The most persistent sentiment affecting voting behaviour was the perceived trustworthiness of the leader. Ironic, perhaps, that the leader who picked up the nickname "Lyin' Brian" during his first term would win a credibility contest. But it happened, and this implies not the slightest irrationality on the part of the voter. Free trade was complex and inherently unfathomable. It possessed no meaning other than what was imposed upon it. When the imposed meanings collided, the question came down to one of trust — who's believable? Or, more accurately perhaps, who's most nearly believable? The voters, however little they understood the actual agreement, made their choice in the wisest, most informed manner available to them. In the end, using nothing more than a sort of popular wisdom, they found their way through the 1988 campaign — the muddle of semantic chaos and political illusion, of tangential motive and opaque reasoning — just as Donald Johnston had predicted they would.

IT WAS A FRIDAY afternoon in December, and Johnston was in his office in the East Block of Parliament Hill. He preferred these older offices to the newer, more spacious quarters across the road — they still echoed with the ghosts of high-collared finance ministers and scratch-fingered clerks. Not that it mattered any more. This would be Johnston's last visit to this office. He had not lost the election; he had not cared to run.

The bookshelves along one wall had been emptied, save for a few scraps of paper and regular rows of dust, marking the shadows of the books. On the walls, the photographs and testimonials of a political career had been removed, leaving only holes in the plaster and rectangles of less-faded paint. More shadows. His staff hovered outside his door, waiting, speaking in lowered voices, hoping there was something they could do. It was as hopeless as a deathbed. There was nothing they could do. Johnston gamely offered his visitor a coffee. The coffee machine was still working, but someone had taken away the cream and sugar. Do you mind it black?

Johnston had just held a news conference, to promote a book he had compiled. The book was an edited series of speeches by Pierre Trudeau about the Meech Lake agreement, *With a Bang, Not a Whimper*. The title came from a poem by T. S. Eliot, which Trudeau had quoted in his appearance before the Senate Submissions Group on the Meech Lake Constitutional Accord. Trudeau had begun by saying he intended to speak primarily in English, since his last appearance had been conducted mainly in French. He would be happy, he added, to field questions in both official languages.

From the parliamentary press gallery, a francophone Quebec columnist, Michel Vastel, rose to his feet and shouted at Trudeau, in a voice loaded with venom: "Parlez en français!" The man was removed by Senate security.

Trudeau proposed that the Senate amend the Meech Lake Accord, to clarify its meaning. "The stock in trade of legislatures, from time immemorial, has been to vote on something the meaning of which they assume they know and then, when they realize they do not know, they clarify," he said. "Let the people decide once they know what it means."

If Canadians decided they wanted it, being clear on what it meant, "I, for one, will be convinced that the Canada we know and love will be gone forever. But then, Thucydides wrote that Themistocles' greatness lay in the fact that he realized Athens was not immortal. I think we have to realize that Canada is not immortal; but, if it is going to go, let it go with a bang rather than a whimper."

Johnston held a copy of the book in his hands. He looked around the empty room, glancing at the bare walls.

Some workmen arrived, to move the piano. Johnston's piano had been in his office as long as anyone could remember. In other times, his office had often been filled with music. He liked to play and sing, and they called him "The Piano Man." Many nights, after a late sitting or some difficult House business, people would drift into Johnston's office, sip some wine, and crowd around the piano. The security guard from down the hall would drop in, too, and give a reverberant version of "O Sole Mio."

"Be careful with that," he said to the movers.

"Oh, we will," one of them said, in French. "It's a fine piece, that."

The movers admired the piano's workmanship, peering inside to see when and where it had been built. With an exaggerated show of delicacy, they loaded the piano on a trolley and carted it out the door.

"It's hard, eh?" one of the movers said to a member of Johnston's staff, as he passed through the doorway.

"Yes," she said. "It's hard."

The visitor was eager to talk about the hundred-monkeys idea that Johnston had raised the previous summer. As it turned out, it wasn't fiction. Something had indeed happened on the island of Koshima in 1953, when a group of macaques were given a new food — sweet potatoes — by a group of scientists observing their behaviour. One day, a sixteen-month-old macaque named Imo dipped her potato in a stream, and washed the dirt off it with her other hand. This knowledge was not transferred overnight. It took five years for the younger monkeys to follow the pattern, and another four years for it to spread to adults.

The macaques invented other tricks — walking on their hind feet, swimming in the ocean, and dipping their potatoes in salt water to improve the taste — that were soon transmitted to all the other macaques in the group. The scientific literature is divided on how, and even whether, these habits spread to other colonies of macaques on other islands. Some books say it did, some do not mention it. Certainly, the "hundred" number is arbitrary — there were only thirty monkeys in Imo's colony.

But the idea of the hundred-monkeys phenomenon spread through the literature, perhaps evidence in itself of the hundred-monkeys effect at work. Ken Keyes, a peace activist, wrote a tract called "The Hundredth Monkey" (no copyright, priced to give to your friends) in which he quoted the eminent scientist Lyall Watson's references to the Koshima Island happening. According to this, the habit of washing sweet potatoes was observed spontaneously in a mainland troop of monkeys at Takasakiyama. (This is not mentioned in the field guide by Michael Kavanagh; neither is Keyes' assertion that the behaviour spread through the adults overnight.) It was Keyes who attached the number "one hundred" to the phenomenon. "Let us suppose that when the sun rose one morning there were 99 monkeys on Koshima Island who had learned to wash their sweet potatoes," he wrote. "Let's further suppose that later that morning, the hundredth monkey learned to wash potatoes. Then it happened! By that evening, almost everyone in the tribe was washing sweet potatoes before eating them."

Photographs of Imo at work appear in a book called *The Tree of Knowledge: The Biological Roots of Human Understanding*, by Humberto Maturana and Francisco Varela, two new-wave biologists. The authors also cite, as another example of spontaneous learning, the better-known incident of the blue titmice in

England. These birds rapidly acquired and transmitted the behaviour of puncturing milk-bottle caps for the cream inside.

These various observations were not placed in the context of a comprehensive theory by a reputable scientist until the appearance of *A New Science of Life*, by Rupert Sheldrake. Like Teilhard, Sheldrake was fully satisfied neither by Darwinism nor by much of the scientific way of looking at things. He put forth the theory of "formative causation." Sheldrake maintains that species can learn, develop and adapt through a process he calls morphic resonance — which means, roughly, "form echoing." In simplest terms, the theory holds that, after rats in one location have learned to run a maze, all other rats at other locations should be able to run the same maze faster.

Sheldrake's theory attacks not only the conventional wisdom but the very foundations of science. It holds that nature is not so much governed by laws, as the *New Scientist* put it, "but [instead] because of all the things that could happen, only one does — and that one then influences all things. . . that come afterwards."

This notion was welcomed by the scientific establishment with the same enthusiasm initially displayed for the idea that the earth revolves around the sun, rather than the other way round. *Nature* magazine concluded: "His book is the best candidate for burning there has been for many years." This widespread condemnation of his work was tempered by widespread respect for Sheldrake as a scientist: "Of course, within the context of modern science, such an idea is completely scatty," the *New Scientist* commented. Nonetheless, the respected science journal said there were three reasons for taking him seriously. "First, Sheldrake is an excellent scientist; the proper, imaginative kind. . . Second, [the] science in his ideas is good, [but] to absorb what he says involves. . . putting aside our assumptions on how the world works. . . The third reason for taking Sheldrake seriously is that other people do. . . the scientists who take him most seriously and sit up at nights working through the implications are the ones who ought to be the most affronted: the physicists."

Prizes were offered to anyone who could come up with an experiment that met the basic requirements of science — it had to be controlled and repeatable — to prove or disprove Sheldrake's theory. Some imaginative experiments were tested, with promising results. The great difficulty lay in designing an experiment that could be repeated or controlled; Sheldrake's own theory, after all, holds that the reality under investigation would change with each experiment. In 1985, in his last revision of the book, Sheldrake wrote: "I expect that within a few years it should be possible to know whether or not the hypothesis. . . is pointing in the right direction."

DONALD JOHNSTON's phone rang. He took the call, lowering his voice to say something about John Turner. When he sat down again, his face was dark. He could have been brooding, or plotting. Everything was all so mixed up with his own obvious mourning that it was hard to tell.

Johnston's visitor raised the hundred monkeys. It seemed there might be something to it; at least it was something to talk about, there in the empty office. Johnston was asked whether he recalled that afternoon at his cottage the previous summer, peaches-and-cream corn, chianti on the patio, the thing about the hundred monkeys?

He registered a look of recognition and mild surprise, as though reminded of a long-dead relative: "Oh yes, sure. My researcher told me about that. She knows all about it. If you have any questions, ask her."

A workman poked his head in the door. "Sir?" he said tentatively. "We've found a place for it, out back. It should be safe enough there — we've put a blanket on it. You can come and look, if you like."

It was an old mahogany Heintzman, built in the roaring twenties, passed from Johnston's aunt to his mother, then on to him. Back in the days when Don Johnston served his vision of the country and played and sang, you'd have said it was just a piano. But it was more than that, of course. It was one of those intangible bonds that hold people and places together — the sort of thing you miss only when it's gone.

Johnston excused himself, and went to see what they'd done with his piano.

# INDEX

Abella, Rosalie 204
Atkins, Norman 39, 214, 217, 247-51, 264
Atwood, Margaret 50-9
Axworthy, Lloyd 55, 160

Bailey, Angela 180
Barnett, Lincoln 166
Bauch, Herbert 205
Beck, J. Murray 31
Bellemare, Eugène 266
Bentsen, Lloyd 200
Bertrand, Gabrielle 125
Bissonnette, André 86
Blaikie, Bill 45, 58
Blais, André 13, 268-70
Blais-Grenier, Suzanne 86
Blakeney, Allan 193
Blenkarn, Donald 48
Bouchard, Lucien 56, 182-3
Bourassa, Robert 58
Bowker, Marjorie 223
Bozinoff, Lorne 206-7, 247
Brady, Henry 13, 268-70
Broadbent, Ed:
    image of, 25-7, 177; on
    ethics, 101; lists assets, 102;
    campaign methods, 81-3,
    122, 135-6, 173-4, 190;
    and Paul Vachon, 129-30;
    in polls, 132, 183;
    televised debate, 195-7, 202;

resigns, 259
Broadbent, Lucille 83
Brown, Ian 177
Burke, Edmund 103
Burney, Derek 217, 249
Bush, George 22, 76, 260

CTV Television 170, 235
Cameron, Bill 162
Camp, Dalton 30-3, 36
Campaigns and Elections
    (magazine) 18-24
Canadian Alliance for Free
    Trade 222
Canadian Broadcasting
    Corporation 69, 154, 157,
    189-90, 194, 204, 206, 219, 227,
    232, 243; "coup" report,
    158-72
Canadian National Election
    Study 13, 209-11, 268-70
Capone, Al 239
Carney, Pat 116
Carr, Shirley 15, 56, 58
Cassidy, Michael 254, 257
Chatelaine (magazine) 141-6
Chicago Mercantile Exchange
    232-5
Chomiak, John 248
Chrétien, Jean 217
Christian, William 117
Clark, Eric 42

279

Clark, Joe **141-52, 182, 202, 217, 265**
Clarke, Harold **40**
Coates, Robert **84**
Cole, John **123**
Comor, Henry **191**
Computers:
impact on campaign methods, **19, 28, 39, 149, 260-4**; on polling, **33, 74-6, 229**; and markets, **77-8, 235-40**; and patronage, **87**; and party communications, **248-9**
Connolly, Peter **160, 165, 169-70, 192, 203-4**
Conservative Party:
*see* Progressive Conservative Party
Cooke, Janet **167**
Cooper, Albert **45**
Cooper, Sherry Atkinson **232**
Côté, Clément **56-8**
Côté, Michel **87**
Copps, Sheila **57, 62**
Crête, Jean **13, 268-70**
Crosbie, John **182**
Crow, John **238**

Davey, Keith **34, 41**
De Kerckhove, Derek **194**
Den Hertog, Johanna **116**
Der Hoi Yin **232**
Diefenbaker, John **30-3, 64**
Domm, Bill **264**
Douglas-Home, Sir Alec **175**
Downing, Dorothy **30**
Dubow, Joel S. **42**
Dukakis, Michael **76, 137-8**
Dylan, Bob **78**

Edmonston, Phil **130**
Enemark, Tex **115-16**
Enemark, Kirsten **116**
Estey, Willard **219**
Evry, Hal **121-2**
Ewing, J.R. **187**

Fife, Robert **144**
Fingerhut, Vic **133-4, 136**
Fortier, Pierre **18, 261-5**
Fowler, Rod **236**
Fox, Bill **195**
Francis, Charlie **180**
Franks, C.E.S. **49**
Fraser, John **85**
Free Trade **3, 44, 82**; importance of name, **12-15**; parl'y review, **48-59**; talismanic nature, **60-4, 201, 211-4**; in televised debate, **195, 198-200**; and special-interest groups, **222-3**; explained by Mulroney, **266**; and election result, **269-70**
Frith, Doug **217**
Fulton, Davie **30**

Gardiner, Chauncey **107**
Garneau, Raymond **160, 162-3**
Gaulle, Charles de **32**
Gitlin, Todd **73-4, 76**
Gleddie, Graham **175**
Global Television **102, 173**
*Globe and Mail* **57, 146, 205, 236-7, 243**
Goar, Carol **205**
Goldfarb, Martin **34, 36, 160, 226**
Gorbachev, Mikhail **189, 223**

Gordon, Charles 196
Gossage, Patrick 193-4
Graham, Alasdair 159, 192
Graham, Bill 264
Gratton, Michel 220
Gray, Herb 160, 165
Gregg, Allan 41, 90, 123, 133-4, 203, 208-14, 228-30, 250, 264; methods described, 70-82
Griffiths, Bryan 236
Guinness, Sir Alec 177

Hall, Emmett 219
Halton, David 90, 206
Harb, Mac 252-7
*Harper's* (magazine) 71
Harris, Lou 33-4, 260
Hodson, Peregrine 78
Hoy, Claire 155
Humpty Dumpty 9, 10, 17
Hurtig, Mel 60-2
Huxley, Sir Julian 186

Inuit Defence Force 61-2
Issajenko, Angella 180
Istona, Mildred 143

Jamieson, Nancy 135
Jenson, Jane 40
Johnson, Ben 180-9
Johnston, David 131
Johnston, Donald 1-6, 10, 16, 217; and John Turner 2, 11, 15; and one hundred monkeys, 17, 184, 276; departure, 271-3, 276-7
Johnston, Heather 2-3
Johnston, Richard 13-4, 209-13, 268-70
Jung, Carl 185

Kaplan, Bob 160
Kapuściński, Ryszard 231
Kavanagh, Michael 273
Keyes, Ken 273
Kirby, Michael 36, 159-60, 170-1, 246
Kirkpatrick, Doug 194, 204
Koppel, Ted 187

Lalonde, Marc 161
Landon, Alf 242
LaSalle, Roch 86
LeBreton, Marjorie 248
Leclerc, Gilbert 152
LeDuc, Lawrence 40
Lemieux, Mario 148
Lennon, John 54
Lewis, Carl 183
Liberal Party 3, 33, 35-8, 65, 175-8; leadership "coup," 158-71; advertising, 226-7; election results, 257
*Life* (magazine) 122
*Literary Digest* 240-4
*Literary Gazette* 225
Locke, Lt. Col. A. 63
Lortie, Marc 155, 157, 217, 249
Lougheed, Peter 222
Lucas, Pierrette 146

MacDonald, David 264
Macdonald, Donald 217
MacDonald, Flora 182, 193
MacGregor, Roy 223
*Maclean's* (magazine) 55, 195
Mansbridge, Peter 158-62, 194, 206, 232
Masse, Marcel 86, 182
Maturana, Humberto 274
Mazankowski, Don 182

McClung, Nellie **144**
McDougall, Barbara **142, 149, 264**
McFerrin, Bobby **76**
McGillivray, Donald **191**
McGuinty, Dalton **253-7**
McLoughlin, Bill **152-3**
McGrath, James **46-7**
McLuhan, Marshall **26, 178, 194**
McTeer, Maureen:
  columnist, **141-6**; other
  achievements, **146-7**;
  campaign methods,
  **148-53, 264-5**; loses, **266**
McNeely, Jeffrey **62**
Medhurst, Mr. Justice Donald **221**
*Media File* **168**
Meech Lake Accord:
  described, **3-8**; importance
  of name, **4, 7**; explained by
  Mulroney, **266**
*Mein Kampf* **225**
Miller, Mary Ellen **260**
Milligan, Pat **122-3**
Montreal *Gazette* **128, 131, 205, 222**
Morrow, Lance **157**
Morton, David **226-7**
Mosher, Terry (Aislin) **222**
Mulroney, Brian:
  and Meech Lake, **5, 6, 10, 266**; image of, **26-7, 43, 177**;
  and parliament, **46**;
  patronage and scandals,
  **78, 84-91, 182**; at Great
  Wall, **85-6**; removes Sinclair
  Stevens, **92-3**; campaign
  methods, **65, 81, 153-7, 173,**
  **215-17, 219-20, 238, 249**; in
  polls, **183, 208-14**; televised
  debate, **195-206**; accepts
  victory, **266-7**
Mulroney, Mila **85-6, 143**;
  appraised by McTeer, **146**
Murphy, Peter **62**
Murray, Lowell **6-7, 214**

National Citizens' Coalition **220-1**
Naumetz, Tim **173**
Near, Harry **214, 217, 248-50**
Neville, Bill **265**
New Democratic Party **37, 64**;
  campaign organization,
  **132-5**; advertising, **137**;
  election results, **259**
*New Scientist* (magazine) **274**
Nicholson, Aideen **264**
Nicholson, Rob **264**
Nielsen, Erik **31**
Nixon-Kennedy debates **27, 201-2, 229**
Nöosphere **184-90, 201, 239**

Obando y Bravo, Cardinal
  Miguel **147**
O'Donnell, Joe **205**
Ortega, Daniel **147**
One Hundred Monkeys **17, 44, 184, 201, 207, 273-5**
O'Rourke, Mickey **85**
*Ottawa Citizen* **196, 205-6, 223**
Ouellet, André **159, 163, 192**
Owen, John **157, 168-9**

Pammett, John **40**
Parizeau, Jacques **259**
Pavlov, Ivan **42**

Pearson, Lester B. **34**
Pedersen, Lissie **95**
Peterson, David **10, 116, 253**
Pharoah, Ethel **151**
Phillips, Bruce **191, 193**
Piggott, Jean **149, 152**
Pillitteri, Gary **264**
Pollies, The **20**
Polling and pollsters:
  impact on campaign
  methods, **19-20, 28-40, 73-6**;
  rel'nship with product
  marketing, **41-2**; Kendall
  equation explained, **75,
  213-14**; validity and
  methodology, **183, 240-7**;
  election law, **221-2**; future
  trends, **268**
Poll results:
  free trade, **13-14, 209-14**;
  Meech Lake, **16**; and
  Liberal strategy, **36**; and
  Conservative strategy,
  **72-81**; and New Democrat
  strategy, **132-5**; Turner,
  **159**; Ben Johnson, **181, 183**;
  federal-cabinet recognition,
  **181-2**; attachment to
  politics, **182**; to
  issues/leaders, **183**; of 1984
  televised debate, **202**; of
  1988 televised debate,
  **206-7, 208-14**; and value of
  dollar, **235-40**; "rogue"
  Gallup, **247**
Postman, Neil **25**
Pro-Canada Network **222**
Progressive Conservative
  Party **28, 30, 37, 39, 65**;
  advertising, **43, 224-8**;

whiteshirts, **173**;
Confederation Club, **218**;
organization, **247-50**;
election results, **259-60**

Quammen, David **186-7**
Quayle, Dan **22-4, 237**
Quayle, Oliver **34**

Rae, Bob **193**
Ralfe, Tim **265**
Rather, Dan **186**
*Ready, Set, Go!* **38**
Reinsch, J. Leonard **34, 201-2**
Reisman, Simon **219**
Retton, Mary Lou **181, 187**
Robertson, Pat **21, 260**
Roebuck, Arthur **29, 33, 252,
  255-6**
*Romper Room* **227**
Roosevelt, Franklin Delano
  **242**
Rose, Jeff **62**
Rosen, Harry **150**
Russell, Sylvia **116**

Saint-Basile-le-Grand **68**
Saint-Laurent, Louis **31-3**
Sauvé, Jeanne **117**
Sawyer, Diane **22**
Schlesinger, Arthur, Jr. **37**
Sears, Robin **18, 137-8, 191**
Sears, Val **243**
Segal, Gary **234**
Segal, Hugh **154, 214**
Seoul Olympics **135, 178-83**
Shaw, George Bernard **56**
Sheldrake, Rupert **274-5**
Simon, Paul **153, 239**
Simpson, Jeffrey **205**

Small, David **149-50, 265**
Small, Doug **102**
Southam News **155, 161, 190**
Sparrow, Barbara **46**
Spitz, Mark **181**
*Spy* (magazine) **143**
Squire, Peverill **242-4**
Stevens, Sinclair **87**; removed
from race, **92-3**; demeanour,
**94**; compares self with Joe
Clark, Robert Stanfield, **96**,
with Oliver North, Rick
Hansen, **98**, with Ben
Johnson, Gary Hart, **99**;
Parker Commission, **96-7**;
explains conspiracy, **97-8**;
accepts fate, **99-103**
Straps (RCMP dog) **155**
Stronach, Frank **97, 102, 218**;
and Sinc Stevens, **105** ;
Beechwood Farm, **105-6**;
appearance, **106**; explains the
Magna Way, **107-11**; practical
applications of Way, **112-14**;
describes self, **114-15**;
receives Liberal nomination,
**120-1**; campaigns, **123**;
loses, **258**
*Stürmer, Der* **225**
*Sunday Morning* **227**

Taft, William Howard **25**
Taylor, Tom **121**
Teilhard de Chardin, Pierre
**184-7, 239**
Television:
impact on campaign
methods, **21-44**; on
perception, **165-7, 172**;
and hecklers, **174-80**;

debates, **27, 90, 184, 188,
191-207**; as events broker,
**189-91**
Terry, John **241**
Thatcher, Margaret **189**
Thibault, Laurent **197**
Thomson, Oliver **225**
Thompson, Robert **138**
Tigers **7-8, 63**
*Time* (magazine) **24-5**
Toronto:
bourgeoisie, **51, 59**; hot,
**66-70**; arrogant, **182**
*Toronto* (magazine) **69**
*Toronto Life* (magazine) **69**
*Toronto Star* **57, 147, 156, 195,
204-5, 243**
*Toronto Sun* **57, 173, 205**
*Toronto Telegram* **243**
Trudeau, Pierre **4, 5, 10, 64,
202, 246, 272-3**
Truman, Harry S **31**
Turcotte, Sheldon **158-9**
Turner, Geills **63, 83**
Turner, John:
campaign methods **35-7, 65,
82-3, 123, 174-8, 190**; image
of, **26-7, 177**; patronage, **87**;
use of Senate, **116-18**;
Quadra speech, **118-20**; and
CBC report, **159-72**; in
polls, **159, 183, 208-14**;
televised debate, **192-206**;
assailed as liar, **214-18**; as
traitor, **219-20**; defends
record, **236**; resigns, **257-8**

Vachon, Paul:
and Mad Dog, **126, 128-9**;
becomes "The Butcher,"

126; assumes Russian
identity, 126-7; adventures
in India, 127; and
Broadbent, 129-30, 140;
campaign methods, 129-32,
138-40; loses, 258
*Vancouver Sun* 205
Vander Zalm, Bill 142
*Vanity Fair* (magazine) 23
Varela, Francisco 274
Vastel, Michel 273
*Vogue* (magazine) 27

Wachtel, Paul Spencer 63
Walker, David C. 34
Walley, Don (fictional
  candidate) 20, 21
*Washington Post* 23, 189
Webster, John 18, 159
Whelan, Eugene 223
White, Bob 51
White, Jodi 265
Will, George F. 23
Willis, Harry 30
Wilson, Harold 174-5
Wilson, Michael 12, 53, 182,
  193, 197, 218-19, 236
Winegard, William 48, 50, 58
Winser, Joan Price 146
Winsor, Hugh 167,170

# A NOTE ON THE TYPE

This book is set in Trump Mediaeval, an old style serif typeface designed in 1954 by Georg Trump (1896-1985), originally for the typefounder C.E. Weber of Stuttgart, West Germany. An excellent example of modern design reworking classical form, this type possesses a timeless appearance. The letterform can be reproduced on any kind of paper by any method of printing and still retain its integrity.

BOOK DESIGN BY
*Derek Ungless and Noel Claro*

*Type set by Tony Gordon Limited*